Pliny's natural history in thirty-seven books

Pliny, the Elder, Wernerian Club, Philemon Holland

only
Vols 1 & 2 rpt & 3 pub.

Clar
ind

PLINY'S
NATURAL HISTORY.

IN

THIRTY-SEVEN BOOKS.

A TRANSLATION

ON THE BASIS OF THAT BY DR. PHILEMON HOLLAND.
ED. 1601.

WITH CRITICAL AND EXPLANATORY NOTES.

VOL. II.

Edited by the Wernerian Club

PRINTED FOR THE CLUB

BY

GEORGE BARCLAY, CASTLE STREET, LEICESTER SQUARE.

1848-49.

PURSUANT to a Resolution to the following effect, passed at a meeting of the Committee held on Wednesday, the 15th March, 1848,—

"The best thanks of the Club are hereby presented to—

JONATHAN COUCH, Esq. F.L S , *the Superintending Editor of this Publication, and Translator of the Work*

Also to the following Gentlemen, viz ·—

In the Department of Classics,

W G V. BARNEWALL, Esq. M A.
Rev. GEORGE MUNFORD.

In the Department of Geography,

W. H F PLATÉ, Esq. LL D.
GEORGE ALEXANDER, Esq F.S.A.
CHARLES MOXON, Esq

In the Department of Natural History and Physiology,

C J. B. ALDIS, Esq. M.D.
C. R. HALL, Esq. M.D.
JONATHAN COUCH, Esq. F.L.S.
JOHN CHIPPENDALE, Esq. F.R.C.S.

For the Editorial Assistance rendered by them in the preparation of the accompanying Work."

IN THE FOURTH BOOK

ARE COMPRISED

REGIONS, NATIONS, SEAS, TOWNS, MOUNTAINS, PORTS, RIVERS,
WITH THEIR DIMENSIONS, AND PEOPLE, EITHER NOW
OR IN TIMES PAST KNOWN; VIZ.:—

Herein are contained many principal Towns and Countries, famous Rivers and Mountains; Islands, also, besides Cities or Nations that are perished: in sum, Histories and Observations.

LATIN WRITERS ABSTRACTED:

M. Varro, Cato Censorius, M. Agrippa, Divus Augustus, Varro Atacinus, Cor. Nepos, Hyginus, L. Vetus, Pomponius Mela, Licinius Mutianus, Fabricius Thuscus, Atteius Capito, and Atteius Philologus.

FOREIGN AUTHORS:

Polybius, Hecatæus, Hellanicus, Damastes, Eudoxus, Dicæarchus, Timosthenes, Ephorus, Crater the Grammarian, Serapion of Antioch, Callimachus, Artemidorus, Apollodorus, Agathocles, Eumachus Siculus the Musician, Alexander Polyhistor, Thucydides, Dosiades, Anaximander, Philistides, Mallotes, Dionysius, Aristides, Callidemus, Menæchmus, Ædasthenes, Anticlides, Heraclides, Philemon, Menephon, Pythias, Isidorus, Philonides, Xenagoras, Astyonomus, Staphylus, Aristocritus, Metrodorus, Cleobulus, and Posidonius.

THE FOURTH BOOK

OF THE

HISTORY OF NATURE.

WRITTEN BY

C. PLINIUS SECUNDUS.

From whence first arose all the fabulous Lies, and the excellent Learning of the Greeks.

THE third Bay of Europe beginneth at the Mountains of Acroceraunia, and endeth in the Hellespont. It containeth, besides 19 smaller Bays, 25,000 Miles. Within it are Epirus, Acarnania, Ætolia, Phocis, Locris, Achaia, Messania, Laconia, Argolis, Megaris, Attica, Bœotia. And again, from another Sea, the same Phocis and Locris, Doris, Phthiotis, Thessalia, Magnesia, Macedonia, Thracia. All the fabulous Vein, as well as the illustrious learning of Greece, proceeded first out of this quarter; on which account we will therein stay somewhat the longer. The Country Epirus, generally so called, beginneth at the Mountains of Acroceraunia. In it are, first, the Chaones, of whom Chaonia taketh the Name : then the Thesproti, and Antigonenses : the Place Aornus, and Exhalation so deadly to Birds. The Cestrini, and Perrhœbi, with their Mountain Pindus : the Cassiopæi, the Dryopes, Selli, Hellopes, and Molossi, among whom is the Temple of *Jupiter*

Dodonæus, so famous for the Oracle . the Mountain To-marus, celebrated by *Theopompus* for the hundred Fountains about its foot.

Chapter I.

Epirus.

Epirus itself reaching to Magnesia and Macedonia, hath behind it the Dassaretæ above named, a free Nation ; but presently the savage People of the Dardani On the left side of the Dardani, the Tieballi and Nations of Mœsia lie ranged : from the Front are joined to them, the Medi and Denthelatæ, upon whom the Thraces border, who reach as far as to Pontus. Thus it is environed with Rhodopè, and is fenced presently also with the Heights of Hæmus. In the Coast of Epirus, among the Acroceraunia, is the Castle Chimæra, under which is the Spring of the King's Water. The Towns are Mæandria and Cestria · the River of Thesprotia, Thyamis : the Colony Buthrotium . and the Gulf of Ambracia, above all others most famous, receiving at its Mouth the wide Sea, 39 Miles in Length and 15 in Breadth. Into it runneth the River Acheron, flowing out of Acherusia, a Lake of Thesprotia, 36 Miles from thence : and the Bridge over it, 1000 Feet long, ad-mirable to those that admire all Things of their own. In the Gulf is the Town Ambracia The Rivers of the Molossi, Aphas and Arachtus. The City Anactoria, and the Lake Pandosia The Towns of Acarnania, called formerly Curetus, are Heraclea and Echinus : and in the very entrance, Actium, a Colony of *Augustus*, with the noble Temple of *Apollo*, and the free City Nicopolis. When out of the Ambracian Gulf and in the Ionian Sea, we meet with the Leucadian Coast and the Promontory of Leucatè. Then the Bay, and Leu-cadia itself, a Peninsula, once called Neritis, but by the Labour of the neighbouring Inhabitants cut off quite from the Continent, but joined to it again by means of the Winds

blowing together heaps of Sand; which Place is called
Dioryctus, and is in Length half a mile. A Town in it is
called Leucas, formerly Neritum. Then the Cities of the
Acarnani, Halyzea, Stratos, Argos, surnamed Amphilo-
chicum. The River Achelous running out of Pindus, and
dividing Acarnania from Ætolia; and by continual addition
of Earth joining the Island Artemita to the main Land.

Chapter II.

Ætolia.

The Ætolian People are the Athamanes, Tymphei,
Ephiri, Ænienses, Perrhœbi, Dolopes, Maraces and Atraces,
from whom the River Atrax falleth into the Ionian Sea.
The Town Calydon in Ætolia is seven Miles and a half from
the Sea, near to the River Evenus. Then followeth Ma-
cynia and Molychria; behind which Chalcis standeth, and
the Mountain Taphiassus. But in the Borders, the Promontory Antirrhium, where is the Mouth of the Corinthian
Gulf, not a Mile broad where it runneth in and divideth
the Ætoli from Peloponnesus. The Promontory that shooteth
out against it is named Rhion: but in the Corinthian Gulf
are the Towns of Ætolia, Naupactum, and Pylenè. and in
the Midland parts, Pleuron, Halysarna. The Mountains of
name: in Dodonè, Tomarus: in Ambracia, Grania: in
Acarnania, Aracynthus: in Ætolia, Acanthon, Panætolium,
and Macinium.

Chapter III

Locri.

Next to the Ætoli are the Locri, surnamed Ozolæ, free:
the Town Oeanthè: the Port of *Apollo Phæstius*: the Bay
Crissæus. Within, the Towns Argyna, Eupalia, Phæstum,
and Calamissus. Beyond are Cirrhæi, the Plains of Phocis,
the Town Cirrha, the Port Chalæon: from which, seven
Miles within the Land, is the free City Delphi, under the

Mountain Parnassus, the most illustrious Place upon Earth for the Oracle of *Apollo*. The Fountain Castalius, the River Cephissus, running before Delphos, which ariseth in a former City, Lilœa. Moreover, the Town Crissa, and together with the Bulenses, Anticyra, Naulochum, Pyrrha, Amphissa, a free State, Trichonè, Tritea, Ambrysus, the Region Drymæa, named Daulis. Then, at the bottom of the Bay, the Angle of Bœotia is washed by the Sea, with the Towns Siphæ and Thebæ, which are surnamed Corsicæ, near to Helicon The third Town of Bœotia from this Sea is Pagæ, from whence projecteth the Neck of Peloponnesus

Chapter IV.

Peloponnesus.

Peloponnesus, called formerly Apia and Pelasgia, is a Peninsula, worthy to come behind no other Land for nobleness, lying between two Seas, Ægeum and Ionium like the Leaf of a Plane Tree[1], in regard of the indented Creeks thereof. it beareth a circuit of 563 Miles, according to *Isidorus*. The same, if you comprise the Creeks, addeth almost as much more. The Straits whence it passeth is called Isthmos. In which Place the Seas above-named, bursting from various ways, from the North and the East, devour all the Breadth of it there: until, by the contrary running in of such Seas, the Sides on both hands being eaten away, and leaving a Space between, five Miles over, Hellas, with a narrow Neck, meeteth with Peloponnesus. The one Side thereof is called the Corinthian Gulf, the other, the Saronian. Lecheum on the one hand, and Cenchreæ on the other, are the Bounds of the Straits where such Ships as for their bigness cannot be conveyed over upon Waggons, make a great compass about with some Danger. For which cause, *Demetrius* the King, *Cæsar* the Dictator,

---

[1] Dionysius, the geographer, also compares the form of the Morea, or ancient Peloponnesus, to the leaf of a plane-tree, making the footstalk to be the isthmus by which it is joined to Greece And in Martyn's "Virgil," a figure of this leaf is engraved to illustrate the subject — *Wern. Club*

Prince *Caius*, and *Domitius Nero*, endeavoured to cut
through the narrow portions, and make a navigable Channel :
but the attempt was unhappy, as appeared by the issue of
them all.   In the midst of this narrow Strait which we
have called Isthmos, the Colony Corinthus, formerly called
Ephyra, situated on a little Hill, is inhabited, three score
Stadia from each Shore : which from the top of its Citadel,
which is named Acrocorinthus, wherein is the Fountain
Pirenè, hath a prospect into both those opposite Seas.
Through the Corinthian Gulf is a Passage from Leucas to
Patræ, of 87 Miles.   Patræ, a Colony, built upon the Promontory of Peloponnesus that shooteth furthest into the
Sea, over against Ætolia and the River Evenus, of less dis-
tance, as hath been said, than a Mile, in the very entrance,
sendeth out the Corinthian Gulf 85 Miles in Length, even
as far as Isthmos.

Chapter V.

Achaia.

ACHAIA, the name of a Province, beginneth at the
Isthmus : formerly it was called Ægialos, because of the
Cities disposed in order upon the Strand.   The first there is
Lecheæ above named, a Port of Lecheæ of the Corinthians.
Next to it Oluros, a Castle of the Pellenæi.   The Towns,
Helicè, Bura, and (into which the Inhabitants retired when
these before-named were swallowed up in the Sea) Sicyon,
Ægira, Ægion, and Erineos.   Within, Cleonè and Hysiæ.
Also the Port Panhormus, and Rhium, described before :
from which Promontory, five Miles off, standeth Patræ,
above mentioned, and the Place called Pheræ.   Of nine
Mountains in Achaia, Scioessa is most known ; also the
Spring Cymothoè   Beyond Patræ is the Town Olenum, the
Colony Dymæ.   Places called Buprasium and Hirmenè·
and the Promontory Araxum.   The Bay of Cyllenè, the
Cape Chelonates : from whence to Cyllene is two Miles.
The Castle Phlius.   The Tract also by *Homer* named
Arethyrea, and afterwards Asophis · then the Country of

the Elii, who before were called Epei. Elis itself is in the Midland, 12 Miles from Pylos. Within is the Shrine of *Jupiter Olympius*, which, for the fame of the Games there, containeth the Calendars of the Greeks (fasti) · also, the former Town of the Pisæi, before which the River Alpheus runneth but in the Borders, the Promontory Icthys. The River Alpheus is navigated to the Towns Aulos and Leprion. The Promontory Platanestus. All these lie Westward. But towards the South, the Bay Cyparissius, the City Cyparissa, 72 Miles in circuit. The Towns, Pylos, Methonè, a Place called Helos: the Promontory Acritas: the Bay Asinæus of the Town Asinum, and Coronæus of Coronè and these are bounded by the Promontory Jænarus. There also is the Region Messenia with 22 Mountains: the River Paomisus. But within, Messene itself, Ithomè, Occhalia, Arenè, Pteleon, Thryon, Dorion, Zanclum, famous at various times. The Compass of this Bay is 80 Miles, the Passage over 30 Miles Then from Tænarus, the Laconian Land pertaining to a free People, and a Bay there in circuit about 206 Miles, but 39 Miles over. The Towns Tænarum, Amiclæ, Pheræ, Leuctra, and within, Sparta, Theranicum: and where stood Cardamylè, Pitanè, and Anthanè. The Place Thyrea, and Gerania: the Mountain Taygetus: the River Eurotas, the Bay Ægylodes, and the Town Psammathus. The Bay Gytheates, of a Town thereby (Gythæum), from whence to the Island Creta there is a very direct course All these are enclosed within the Promontory Maleum. The Bay next following to Scyllæus is called Argolicus, and is 50 Miles over, and 172 Miles round. The Towns upon it, Bœa, Epidaurus, Limera, named also Zarax: the Port Cyphanta Rivers, Inachus, Erasinus between which standeth Argos, surnamed Hippium, upon the Lake Lernè, from the sea two Miles, and, nine Miles further, Mycenæ. Also, where they say Tiryntha stood, and the Place Mantinea. Mountains, Artemius, Apesantus, Asterion, Parparus, and 11 others besides Fountains, Niobè, Amymonè, Psammothè. From Scyllæum to the Isthmus, 177 Miles Towns, Hermionè, Trœzen, Coryphasium, and Argos, called of some Inachium,

of others Dipsium.   The Port Cænites, the Bay Saronicus,
encircled in old Time with a Grove of Oaks, from whence it
had the Name, for so old Greece called an Oak.   Within it
the Town Epidaurum, celebrated for the Shrine of *Æscu-
lapius*, the Promontory Spiræum, the Harbours Anthedon
and Bucephalus : and likewise Cenchreæ, which we spoke of
before, being the other limit of the Isthmus, with the Shrine
of *Neptune*, famous for its Games every five Years.   So
many Bays cut up the Peloponnesian Coast so many Seas
roar against it.   For on the North side the Ionian Sea
breaketh in : on the West it is beaten upon by the Sicilian.
From the South the Crethean Sea driveth against it : the
Ægean from the South-east, and Myrtoan on the North-
east, which beginning at the Megarian Bay, washeth all
Attica.

Chapter VI.

Of Arcadia

The midland Parts of this, Arcadia most of all taketh
up, being every way remote from the Sea : at the beginning
it was named Drymodis, but soon after Pelasgis.   The
Towns in it are Psophis, Mantinea, Stymphalum, Tegea,
Antigonea, Orchomenum, Pheneum, Palatium, from whence
the Mount Palatium at Rome took the Name, Megalepolis,
Catina, Bocalium, Carmon, Parrhasiæ, Thelphusa, Melanæa,
Heræa, Pilè, Pellana, Agræ, Epium, Cynætha, Lepreon of
Arcadia, Parthenium, Alea, Methydrium, Enespè, Macistum,
Lampè, Clitorium, Cleonè ; between which Towns is the
Tract Nemea, usually called Berubinadia.   Mountains in
Arcadia, Pholoe, with the Town also Cyllenè, Lyceus,
wherein the Shrine of *Jupiter Lyceus*, Mænalus, Artemisius,
Parthenius, Lampeus, and Nonacris : and eight besides of
base account.   Rivers, Ladon, issuing out of the Fens of
Pheneus, Erymanthus out of a Mountain of the same Name,
running both down into Alpheus.   The rest of the Cities to
be named in Achæa, Aliphiræi, Albeatæ, Pyrgenses, Pareatæ,
Paragenitiæ, Tortuni, Typanæi, Thryasii, Trittenses.   All

Achæa *Domitius Nero* endowed with Freedom.   Peloponnesus, from the Promontory of Malea to the Town
Lechæum upon the Corinthian Bay, lieth in Breadth 160
Miles but across, from Elis to Epidaurum, 125 Miles:
from Olympia to Argos, through Arcadia, 63 Miles: from
the same Place to Phlius is the said measure.   And the
whole, as if Nature weighed out a Recompense for the
irruptions of the Seas, riseth up into three score and sixteen
Mountains.

CHAPTER VII.

Greece and Attica.

FROM the Straits of the Isthmus beginneth Hellas, by our
Countrymen called Græcia.   The first Tract thereof is Attica,
in old Time named Actè.   It reacheth the Isthmus on that
Part of it which is called Megaris, from the Colony Megara,
from the Region of the Pagæ.   These two Towns, as Peloponnesus lieth out in Length, are seated on either Hand, as
it were, upon the Shoulders of Hellas.   The Pagæi, and
more especially the Ægosthenienses, lie annexed to the
Magarensians.   In the Coast is the Harbour Schœnus.
Towns, Sidus, Cremyon, the Scironian Rocks for three Miles
long, Geranea, Megara, and Elcusin.   There were besides,
Œnoa and Probalinthus, which now are 52 Miles from
the Isthmus.   Pyræeus and Phalera, two Ports joined to
Athens by a Wall, within the Land five Miles.   This City
is free, and needeth no more any Man's praise: so abund-
antly noble it is.   In Attica are these Fountains, Cephissia,
Larinè, Callirrhoe, and Enneacreunos.   Mountains, Brilessus,
Megialcus, Icarius, Hymettus, and Lyrabetus: the River
Ilissos.   From Pyræeus 42 Miles is the Promontory
Sunium; likewise the Promontory Doriscum.   Also Po-
tamos and Brauron, Towns in time past.   The Village
Rhamnus, the Place Marathon, the Plain Thriastius, the
Town Melita and Oropus, in the Border of Bœotia.   To
which belong Anthedon, Onchestos, Thespræ, a free Town,
Lebadea: and Thebes, surnamed Bœotia, not inferior in

Fame to Athens, as being the native Country (as Men will
have it) of two Gods, *Liber* and *Hercules*. Also, they attribute
the Birth of the Muses to the Grove Helicon. To this Thebes
is assigned the Forest Cithæron and the River Ismenus.
Moreover, Fountains in Bœotia, Œdipodium. Psammatè,
Dircè, Epigranea, Arethusa, Hippocrenè, Aganippè, and
Gargaphiæ. Mountains, besides the forenamed, Mycalessus,
Adylisus, Acontius. The rest of the Towns between Megara
and Thebes, Eleutheræ, Haliartus, Plateæ, Pheræ, Aspledon,
Hylè, Thisbè, Erythræ, Glissas, and Copæ. Near the River
Cephissus, Lamia and Anichia : Medeon, Phligonè, Grephis,
Coronæa, Chæronia. But in the Borders, beneath Thebes,
Ocalè, Elæon, Scolos, Scœnos, Peteon, Hyrie, Mycalessus,
Hyreseon, Pteleon, Olyros, Tanagia, a free People ; and in
the very Mouth of Euripus, which the Island Eubœa maketh
by its opposite Site, Aulis, renowned for its large Har-
bour. The Bœotians in old Time were named Hyantes.
The Locrians also are named Epicnemidii, in Times past
Letegetes, through whom the River Cephissus runneth into
the Sea. Towns, Opus (whereof cometh the Opuntinean
Bay), and Cynus. Upon the Sea-coast of Phocis, one
Daphnus. Within, among the Locrians, Elatea, and upon
the Bank of Cephissus (as we have said) Lilæa : and toward
Delphos, Cnemis and Hiampolis. Again, the Borders of
the Locrii, wherein stand Larymna and Thronium, near
which the River Boagrius falleth into the Sea. Towns,
Narycion, Alopè, Scarphia. After this, the Vale, called
by the People there dwelling, Maliacus Sinus, wherein are
these Towns, Halcyonè, Econia, and Phalara. Then Doris,
wherein are Sperchios, Erineon, Boion, Pindus, Cytinum
On the Back of Doris is the Mountain Œta. Then followeth Æmonia that so often hath changed Name : for
the same hath been called Pelasgicum, Argos, and Hellas,
Thessalia also, and Dryopis, and evermore it took the Name
of the Kings. In it was born a King called *Græcus*, from
whom Greece was named : there also was *Hellen* born,
from whence came the Hellenes. These being but one
People, *Homer* hath called by three Names : Myrmidons,

Hellenæ, and Achæi. Of these, they are called Phthiotæ
who inhabit Doris. Their Towns are Echinus, in the entrance
of the River Sperchius: and the Straits of Thermopylæ, so
named by reason of the Waters: and, four Miles from
thence, Heraclea was called Trachin. There is the Mountain
Callidromus. and the famous Towns, Hellas, Halos, Lamia,
Phthia, and Arnè.

CHAPTER VIII

Thessalia.

MOREOVER, in Thessalia, Orchomenus, formerly called
Minyeus; and the Town Almon, by some Elmon; Atrax,
Pelinnâ, and the Fountain Hyperia. Towns, Pheræ, behind
which Pierius stretcheth forth to Macedonia: Larissa, Gomphi,
Thebes of Thessalia, the Grove Pteleon, and the Bay Pagasicus. The Town Pagasa, the same named afterwards
Demetrias; Tricca, the Pharsalian Plains, with a free City:
Cranon, and Iletia. Mountains of Phthiotis, Nymphæus,
beautiful for the natural Harbours and Garden-works there:
Buzigæus, Donacesa, Bermius, Daphista, Chimerion, Athamas, Stephanè. In Thessalia there are 34, of which the
most famous are Cerceti, Olympus, Pierus, Ossa: over
against which is Pindus and Othrys, the Seat of the Lapithæ;
and those lie toward the West. but Eastward, Pelios; all of
them bending in the manner of a Theatre: and before them,
in form of a Wedge, 72 Cities. Rivers of Thessalia,
Apidanus, Phœnix, Enipeus, Onochomus, Pamisus: the
Fountain Messeis, the Lake Bœbeis: and illustrious above
all the rest, Peneus, which, rising near Gomphi, runneth
for 500 Stadia in a woody Dale between Ossa and Olympus,
and half that Way is navigable. In this Course are the
Places called Tempè, five Miles in Length, and almost an
Acre and a half Broad, where on both Hands the Hills arise
by a gentle Ascent above the reach of Man's Sight. Within,
Peneus glideth by, in a fresh green Grove, clear as Crystal,
over the gravelly Stones, pleasant for the Grass upon the
Banks, and melodious with the Harmony of Birds.   It

taketh in the River Eurotas, but receiveth him not, but, as
Homer expresseth it[1], floweth over him like Oil. and within a
very little while rejecteth the Burden, as refusing to mingle
with his own silver Streams those penal and cursed Waters
so direfully produced.

Chapter IX.

Magnesia.

To Thessalia, Magnesia is annexed · the Fountain there
is Libethra. The Towns, Iolchos, Hirmenium, Pyrrha,
Methonè, Olizon. The Promontory Sepias. Towns, Cas-
tana, Sphalatra, and the Promontory Ænantium. Towns,
Melibœa, Rhisus, Erymnè. The Mouth of Peneus. Towns,
Homolium, Orthè, Thespiæ, Phalanna, Thaumaciæ, Gyrton,
Cranon, Acarnè, Dotion, Melitæa, Phylacè, Potinæ. The
Length of Epirus, Achaia, Attica, and Thessalia, lying strait
out, is by report 480 Miles, the Breadth 287.

Chapter X.

Macedonia.

Macedonia, so called afterwards (formerly it was named
Emathia) is a Kingdom, consisting of 150 several People,
renowned for two Kings, and once ennobled for the Empire
of the World. This Country passing behind Magnesia and
Thessalia toward the Nations of Epirus Westward, is much
troubled with the Dardani. The North Parts thereof are
defended by Pæonia and Pelagonia, against the Triballi.
The Towns are these, Ægè, wherein it was the Custom to inter

---

[1] As Homer expresseth it.   See " Iliad," b. 750 ·—

> " To these were join'd, who till the pleasant fields
> Where Titaresius winds   the gentle flood
> Pours into Peneus all his limpid stores,
> But with the silver-eddied Peneus flows
> Unmixt as oil , for Stygian is his stream,
> And Styx is the inviolable oath
>   Cowper's *Homer.— Wern. Club.*

their Kings : Berœa, and Æginium, in that Quarter which, from the Wood, is called Pieria. In the Borders, Heraclea, and the River Apilas · Towns, Phina and Oloros : the River Haliacmon. Within are the Haloritæ, the Vallei, Phylacei, Cyrrhestæ, Tyrissæi : Pella, the Colony : the Town Stobi, of Roman Citizens. Presently, Antigonia, Europus, upon the River Axius, and another of the same Name, through which Rhædias runneth : Heordeæ, Scydra, Mieza, Gordiniæ Soon after, in the Borders, Ichnæ ; and the River Axius   To this Extremity the Dardani : Treres and Pieres border upon Macedonia. From this River are the Nations of Pæonia, Parorei, Heoidenses, Almopii, Pelagones, and Mygdones. The Mountains Rhodopè, Scopius, and Orbelus. Then the Lap of the Earth spreading along, Arethusii, Antiochienses, Idomenenses, Dobeiienses, Trienses, Allantenses, Andaristenses, Moryllii, Garesci, Lyncestæ, Othrionei, and the free States of the Amantini and Orestæ. Colonies, Bulledensis and Diensis. Xilopolitæ, Scotussæi, free ; Heraclea, Sintica, Tymphei, and Coronæi. In the Coast of the Macedonian Bay, the Town Calastra, and within, Phileros, and Letè. and in the middle bending of the Coast, Thessalonica, of free condition. To it from Dyrrhachium, is 114 Miles ; Thermæ. In the Bay Thermaicus, are these Towns, Dicæa, Pydna, Derrha, Scionè : the Promontory Canastræum. Towns, Pallenè, Phlerga. In which Region these Mountains, Hypsizorus, Epitus, Alchionè, Leuomnè. Towns, Nissos, Brygion, Eleon, Mendæ, and in the Isthmus of Pallenè, the Colony sometime called Potidæa, and now Cassandria ; Anthemus, the Bay Holophyxus, and Mecyberna ; Towns, Phiscella, Ampelos, Toronè, and Singos : the Creek (where *Xerxes*, King of the Persians, cut the Mountain Athos from the Continent), in Length a Mile and a half. The Mountain itself shooteth out from the Plain into the Sea, 75 Miles. The Compass of the Foot thereof taketh 150 Miles. A Town there was on the Summit, Acroton. Now there be Vranopolis, Palæotrium, Thyssus, Cleonè, Apollonia, the Inhabitants whereof are named Macrobii. The Town Cassera, and a second Gullet of the Isthmus, Acanthus, Stagira, Sitonè, Heraclea, and the Region lying under Mygdonia, wherein are, receding from the Sea, Apollonia and Arethusa Again, in the Coast, Posidium, and a Bay, with the Town Cermorus: Amphipolis, a free State, and the Nation Bisaltæ. Then, the River Strymon, which is the Bound of Macedonia, and which springeth in Hæmus: of which this is worthy to be remembered, that it runneth into seven Lakes before it keepeth a direct Course. This is Macedonia, which once obtained the Dominion over all the Earth: this overran Asia, Armenia, Iberia, Albania, Cappadocia, Syria, Egypt, Taurus, and Caucasus· this ruled over the Bactri, Medi, and Persi, and possessed all the East: this having the Conquest of India, wandered through the Tracts of Father *Liber* and *Hercules*. This is the very same Macedonia, of which in one Day *Paulus Æmylius*, our Imperator, sold 72 plundered Cities. So great a Difference of Fortune befel two Men.

Chapter XI.

Thracia

Now followeth Thracia, among the most valiant Nations of Europe, divided into 52 Regiments (strategias) of Soldiers. Of those People in it, whom it does not grieve me to name, the Denseletes and Medi inhabit near the River Strymon, on the right Side, as far as to the Bisaltæ above-named: on the left, the Digeri, and many Names of the Bessi, to the River Nestus, which environeth the Bottom of the Mountain Pangæus, between the Eleti, Diobesi, and Carbilesi; and so forward to the Brysæ and Capæi. Odomanta, a Nation of the Odrysæ, poureth out the River Hebrus to the Neighbour-borderers, the Carbiletes, Pyrogeri, Drugeri, Cænici, Hypsalti, Beni, Corpilli, Botiæi, and Edoni. In the same Tract are the Selletæ, Priautæ, Diloncæ, Thyni, Celetæ, the greater under Hæmus, the less under Rhodopæ· between whom runneth the River Hebrus. The Town situate beneath Rhodopè, before-time named Poneropolis; soon after by the Founder, Philippopolis; but now, from its Site, Trimontium.

The Elevation of Hæmus taketh six Miles the Back and
declining thereof down to Ister, the Mœsi, Getæ, Aoti,
Gaudæ, and Clariæ, and under them the Arræi, Sarmatæ,
whom they call Areatæ, and Scythæ : and about the Sea-
coast of Pontus, the Moriseni and Sithonii, from whom the
Poet *Orpheus* descended, do inhabit. Thus Ister boundeth
it on the North : in the East, Pontus and Propontus : Southward, the Sea Ægæum, in the Coast of which, from Strymon,
stand Apollonia, Œstima, Neapolis, and Polis. Within, the
Colony of *Philip ;* and 325 Miles from Dyrrhachium, Sco-
tusa, Topiris, and the Mouth of the River Nestus. The
Mountain Pangæus, Heraclea, Olynthos Abdera, a free City,
the Marsh and Nation of the Bistoni. There stood the Town
Tinda, terrible for the Stables of the Horses of *Diomedes.*
Now there are the Diceæ, Ismaron, the Place Parthenion,
Phalesina, Maronea, called Ortagurea before-time. The
Mountain Serrium and Zonæ · then, the Place Doriscus,
able to receive 10,000[1] Men : for so there *Xerxes* numbered
over his Army. The Mouth of Hebrus : the Port of Stentor·
the free Town Ænea, with the Tomb of *Polydorus ;* the
Region, sometime, of the Cicones. From Doriscus, the
Coast bendeth to Macron-Tichos for 122 Miles. About
which Place the River Melas, from which the Bay taketh its
Name. Towns, Cypsella, Bisanthè, and that which is called
Macron-Tichos, whence stretching forth the Walls from Propontis to the Bay Melanes, between two Seas, it excludeth
Cherronesus as it runneth out. For Thracia, on one Side,
beginning at the Sea-coast of Pontus, where the River Ister
is discharged, hath in that Quarter the very beautiful Cities,
Istropolis of the Milesii, Tomi, and Calatis, which before
was called Acernetis. It had Heraclea and Bizon, which
was destroyed in a Chasm of the Earth ; now it hath Dionysopolis, formerly called Crunos. The River Ziras runneth by
it. All that Tract, the Scythians named Aroteres possessed.
Their Towns, Aphrodisius, Libistos, Zigerè, Borcobè, Eumenia, Parthenopolis, Gerania, where it is reported were the

[1] Or 100,000.

Nation of the Pygmei[1], whom the Barbarians call Catizi, and they believe that they were chased away by Cranes. In the Borders from Dionysopolis is Odessus of the Milesii; the River Pomiscus, the Town Tetranaulochos. the Mountain Hæmus bending down with a huge Top into Pontus, had in the Summit the Town Aristæum. Now in the Coast is Mesembria and Anchialum, where Messa was. The Region Asticè. There was the Town Anthium, now there is Apollonia. The Rivers Panissa, Rira, Tearus, Orosines. Towns, Thynnias, Almedessos, Develton, with the Marsh which now is called Deultum, belonging to the Veterans. Phinopolis, near which is Bosphorus. From the Mouth of Ister to the Entrance of Pontus others have made 555 Miles. *Agrippa* hath added 40 Miles more. From thence to the Wall above-named, 150: and from it to Cherronesus, 126. But from the Bosphorus is the Bay Gasthenes. The Port Senum, and another which is called the Port Mulierum. The Promontory Chrysoceras, whereon standeth the Town Bizantium of free Condition, and formerly called Lygos. From Dyrrhachium it is 711 Miles. Thus much lieth out the Length between the Adriatic Sea and Propontis Rivers, Bathynias, Pydaras, or Atyras. Towns, Selymbria, Perinthus, annexed to the Continent, 200 Paces broad. Within, Byzia, the Castle of the Thracian Kings, hated by Swallows[2] for the horrible Crime of *Tereus.* The Region Camica: the Colony Flaviopolus, where formerly the Town was called Zela. And 50 Miles from Byria, the Colony Apros, which is from Philippi 188 Miles. But in the Borders, the River Erginus, where was the Town Gonos. And there you leave Lysimachia,

---

[1] The Pygmies are frequently spoken of by ancient writers, and the existence of the diminutive race was never doubted   We defer the particular consideration of the monstrous races of mankind to the 7th Book, c. 2, where they are all mentioned together, but the Pygmies appear to have attracted more of the imagination of the poets than any of the others. The origin of their royal tyrant, the crane, is referred to by Ovid, "Metamorphoses," b vi — *Wern. Club*

[2] See the story of Tereus, Procnè, and Philomela, in Ovid's "Metamorphoses," lib. vi.—*Wern. Club.*

now in Cherronesus.   For there is another Isthmus of like
Straightness, of the same Name, and of equal Breadth.
On both Sides two Cities beautify the Shores, which they
hold in a Manner not unlike : Pactiæ from Propontis, and
Cardia from the Bay Melanè . this taketh its Name from the
Appearance of the Place : and both, afterwards, were en-
closed within Lysimachia, three Miles from the long Walls[1].
Cherronesus from Propontis had Tiristasis and Crithotes,
also Cissa, upon the River Ægos : now it hath from the
Colony Apros 32 Miles ; Resistos, over against the Colony
Pariana.   And Hellespontus, dividing Europe from Asia by
seven Stadia (as we have said), hath four Cities, opposite one
against another : in Europe, Calippolis and Sestos ; in Asia,
Lampsacum and Abydos   Then, is the Promontory of Cherronesus, called Mastisia, opposite to Sigeum, in the crooked
Front whereof is Cynossema : for so is *Hecuba's* Tomb
named, the Station of the Achæi.   The Tower and Shrine
of *Protesilaus ·* and in the utmost Front of Cherronesus,
which is called Æolium, the Town Elæus.   After it, as a
Man goeth to the Bay Melanè, the Port Cælos, Panhormus,
and the above-named Cardia.   The third Bay of Europe is in
this Manner shut in   Mountains of Thracia above those
before rehearsed, Edonus, Gigemorus, Meritus, and Melam-
phyllon, Rivers falling into Hebrus, Bargus, and Suemus.
The Length of Macedonia, Thracia, and Hellespontus, is set
down before   Some make it 720 Miles.   The Breadth is 380
Miles.   The Sea Ægeum took that Name from a Rock, between Tenedos and Chios, more truly than from an Island
named Æx, resembling a Goat, and therefore so called of the
Greeks ; which suddenly riseth out of the midst of the Sea
The People that sail from Achaia to Andros, discover it on
the right Hand, dreadful and mischievous.   Part of the
Ægean Sea is given to Myrtoum, and is so called from a
little Island which sheweth itself to them that sail from
Gerestus to Macedonia, not far from Charystos in Eubœa.
The Romans comprehend all these Seas in two Names :

[1] Macron-Tichos.

Macedonicum, all that which toucheth Macedonia and
Thracia : and Græciensum, where it beateth upon Greece.
For the Greeks divide the Ionian Sea, into Siculum and
Creticum, from the Islands.   Also, Icarius (they call that),
between Samos and Mycionus.   The other Names are given
by Bays, of which we have spoken.   And thus much, indeed,
of the Seas and Nations contained in this Manner within the
third Bay of Europe.

<h2 style="text-align:center">CHAPTER XII.</h2>

Islands between those Lands, among which, Creta, Euboea,
Cyclades, and Sporades: also, of Hellespont, Pontus,
Maeotis, Dacia, Sarmatia, and Scythia

ISLANDS over against Thresprotia, Corcyra : 12 Miles from
Buthrotus, and the same from Acroceraunia, 50 Miles, with
a City of the same Name, Corcyra, of free Condition ; also,
the Town Cassiopè, and the Temple of *Jupiter Cassiopæus*.
it lieth out in Length 97 Miles.   *Homer* called it Scheria
and Phæacia: *Callimachus* also, Drepanè.   About it are
some others : but verging toward Italy, Thoronos   and toward Leucadia, the two Paxæ, five Miles divided from Corcyra.   And not far from them before Corcyra, Ericusa,
Maratè, Elaphusa, Malthacè, Trachiæ, Pytionia, Ptychia,
Tarachiè.   And beyond Pholachrum, a Promontory of Corcyra,
the Rock into which it is feigned that the Ship of *Ulysses* was
turned, on Account of its Resemblance.   Before Leucadia,
Sybota.   But between Leucadia and Achaia there are very
many : of which are Teleboides, the same as Taphiæ   of the
Inhabitants before Leucadia, they are called Taphias ; Oxiæ
and Prinoessa : and before Ætolia, the Echinades, Ægialia,
Cotonis, Thyatira, Geoaris, Dionysia, Cyrnus, Chalcis,
Pinara, and Mystus   Before them in the deep Sea, Cepha-
lenia and Zacynthus, both free States.   Ithaca, Dulichium,
Samè, Crocylea, and Paxos.   Cephalenia, formerly called
Melæna is 11 Miles off, and 44 Miles in Circuit.   Samè was
destroyed by the Romans   nevertheless, it hath still three
Towns : between it and Achaia is Zacynthus, with a Town, a

stately Island, and remarkably fertile.   In Times past it was
called Hyriè, and is 22 Miles distant from the South-coast of
Cephalenia.   The famous Mountain of Elatus is there   The
Island itself is in Circuit 25 Miles.   Twelve Miles from it is
Ithaca, wherein is the Mountain Neritus.   And in the whole
it taketh up the Compass of 25 Miles   From it 12 Miles off
is Araxum, a Promontory of Peloponnesus.   Before this, in
the main Sea, Asteris and Protè.   Before Zacynthus, 35
Miles in the Wind Eusus, are the Strophades, called by
others, Plotæ : and before Cephalenia, Letoia   Before Pylos,
three Sphagiæ, and as many before Messenè, called Œnussæ.
In the Bay Asinæus, three Thyrides   in the Laconian Gulf,
Teganusa, Cothon, Cythera, with the Town formerly named
Porphyris.   This lieth five Miles from the Promontory of
Malea, doubtful for Ships to come about it, by Reason of the
Straits there.   In the Argolic Sea are Pityusa, Irinè and
Ephyrè : and against the Territory Hermonium, Typarenus,
Epiropia, Colonis, Aristera.   over against Trœzenium Ca-
lauria, half a Mile from Platcæ : also, Belbina, Lacia and
Baucidias.   Against Epidaurus, Cecryphalos, and Pytionesos,
six Miles from the Continent.   Next to it is Ægina, of free
Condition, 17 Miles off, and the Navigation of it is 20 Miles
about.   The same is distant from Pyræeum, the Port of the
Athenians, 12 Miles, and in old Time it was usually called
Œnonè.   Over against the Promontory Spiræum, lie Eleusa,
Dendios, two Craugiæ, two Cæciæ, Selachusa, Cenchreis, and
Aspis.   Also, in the Megarian Bay, there are four Methu-
rides.   But Ægilia is 15 Miles from Cythera ; and the same
is from Phalasarna, a Town in Creta, 25 Miles.   And Creta
itself, lying with one Side to the South, and the other to the
North, stretcheth forth in Length East and West ; famous
and noble for 100 Cities.   *Dosiades* saith it took that Name
from the Nymph *Creta*, Daughter of *Hesperis*. but according
to *Anaximander*, from a King of the Curetes   *Philistides*,
Mallotes, *Crates*, have thought it was called first Æria, and
afterwards Curetis, and some have thought it was named
Macaros, on Account of the excellent Temperature of the
Air.   In Breadth it exceedeth in no Place 50 Miles, and in

the middle Part it is broadest: in Length it is full 270
Miles: in Circuit, 589 Miles: and bending itself into the
Cretic Sea, so called from it, where it stretcheth out furthest
Eastward, it putteth forth the Promontory Sammonium,
opposite Rhodos; and Westward, Criu-Metopon, toward
Cyrenæ. The principal Towns are Phalasarnæ, Elæa, Cysa-
mum, Pergamum, Cydon, Minoum, Apteron, Pantoma-
trium, Amphimalla, Rhythymna, Panhormum, Cyteum,
Apollonia, Matium, Heraclea, Miletos, Ampelos, Hiera-
pytna, Lebena, Hierapolis. And in the midland Parts, Cor-
tyna, Phæstum. Gnossus, Potyrrhenium, Myrina, Lycastus,
Rhamnus, Lyctus, Dium, Asum, Pyloros, Rhytion, Clatos,
Phalæ. Holopyxos, Lasos[1], Eleuthernæ, Therapnè, Mara-
thusa, Mytinos. And other Towns to about the Number of
60 stand yet upon Record. The Mountains: Cadiscus,
Idæus, Dictæus, and Morycus. The Isle itself, from the
Promontory in it called Criu-Metopon, as *Agrippa* reporteth,
is distant from Phycus, a Promontory of the Cyrenæ, 225
Miles. Likewise to Capescum from Malea in Peloponnesus,
it is 80 Miles. From the Island Carpathus, from the Promontory Sammonia, in the Favonian Wind, 60 Miles. This
Island lieth between it and Rhodos. The Rest about it are
these: before Peloponnesus two Coricæ, and as many Mylæ,
and on the North Side, with Creta on the right Hand, there
appeareth Leucè over against Cydonia, with the two Budoræ;
against Matium, Cia against the Promontory Itanum Onisa
and Leucè: against Hierapytna, Chrysa, and Caudos. In
the same Tract are Ophiussa, Butoa, and Rhamnus: and
doubling Criu-Metopon, the Isles called Musagores. Before
the Promontory Sammonium, Phocæ, Platiæ, Sirnides, Nau-
lochos, Armedon, and Zephyrè. But in Hellas, yet still in
Ægeum, Lichades, Scarphia, Maresa, Phocaria, and very
many more over against Attica; but without Towns, and
therefore obscure: but against Eleusina, the noble Salamis,

---

[1] Dr Bloomfield ("Recens Synop" *in loco*) thinks this place was the
Lasea of Acts xxvii 8. Pliny makes it an inland town, but by inland
towns he only means such as were not ports, and that Lasea was not a
port is clear, the Fair Havens being its port — *Wern Club.*

and before it Psytalia · and from Sunium, Helenè, five Miles off : and Ceos, from thence as many ; which our Countrymen have named Cæa , but the Greeks Hydrussa cut off from Eubœa. In Times past it was 500 Stadia long : but soon after, almost four Parts, which verged towards Bœotia, were devoured by the same Sea : and now the Towns remaining are Julis and Carthæa. For Coressus and Pæcessa are perished. From hence, as *Varro* saith, came the more delicate Dress that Women use. Eubœa itself hath been torn from Bœotia, being divided with so little a Euripus, that a Bridge joineth the one to the other it is well marked by Reason of two Promontories in the South Side, which are, Genestum, bending toward Attica ; and Caphareus to Hellespontus : and upon the North Side, Cæneus. In no Part doth it extend broader than 40 Miles ; and no where doth it contract beyond 20. But in Length from Attica, as far as Thessalia, it lieth along Bœotia for 150 Miles , and containeth in Circuit 365. From Hellespont, on the Part of Caphareus, it is 225 Miles. In Times past it was illustrious for these Cities : Pyrrha, Porthmos, Nesos, Cerinthus, Oreum, Dium, Ædepsum, Ocha, Œchalia, now Calcis, over against which standeth Aulis on the Continent : but now noble for Gerestum, Eretria, Carystus, Oritanum, Artemisium, the Fountain Arethusa, the River Lelantum, the hot Waters called Hellopiæ ; but yet more known for the Marble of Carystus. In former Time it was called commonly Chalcodontis or Macris, as *Dionysius* and *Ephorus* say ; but Macra, according to *Aristides :* and according to *Callidemus,* Chalcis, from the Brass there first found : and as *Menœcmus* saith, Abantias : and Asopis, as the Poets commonly name it Beyond, in the Myrtoom Sea, are many Isles, but those principally famous are Glauconnesus and Ægilia And from the Promontory Gerestum, about Delos, some lying in a Circle together, whence they took their Name Cyclades. The first of them, Andrus, with a Town, is from Gerestum, 10 Miles ; and from Ceum, 39. *Myrsilius* saith it was called Cauros, and afterwards Antandros *Callimachus* nameth it Lasia, others Nonagria, Hydrussa, and Epagris. It lieth in Compass 93 Miles. A Mile from the same Andros, and 15 from

Delos, lieth Tenos, with a Town stretched out 15 Miles in
Length which, for the Plenty of Water, *Aristotle* saith, was
called Hydrussa, but others name it Ophiussa The Rest are
these: Myconos, with the Mountain Dimastos, 15 Miles
from Delos. Scyros Syphnus, formerly named Meropia and
Acis, in Circuit 28 Miles: Seriphus, 12 Miles, Præpesinthus,
Cythnus. And Delos itself, of all others the most illustrious,
the midmost of the Cyclades, celebrated for the Temple of
Apollo, and for Merchandise; which, having a long Time
floated up and down (as it is reported), was the only Island
that never felt an Earthquake [1] unto the Time of *M. Varro*
Mutianus hath recorded that it was twice shaken. *Aristotle*
giveth a Reason of the Name in this Sort, because it was
produced and discovered on a sudden. *Æglosthenes* termeth
it Cynthia · others Ortygia, Asteria, Lagia, Chlamydia,
Cynethus, and Pyrpilè; because in it Fire was first found
out. It is but five Miles about, and riseth up by the Mountain Cinthus. Next to it is Rhenè, which *Anticlides* calleth
Celadussa, and *Helladius*, Artemitè. Moreover, Syros, which
ancient Writers have reported to be in Circuit 20 Miles,
and Mutianus, 160. Oliatos, Paros, with a Town, 38 Miles
from Delos, of great Name for white Marble, which at
first they called Pactia, but afterwards Minois From it
seven and a half Miles is Naxus, 18 Miles from Delos;
with a Town, which they called Strongylè, afterwards Dia,
soon after Dionysius, from its Fertility of Vines, and by
others, Sicily the Less, and Callipolis It reacheth in Circuit 75 Miles, and is half as long again as Paros. And thus
far, indeed, they note for the Cyclades: the Rest that follow,
for the Sporades. And these are Helenum, Phocussa, Phæ-
casia, Schinussa, Phalegandros; and 17 Miles from Naxos,
Icaros · which gave Name to the Sea, lying out as far in
Length, with two Towns, for the third is lost. beforetime
it was called Dolichum, Macris, and Ichtyœssa · It is situated

---

[1] Thucydides, book ii, says "There was also a little before the time
of the Peloponnesian war, an earthquake at Delos, which, in the memory
of the Grecians, never shook before, and was interpreted for, and seemed
to be a sign of, what was to come afterwards to pass"— Hobbes.— *Wern*
Club

North-east, from Delos 50 Miles · and from Samos it is 35
Miles. Between Eubœa and Andros there is a Strait 12
Miles over. From it to Gerestum is 112½ Miles. And then
no Order forward can be kept; the Rest, therefore, shall be
set down promiscuously. Ios from Naxos is 24 Miles, vene-
rable for the Sepulchre of *Homer* it is in Length 25 Miles,
and in former Time was called Phænicè. Odia, Letandros;
Gyaros, with a Town, in Circuit 12 Miles It is distant from
Aneros, 62 Miles. From thence to Syrnus, 80 Miles Cyne-
thussa, Telos, famous for costly Ointment, and called by
Callimachus, Agathussa. Donysa; Pathmos, in Circuit 30
Miles. Corasiæ, Lebinthus, Leros, Cynara, Sycinus, which
beforetime was Œnœ, Heratia, the same as Onus; Casus,
otherwise Astrabè; Cimolus, otherwise Echinussa; Melos,
with a Town, which *Aristides* nameth Byblis; *Aristotle,* Ze-
phyria; *Callimachus,* Himallis, *Heraclides,* Syphnus and
Acytos. And this, of all the Islands, is the roundest After it
Machia; Hyperè, sometime Patagè, or after some Platagè,
now Amorgos; Potyægos, Phylè, Thera; when it first
appeared, called Callistè. From it afterwards was Therasia
torn away. and between those two soon after arose Auto-
matè, the same as Hiera : and Thia, which in our Days
appeared new out of the Water near Hiera. Ios is from
Thera, 25 Miles Then follow Lea, Ascania, Anaphè, Hip-
puris, Hippurissusa. Astipalæa of free Condition, in Compass 88 Miles : it is from Cadiscus, a Promontory of Creta,
125 Miles. From it is Platea, distant 60 Miles. And from
thence Camina, 38 Miles. Then Azibnitha, Lanisè, Tragia,
Pharmacusa, Techedia, Chalcia, Calydna, in which are
the Towns Coos and Olymna From which to Carpathus,
which gave the Name to the Carpathian Sea, is 25 Miles :
and so to Rhodes with an African Wind. From Carpathus
to Casos, seven Miles : from Casos to Samonium, a
Promontory of Creta, 30 Miles. Moreover, in the Euboic
Euripus, almost at the first Entrance, are the four Islands,
Petaliæ; and at the Outlet, Atalantè, Cyclades, and Sporades: inclosed on the East with the Icarian Sea-coasts of
Asia; on the West, with the Myrtoan Coasts of Attica;

Northward, with the Ægean Sea; and South, with the Cretic
and Carphacian Seas and they lie in Length 200 Miles.
The Bay Pagasicus hath before it Eutychia, Cicynethus, and
Scyrus abovesaid: but the Outermost of the Cyclades and
Sporades, Gerontia, Scadira, Thermeusis, Irrhesia, Solinnia,
Eudemia, Nea, which is sacred to *Minerva*. Athos before
it hath four; Preparethus, with a Town, sometime called
Euonos, nine Miles off: Scyathus, five Miles: and Imbrus,
with a Town, 88 Miles off. The same is from Mastusia in
Corinthos, 75 Miles. Itself is in Circuit 72 Miles. It is
watered by the River Ilissus. From thence to Lemnos, 22
Miles · and the latter from Athos, 87. In Compass it con-
taineth 22½ Miles. Towns it hath, Hephæstia and Myrina,
into the Market-place of which the Mountain Athos casteth a
Shadow at the Solstice. Thassos, a free State, is from it five
Miles: in Times past, called Æria, or Æthria. From thence
Abdera in the Continent is 20 Miles: Athos, 62: the Isle
Samothracè as much, which is free, and lieth before Hebrus:
from Imbrus, 32 Miles: from Lemnus, 22½ Miles: from the
Borders of Thracia, 28 Miles in Circuit it is 32 Miles, and hath
a Rising of the Hill Saoces for the Space of 10 Miles · and
of all the Rest is fullest of Harbours. *Callimachus* calleth it
by the old Name Dardania: between Cherronesus and
Samothracè is Halomesus, about 15 Miles from either of
them · beyond lieth Gethronè, Lamponia, Alopeconnesus
not far from Cœlos, a Port of Cherronesus: and some
others of no importance. In this Bay are rehearsed also
the deserted Islands, of which the Names only can be discovered: Desticos, Larnos, Cyssicos, Carbrusa, Celathusa,
Scylla, Draconon, Arconesus, Diethusa, Scapos, Capheris,
Mesatè, Æantion, Phaterunesos, Pateria, Caletè, Neriphus,
and Polendus.

  The fourth of those great Bays in Europe, beginning
from Hellespont, endeth in the Mouth of Mœotis But we
are briefly to describe the Form of the whole Sea, that the
Parts may be more easily known The vast Ocean lying
before Asia, and driven out from Europe in that long Coast
of Cherronesus, breaketh into the Land with a narrow

Passage of seven Stadia (as hath been said) dividing Europe
from Asia. The first Straits they call Hellespontus. Over
this, *Xerxes*, King of the Persians, made a Bridge upon
Ships, and so led his Army across. From thence is extended
a small Euripus for the space of 86 Miles, to Priapus, a
City of Asia, where *Alexander* the Great passed over. From
that Place the Sea groweth wide, and again gathereth into
a Strait: the largeness is called Propontis; the Straits, the
Thracian Bosphorus, 500 Paces over : by which *Darius*, the
Father of *Xerxes*, made a Bridge and transported his Forces.
The whole Length from Hellespont is 239 Miles. From
thence the vast Sea called Pontus Euxinus, and in Times
past Axenus, taketh up the space between Lands far remote,
and with a great winding of the Shores, bendeth backward
into Horns, and lieth stretched out from them on both Sides,
resembling evidently a Scythian Bow. In the midst of this
bending, it joineth close to the Mouth of the Lake Mœotis.
That Mouth is called Cimmerius Bosphorus, two Miles and
a half Broad. But between the two Bosphori, Thracius and
Cimmerius, there is a direct Course, as *Polybius* saith, of
500 Miles. But the Circuit of all this Sea, as *Varro* and
almost all the old Writers witness, is 2150 Miles. *Nepos
Cornelius* addeth thereto 350 Miles. *Artemidorus* maketh
it 2919 Miles · *Agrippa*, 2360 Miles : *Mutianus*, 2865
Miles. In like sort, some have determined the Measure
to the Side of Europe to be 4078½ Miles: others, 11,072
Miles. *M Varro* taketh his Measure in this manner: from
the Mouth of Pontus to Apollonia, 188½ Miles: to Calatis,
as much : to the Mouth of Ister, 125 : to Borysthenes, 250 :
to Cherronesus, a Town of the Heracleates, 375 Miles : to
Panticapæus, which some call Bosphorus, the utmost Coast
of Europe, 222½ Miles : the sum of which makes 1336½ Miles.
Agrippa measureth, from Bizantium to the River Ister, 560
Miles : to Panticapæum, 630 : from thence the very Lake
Mœotis, receiving the River Tanais which runneth out of
the Riphæan Mountains, is supposed to be in Compass 1306
Miles ; being the furthest Bound between Europe and Asia.
Others make 11,025 Miles. But it is evident, that from its

Mouth to the Mouth of Tanais, by a straight Course, it is 375
Miles. The Inhabitants of that Bay have been named in
the mention of Thracia, as far as to Istropolis. From thence
the Mouths of Ister. This River riseth among the Hills of
Abnoba, a Mountain of Germany, over against Rauricum, a
Town in Gallia, and passing many Miles beyond the Alps, and
through innumerable Nations, under the Name of Danubius,
with a mighty increase of Waters, and whence he first beginneth to wash Illyricum taking the Name of Ister, after
he hath received 60 Rivers, and almost the one-half of them
navigable, rolleth into Pontus with six vast Streams. The
first Mouth of it is Peuce: soon after, the Island Peucè
itself, from which the next Channel took its name, and is
swallowed up in a great Marsh of 19 Miles. Out of the
same Channel, and above Astropolis, a Lake is produced of
63 Miles' compass; which they call Halmyris. The second
Mouth is called Naracustoma· the third, Calostoma, near
the Island Sarmatica: the fourth, Pseudostoma, and the
Island Conopon Diabasis. After that, Boreostoma, and
Spireostoma. Each of these is so great, that by Report
the Sea, for 40 Miles' length, is overmatched with the
same, and the fresh Water may so far be tasted. From it,
into the inland Parts, the People are all Scythians. but
various other Nations inhabit close on the Coasts: in some
Places the Getæ, called by the Romans Daci: in others the
Sarmatæ, by the Greeks Sauromatæ; and among them, the
Hamaxobii or Aorsi. Elsewhere the degenerate Scythians,
who are sprung from Servants, or the Troglodites. presently,
the Alani and Rhoxalani. But the higher Parts between Danubius and the Forest Hercynius, as far as to the Pannonian
wintering Places of Carnuntum, and the Confines there of
the Germans, the Fields and Plains of Jazygè, the Sar-
matians possess. But the Mountains and Forests, the Daci,
who were expelled by them, inhabit, as far as to the River
Parhyssus from Morus; or this is Duria, dividing them
from the Suevi and the Kingdom of Vanni. The Parts
against these the Bastarnæ hold; and from thence other
Germani. *Agrippa* hath set down that whole Tract, from

the Ister to the Ocean, as amounting to 2000 Miles, and
400 less in Breadth, from the Deserts of Sarmatia to the
River Vistula · the Name of Scythæ everywhere continually
runneth into Sarmatæ and Germani.   Neither hath that old
denomination remained in any others but those, who, as I
have said, live the furthest off of these Nations, almost
unknown to all other Men.   But the Towns next to the
Ister are Cremniscos and Æpolium · the Mountains Ma-
crocrennii   the noble River Tyra, giving Name to the Town,
whereas before time it was called Ophiusa.   Within the same
is a spacious Island, inhabited by the Tyragetæ.   It is from
Pseudostomum, a Mouth of the Ister, 130 Miles.   Soon
after are the Axiacæ, named after the River. beyond whom
are the Crobyzi : the River Rhodè · the Bay Sagaricus, and
the Port Ordesus.   And, 120 Miles from Tyra, is the River
Borysthenes, and a Lake and Nation of that Name :
and a Town 15 Miles within from the Sea, called by the
ancient Names Olbropolis and Miletopolis.   Again, on the
Shore, the Harbour of the Achæans : the Island of Achilles,
famous for the Tomb of that Man.   And from it 135 Miles,
is a Peninsula, lying out across in the Form of a Sword,
and called Dromos Achilleos, upon occasion of his Exercise
there : the Length of which *Agrippa* hath declared to be 80
Miles.   All that Tract, the Taurisci, Scythæ, and Sarmatæ
inhabit.   Then the woody Region gave the name to the Sea
Hylæum, by which it is encircled   The Inhabitants are called
Enæcadloæ.   Beyond is the River Panticapes, which divideth
the Nomades and Georgi : and soon after, Acesinus.   Some
say that Panticapè, with Borysthenes, run together beneath
Olbia, but the more exact name Hypanis : so much they
erred who have described it in a part of Asia.   The Sea
retires with a very great Ebb, until it is distant from Mœotis
with an interval of five Miles, compassing a vast Space, and
many Nations.   There is a Bay called Corcinites, and a
River Pacyris   Towns, Naubarum and Carcinè.   Behind
is the Lake Buges, let out into the Sea by a foss.   And
(Buges) itself is disjoined from Coretus, a Bay of the Lake
Mœotis, by a rocky Back.   It receiveth the Rivers Buges,

Gerrhus, Hypanis, coming from different quarters : for
Gerrhus parteth the Basilides and Nomades   Hypanis
floweth through the Nomades and the Hyleans into Buges,
by a Channel made by Man's Hand, but in his natural
Channel into Coretus. The Region of Scythia is named
Sendica. But in Carcinites, Taurica beginneth : which in
Times past was environed with the Sea, where now there
lie Fields : afterwards it mounteth up with very great Hills.
Thirty People are in it : and of them 24 are within Land.
Six Towns, Orgocyni, Caraseni, Assyrani, Tractari, Archi-
lachitæ, and Caliordi.   The Crest of the Hill the Scytotauri
hold.   They are shut in Westward by Cherronesus ; East-
ward by the Scythian Satarchi.   In the Coast from Car-
cinites are these Towns : Taphræ, in the very Straits of the
Peninsula : then, Heraclea, Cherronesus, endowed with
Liberty by the Romans.   Formerly it was called Megaricè,
and is the most Elegant in all that Tract, as retaining the
Manners of the Greeks ; and it is encompassed with a Wall
of five Miles' extent.   Then the Promontory Parthenium.
A City of the Tauri, Placia   The Harbour Symbolon : the
Promontory Criu-Metopon, over against Charambes, a Promontory of Asia, running through the middle of Euxinus
for the space of 170 Miles : which is the cause especially
that maketh the Form abovesaid of a Scythian Bow.   Near
to it are many Harbours and Lakes of the Tauri.   The
Town Theodosia, distant from Criu-Metopon 122 Miles, and
from Cherronesus 165 Miles.   Beyond, there have been
the Towns Cytè, Zephyrium, Acrè, Nymphæum, and Dia
And by far the strongest of them all remaineth still in the
very entrance of Bosphorus, namely, Panticapæum of the
Milesians, from Theodosia 1035 Miles : but from Cim-
merum, a Town situated beyond the Strait, a Mile and a half,
as we have said.   And this is all the Breadth there that
divideth Asia from Europe : and even that is for the most
part passable on Foot, when the Strait is frozen over.   The
Breadth of Bosphorus Cimmerius is 12 Miles.   It hath the
Towns Hermisium, Myrmecium ; and within it, the Island
Alopecè.   But through Mœotis, from the furthest part of

the Isthmus, which Place is called Taphræ, to the Mouth of
Bosphorus, it containeth 260 Miles. From Taphræ, the
Continent within is inhabited by the Anchetæ, among whom
the Hypanis springeth : and Neuri, where Borysthenes hath
his Head ; also, the Geloni, Thussagetæ, Budini, Basilidæ,
and the Agathyrsi, with blue Hair on their Heads. Above
them, the Nomades , and then the Anthropophagi. From
Buges, above Mœotis, the Sauromates and Essedones dwell.
But along the Borders, as far as Tanais, the Mœotæ, from
whom the Lake was so called , and the last behind them,
the Arimaspi. Within a little are the Riphæan Mountains,
and a Country called Pterophoros, for the resemblance of
Wings (Feathers[1]) occasioned by the continual fall of
Snow : a Part of the World condemned by the nature of
Things, and immersed in thick Darkness, having no shelter-
ing Places but the work of Cold, the produce of the freezing
North Wind.   Behind those Mountains, and beyond the
North Pole, there is a happy Nation (if we may believe it)
whom they call Hyperborei[2], who live exceeding long, and

[1] " A race of men there are, as fame has told,
  Who shivering suffer Hyperborean cold,
  Till nine times bathing in Minerva's lake
  Soft feathers, to defend their naked sides, they take "
  DRYDEN's *Ovid. Metam.* lib. xv.

Herodotus, Melpo 31, says· " In respect to the feathers wherewith
the Scythians affirm the air to be filled, my opinion is this· above that
country snow falls continually, now any one that has seen snow falling
thick, and close to himself, must understand what I say The snow does, in
fact, bear great resemblance to feathers. I think, therefore, that the
Scythians and the surrounding nations compare the snow to feathers.—
LAURENT —*Wern Club.*

[2] The ancients denominated those people and places Hyperborean
which were to the northward of the Scythians They had, indeed, but
very little acquaintance with these regions ; and all they tell us of them
is very precarious, while much of it is false Herodotus, as well as Pliny,
doubts whether or not there were any such nations ; while Strabo professes to believe that they really existed See a very amusing account of
these fabulous Hyperboreans in Herodotus, Melpo. 32–36 From whence
much that Pliny says was borrowed —*Wern. Club.*

are celebrated for fabulous Wonders. There are believed to
be the Poles of the World, and the very Ends of the revo-
lution of the Heavens, having for six Months together one
entire Day, and Night as long, when the Sun is turned from
them: but their Day is not from the Spring Equinox (as
the Ignorant say) to the Autumn for once in the Year, at
the Solstice, the Sun riseth with them · and once likewise
it setteth in Mid-winter. The Region is open to the Sun,
of a happy Temperature, void of all hurtful impulse of Air.
The Woods are their Habitations, and the Groves where
they worship the Gods Man by Man, and in Companies:
Discord and all Disease are unknown, and they never die,
but when they are satiated with Life · when the aged Men,
having feasted and anointed their bodies, leap from a certain
Rock into the Sea. This kind of Sepulture is the most happy.
Some Writers have placed them in the first Part of the Sea-
coast in Asia, and not in Europe, because some are there resembling them in manners and situation, named Atocori,
others have set them in the midst, between both Suns, that
is, the Setting of it with the Antipodes, and the Rising of it
with us: which cannot possibly be, so vast a Sea lying
between. Those that have placed them nowhere but in the
six Months' daylight, have written of them, that they sow in
the Morning, reap at Noon, at Sunset gather the Fruits from
the Trees, and by Night lie within Caves. Neither may we
make doubt of that Nation, since so many Authors testify,
that they were accustomed to send their first Fruits to
Delos, to *Apollo*, whom they chiefly worship. They were
Virgins that conveyed these Fruits; who for certain Years
were venerated and entertained by all Nations, until, upon
breach of Faith, they appointed to bestow those sacred ob-
lations in the next Borders of their Neighbours: and these
again to convey them to those that bordered upon them, and
so on as far as to Delos: and, soon after, this custom wore
out. The Length of Sarmatia, Scythia, and Taurica, and of all
that Tract from the River Borysthenes, is 980 Miles, the
Breadth 717, as *M. Agrippa* hath delivered it. But I judge

that the Measure of this Part of the Earth is uncertain.
But after the appointed Order, the remainder of this Gulf
may be spoken of; and we have already shewn the Seas of it.

CHAPTER XIII.

The Islands of Pontus.

HELLESPONT hath no Islands to be spoken of in Europe.
In Pontus are two, a Mile and a half from Europe, and 14
Miles from the Mouth: Cyaneæ, of others called Symplegades: and by Report of Fables, they ran one into another:
because they being severed by a small Space, to them that
enter the Sea full upon them they seemed a Pan: but if
the Eye be a little turned aside, they made a Show as if they
met together   On this Side the Ister there is one, pertaining
to the Apolloniates, 80 Miles from Bosphorus Thracius. out
of which *M. Lucullus* brought *Apollo Capitolinus*[1]. What
were within the Mouths of the Ister we have declared already. Before Borysthenes is the above-named Achillea, and
the same is called Leucè and Macaron. This the modern
demonstration places 140 miles from Borysthenes: from
Tyra, 120: from the Island Peucè, 50. It is in Compass
about ten Miles. The rest are in the Bay Carcinites. Ce-
phalonnesos, Rhosphodusa, and Macra. I cannot pass by
the Opinion of many Writers, before we depart from Pontus,
who have thought that all the inland Seas arise from that
head, and not from the Straits of Gades, and they lay for
their argument, not without some probability, because out
of Pontus the Tide always floweth, and never returneth.

But now we are to depart thence, that other Parts of

---

[1] Apollonia was a colony of the Milesians in Thrace, the greatest
part of whose chief town was situated in a small island in the Euxine,
and contained a temple dedicated to Apollo   The colossal statue of the
god which Lucullus is said to have removed from thence, and placed in
the Capitol at Rome, is described by Pliny (lib xxxiv c 7), as being 30
cubits high, and costing 500 talents   After its removal, it acquired the
name of Apollo Capitolinus.—(*Note*. HOLLAND's Translation says 150
talents only.)—*Wern Club*

Europe may be spoken of; and passing the Riphæan Mountains, we must proceed along the Shore of the Northern Ocean to the left, until we come to Gades. In which Tract there are reported to be very many Islands without Names, of which, by the Report of *Timæus*, there is one before Scythia called Bannomanna, distant from Scythia one Day's Sailing, into which, in the Time of Spring, Amber is cast up by the Waves. The other Coasts are of uncertain Report. The North Ocean from the River Paropamisus, where it washeth Scythia, *Hecatæus* nameth Amalchium, which Word, in the language of that Nation, signifieth Frozen. *Philemon* writeth, that the Cimbrians call it Morimarusa, that is *Mortuum Mare* [the Dead Sea], even as far as to the Promontory Rubeæ: then beyond, Cronium. *Xenophon Lampsacenus* saith, That in three Days' sailing from the Scythian Coast there is the Island Baltia, of exceeding magnitude The same doth *Pythias* name Basilia. There are reported the Isles Oonæ, wherein the Inhabitants live on Birds' Eggs and Oats. Others also, wherein men are born with the Feet of Horses, and called Hippopodes. Others of the Panoti[1], who, being otherwise naked, have immensely great Ears that cover their whole Bodies. Then begins a clearer Report to open from the Nation of the Ingevoni, the first of the Germans in those Parts. There is the exceeding great Mountain Sevo, not inferior to the high Crags of Riphæus, which maketh a very large Gulf, as far as to the Cimbrians' Promontory, called Codanus, and it is full of Islands, of which the most celebrated is Scandinavia, the Magnitude whereof is not yet discovered. A Part only thereof, as much as is known, the Nation of Helleviones inhabiteth, in 500 Villages: and they call it a second World, and as it is thought Enigia is not less. Some say, that these Parts, as far as to the River Vistula, are inhabited by the Sarmati, Veneti, Scyri, and Hirri : also that

---

[1] Some editions read Fanesii, but Panoti seems the more correct; for as the Oonæ were so called in consequence of their living on *eggs*, and the Hippopodes because they had *horses' feet*, so the Panoti derived their name from having *immensely great ears that covered their whole bodies*

the Gulf of the Sea is called Clylipenus: and that in the Mouth of it is the Island Latris. Also that not far from it, there is another Bay bounding upon the Cimbri. The Promontory of the Cimbrians shooting far into the Seas, maketh a Peninsula, which is called Cartris. Thence three-and-twenty Islands are known by the Roman Armies. The noblest of them are Burchana, called by our countrymen Fabaria, from the Plenty of Vegetables growing there unsown. Likewise Glessaria, so called by the Soldiers from Amber; but by the Barbarians, Austrania; and besides them Actania. Along this Sea, until you come to the River Scaldis, the German Nations inhabit · but the Measure of that Tract can scarcely be declared, such very great Discord there is among Writers   The Greeks and some of our own Writers have described the Coast of Germany to be 2500 Miles. *Agrippa* again, joining with it Rhætia and Noricum, saith, that it is in Length 686 miles, and in Breadth 268.   And of Rhætia alone, the Breadth is almost greater, at least at the time that it was subdued, and the People departed out of Germany   for Germany was discovered many years after, and is not all, even now.   But if it be permitted to guess, there will not be much wanting in the Coasts, from the opinion of the Greeks; nor in the Length as set down by *Agrippa*

CHAPTER XIV.

Germania.

Of Germans, there are five Kinds; the Vindili, a part of whom are the Burgundiones, Varini, Carini, and Gurtones. A second kind, the Ingævones, part of whom are the Cimbri, Teutoni, and the Nations of the Cauchi.   The Istævones are the nearest to the Rhine (Rhenus), and part of them are the Cimbri.   Then the Midland Hermiones, among whom are the Suevi, Hermunduri, Chatti, and Cherusci.   The fifth part are the Peucini, and Basternæ, bordering upon the abovenamed Dacæ.   Notable Rivers that run into the Ocean; Guttalus, Vistillus or Vistula, Albis, Visurgis, Ami-

sius, Rhenus, Mosa. And within, the Hircynium Hill,[1] inferior to none in estimation, is stretched forward.

Chapter XV.

Islands in the Gallic Ocean.

In the Rhine itself, for almost an hundred Miles in
Length, is the most noble Island of the Batavi, Cannenu-
fates; and others of the Frisii, Cauchi, Frisiaboni, Sturii,
and Marsatii, which are spread between Helius and Flevus
For so are the Mouths called, into which Rhenus, as it gushes,
scatters itself: from the North into Lakes; from the West
into the River Mosa. But in the middle Mouth between
these, he keepeth a small Channel, of his own name.

Chapter XVI.

Britannia and Hybernia—England and Ireland.[2]

Over against this Tract lieth the Island Britannia, between the North and West; renowned in Greek and Roman

[1] The Hercynian Hill (jugum) is elsewhere called the Hercynian
Forest (saltus).

Although Pliny had served with the army in Germany, and had
written a history of the war in which he was engaged, yet he makes no
mention, in this work, of any city or region of that country, a proof
that the celebrity of a place as estimated at Rome, was the measure of its
importance with him *— Wern Club*

[2] Different suggestions have been offered in explanation of the word
"Britannia." By some it has been supposed to be derived from the British
word "Brithy"—painted; from a practice by the inhabitants of staining
their skin of a blue colour with woad, to render themselves formidable to
their enemies. But a name thence derived would only be applied by
strangers, who would not have selected a word foreign to their own language to express the custom   It is more likely, therefore, to have been
derived from a foreign source; and it is Bochart's opinion that it was
first applied by the Phœnicians, in whose language the word "Baratanac"
signifies the land of tin   the chief produce which tempted these adven-
turous merchants to visit this country, and make settlements in its most
western extremity, at a very remote period   The word became afterwards translated into the Greek name " Cassiterides," which was applied by

Records.   It is opposite to Germania, Gallia, and Hispania, the greatest Parts by far of Europe, and no small Sea lying between.   Albion was its Name, when all the Islands were called Britanniæ, of which by and by we will speak.   This (Island) is from Gessoriacum, a Coast of the Nation of the Morini, 50 Miles by the nearest Passage.   In Circuit, as *M. Pytheas* and *Isidorus* report, it containeth 3825 Miles.   And now for about 30 Years the Roman Armies growing into further knowledge, yet have not penetrated beyond the neighbour-

the latter people, more particularly to the Scilly Islands and the County of Cornwall   Albion was more properly the Roman name of the country, and was probably derived from its white appearance, as seen on their approach to it from Gaul   This latter name was retained in official documents, even under the Saxon dominion, as appears from a charter of Æthelred in the 10th century, in which he terms himself " Ego Æthelredus, totius Albionis, Dei gubernante moderamine, Basileus " and ending, " Ego Æthelredus Rex Anglorum "—Hearne's *Leland*, vol. ii.

As natives of the British Islands, we cannot but regret that, while the Author has been so minute in the mention of places lying round the borders of the Mediterranean Sea, he has passed over with neglect the regions and towns of Britain and Ireland, as well as those of the north of Europe.   Although his knowledge of these was probably limited, the omission can scarcely have proceeded from ignorance alone, for Suetonius informs us, that the Emperor Vespasian, who was the great patron of Pliny, had subdued twenty cities in Britain, together with the Isle of Wight, and we cannot suppose that Pliny remained unacquainted with the names of any of them   In another place he names Camelodunum, which is believed to be Doncaster, as a station sufficiently known, from which to measure the distance to the Island Mona, or Anglesea; and the city of the Trinobantes had been previously mentioned by Julius Cæsar.   His distribution of the islands lying round Britain is contradictory as well as obscure, but he appears to regard all that are situated west of the ordinary place of passage from the Continent into Britain, (Gessoriacum, which is probably Boulogne on the one side, and the British port of the Morini, whether Dover or Folkestone,) as being necessarily situated between Britain and Ireland   Vectis is admitted to be the Isle of Wight, but by some authors the same name is given to an island to which tin was carried from Cornwall in carts, and from which it was afterwards exported.   From a comparison of ancient authors, Sir Christopher Hawkins was persuaded that this could be no other that St Michael's Mount, in Cornwall, and the argument urged against this supposition, built on the tradition that it once stood within the land, and was surrounded by

hood of the Caledonian Forest. *Agrippa* believeth that it is in Length 800 miles, and in Breadth 300; and also that Ireland is as broad, but not so long by 200 Miles. This Island is seated above it, and but a very short Passage distant; 30 Miles from the Nation of Silures. Of the other Islands there is none, by report, in Compass more than 125 Miles   But there are the Orcades 40, divided from each other by small spaces: Acmodæ 7, and 30 Hæbrides. Also between Britannia and Hibernia are Mona, Monapia, Ricnea,

a wood, may be answered by believing that these facts refer to very different ages of the world   The Mictis of Pliny may be this Cornish island ; his error in the distance having arisen from confounding the place of export for tin with the islands producing it   To the latter, or Scilly Islands, it appears the Britons were accustomed to sail in their wicker boats covered with leather, or coracles , a mode of navigation perhaps not less secure than the somewhat similar vessels at present in use among the Greenlanders   That they were capable of a considerable voyage appears from the fact, that they have been employed in crossing the channel from Armorica to Cornwall so late as about the 7th century   It must have been from misinformation that Pliny assigns the Cassiterides (Chap XXII.) to Spain, but even this great error may be excused, by recollecting that in a preceding age the merchants had succeeded in concealing the situation of this Cornish group from the inquiry of Julius Cæsar, when he was tempted to invade the seat of pearls and tin , and that Cadiz was the Continental port, from which this profitable intercourse with Cornwall and Scilly had from the remotest ages been carried on.

The Islands mentioned by Pliny may be judged the following —

Orcades .	Orkneys
Acmodæ .	probably Zetland
Hæbredes, Hæbrides	Western Islands
Mona . .	Anglesea
Monapia, Monuædia, and by others *Menavia,* Isle of Man.	
Ricnea, qu *Ricina* ? .	Birdsey, between Wales and Ireland
Vectis	Isle of Wight
Silumnus .	?
Andros .	?
Siambis . .	?
Axantos .	?
Mictis . . .	St. Michael's Mount
Glessariæ } *Electrides* }	Nordstant, in the German Sea

Wern. Club

Vectis, Silimnus, and Andros : but beneath Siambis and Axantos. and on the contrary side, toward the German Sea, there lie scattered the Glessariæ, which the later Greek Writers have named Electrides, because Amber was produced there. The farthest of all, which are spoken of, is Thulè , in which there are no Nights, as we have declared, at the Solstice, when the Sun passeth through the Sign Cancer , and on the other hand no Days in Midwinter ; and each of these Times they supposed to last Six Months. *Timæus* the Historiographer saith, That farther within, at Six Days' sailing from Britannia, is the Island Mictis, in which White Lead is produced, and that the Britanni sail thither in Wicker Vessels, sewed round with Leather   Some make mention of others, as Scandia, Dumna, and Bergos , and the biggest of all, Nerigos ; from which Men sail to Thulè.   Within one Day's Sail from Thulè is the Frozen Sea, named by some Cronium.

Chapter XVII

Gallia.

A ll Gallia, by one Name called Comata, is divided into three Kinds of People, and those for the most part divided one from the other by Rivers. Belgica, from Scaldis to Sequana : Celtica, from it to Garumna , and this Part of Gallia is also named Lugdunensis. From thence to the lying out of the Mountain Pyrenæus, Aquitania, formerly called Aremorica. *Agrippa* hath made this Computation of all the Galliæ lying between Rhenus, Pyrenæus, the Ocean, and the Mountains Gebenna and Jura ; whereby he excludeth Narbonensis Gallia ; in Length 420 Miles, and in Breadth 313. Next to Scaldis, the Toxandri inhabit the utmost Borders, under many Names. Then the Menapii, Morini, and Oromansaci ; joining upon that District which is called Gessoriacus, the Brinanni, Ambiani, Bellonici, and Hassi. Within, the Castologi, Atrebates, and the free Nervii. The Veromandui, Sueconi, and free Suessiones, free Ulbanectes, Tungri, Rinuci, Frisiabones, Betasi, free Leuci. The Treviri, free formerly: the Lingones Confederates: the Remi Confederate: the Mediomatrici, the Sequani, the Raurici, and Helvetii. Colonies, Equestris and Rauriaca. But, of German Nations in the same Province, that dwell near the Rhenus, the Nemetes, Tribochi, and Vangiones: then the Ubii, Colonia Agrippensis, Gugerni, Batavi, and those whom we spake of in the Islands of the Rhenus.

Chapter XVIII.

Lugdunensis Gallia

LUGDUNENSIS GALLIA containeth the Lexovii, Velocasses, Galleti, Veneti, Abricatui, Osismii, and the noble River Ligeris: but a remarkable Peninsula running out into the Ocean from the Extremity of the Osismii, having in circuit 625 Miles: with its Neck 125 Miles broad. Beyond it dwell the Nannetes: within, the Hœdui Confederates, the Carnuti Confederates, the Bou, Senones, Auleiici, surnamed Eburovices, and the Cenomannes, and Meldi, free Parrhisii, Trecasses, Andegavi, Viducasses, Vadicasses, Unelli, Cariosvelites, Diablindi, Rhedones, Turones, Itesui, and free Secusiani, in whose Country is the Colony Lugdunum.

Chapter XIX.

Aquitania.

To Aquitania belong the Ambilatri, Anagnutes, Pictones, the free Santones (Bituriges), named also Vibisci, Aquitani, from whom the Province is named, and the Sediboniates. Then such as were enrolled into a Town from various Parts: Begerri, Tarbeli, who came under 4 Ensigns, Cocossati, under 6 Ensigns; Venami, Onobrisates, Belendi, and the Forest Pyrenæus. Beneath them, the Monesi; Osquidates, Mountaineers, Sibyllates, Camponi, Bercorates, Bipedimui, Sassumini, Vellates, Tornates, Consoranni, Ausci, Elusates, Sottiates, the Field Osquidates, Successes, Latusates, Basabocates, Vassei, Sennates, Cambolectri, Agesinates joined to

the Pictones.   Then the free Biturlges, who are also called
Cubɪ.   Next to them, Lemovices, the free Arverni, and Ga-
bales.   Agaɪn, those that border upon the Provɪnce Narbo-
nensɪs , the Rutheni, Cadurci, Autobroges, and the Petro-
gori dɪvided from the Tolosanɪ by the Rɪver Tarnè.   Seas
about the Coast· upon the Rhenus the North Ocean : between
the Rhenus and Sequana, the Brɪtɪsh Ocean : between it and
Pyrenæus, the Gallic Ocean.   Islands : many of the Veneti,
which are called also Veneticæ   and in the Gulf of Aquitaine,
Uliarus.

CHAPTER XX.

The Hither Hispania.

Aт the Promontory of Pyrenæus beginneth Ḣɪspania
(Spaɪn) , narrower not only than Gallɪa, but also than itself
(as we may say), so vast a Quantity is wrought ɪnto it by
the Ocean of the one Coast, and the Iberɪan Sea on the
other.   The Mountains of Pyrenæus, whɪch from the
East spread all the way to the Southwest, make Hispania
shorter on the North Side than the South.   The nearest
Border of thɪs hɪther Provɪnce ɪs the same as the Tract
of Tarracon, from Pyrenæus along the Ocean, to the
Forest of the Vascones   In the Country of the Varduli .
the Towns Olarso, Morosgi, Menosca, Vesperies, the Port
Amanum, where now is Flaviobɪiga, a Colony of nine Cities.
The Region of the Cantabrɪ, the River Sada, the Port of
Victoria, inhabɪted by the Julɪobrigenses.   From that Place
the Fountaɪns of Iberus, 40 Miles.   The Port Biendɪum, the
Origenɪ, intermingled with the Cantabri.   Theɪr Harbours,
Vesei and Veca : the Country of the Astures, the Town
Nœga, in the Penɪnsula Pesicus.   And then the Conventus
Lucensɪs, from the River Navilubio, the Cibarci, Egovarri,
surnamed Namarini, Iadoni, Arrotrebæ, the Promontory
Celticum.   Rivers, Florius and Nelo.   Celtici, surnamed
Nerɪæ : and above the Tamirici, in whose Penɪnsula are
three Altars called Sestɪanæ, dedɪcated to *Augustus ;* Cœpori,
the Town Nœla.   The Celtici, surnamed Præsamarci, Cɪleni.
Of Islands worth the naming, Corticata and Aunios   From

the Cileni, the Conventus of the Bracæ, Heleni, Gravii, the
Castle Tydè, all descended from the Greeks.   The Islands
Cicæ, the distinguished Town Abobrica ; the River Minius
with a broad Mouth, four Miles over ; the Leuni, Seurbi,
Augusta, a Town of the Bracæ and above them, Gallæcia ;
the River Limia   The River Durius, one of the greatest in
Hispania, springing in the Pelendones' Country, and running
by Numantia and so on, through the Arevaci and Vaccæi,
dividing the Vettones from Asturia, and the Gallæci from
Lusitania . and there also it keepeth off the Turduli from the
Bracari.   All this Region abovesaid from Pyrenæus is full
of Mines, of Gold, Silver, Iron, Lead, both black and white
(Tin).

CHAPTER XXI.

Lusitania.

FROM the (River) Durius beginneth Lusitania, wherein
are Turduli the old, Pesuri, the River Vacca. The Town
Talabrica, the Town and River Minium.   Towns, Conim-
brica, Olisippo, Eburo, Britium.   From whence runneth out
into the Sea with a mighty Horn the Promontory, which
some have called Artabrum ; others, the Great ; and many,
Olissoponense, from the Town, making a Division of Land,
Sea, and Sky   By it is the Side of Hispania determined,
and from the Compass of it beginneth the Front.

CHAPTER XXII.

Islands in the Ocean

ON the one hand, is the North and the Gallic Ocean .
on the other, the West and the Atlantic Ocean   The
shooting forth of the Promontory some have reported to
be 60 Miles, others 90.   From thence to Pyrenæus not a
few say it is 1250 Miles ; and that there is a Nation of the
Atabri, which never was, with a manifest Error.   For they
have set the Ariotrebæ, whom we have placed before the
Celtic Promontory, in this place, by exchanging some Letters   They have erred also in certain famous Rivers   From

Minius abovenamed (as *Varro* saith) Æminius is 200 Miles
distant (which some take to be elsewhere, and call it Limæa),
named by the ancients Oblivionis; of which goeth many
a Fable. From Durius to Tagus is 200 Miles, and Munda
cometh between   Tagus is much renowned for Sand that
yieldeth Gold · 160 Miles from it the Promontory Sacrum
(Sacred) runneth out from about the middle Front of Hispania : and *Varro* saith it is 14 Miles from it to the midst of
Pyrenæus. But from Ana, by which we have separated
Lusitania from Bætica, 226 Miles : adding thereto from
Gades 102 Miles   Nations : Celtici, Varduli, and about the
Tagus, the Vettones. From Ana to Sacrum, the Lusitani
Memorable Towns : from Tagus in the Coast Side, Olisippo,
noble for the Mares that conceive there by the Favonius
Wind   Salacia, denominated Urbs Imperatoria, and Mero-
brica : the Promontory Sacrum, and another called Cæneus.[1]
Towns. Ossonoba, Balsa, and Myrtius   The whole Province
is divided into three Conventions : Emeritensis, Pacensis,
and Scalabitanus. It containeth in all five-and-forty People.
wherein are five Colonies, one Municipium of Roman Citizens ; three of Old Latium   Stipendiaries, six-and-thirty.
Colonies, Augusta Emerita : and upon the River Ana,
Metallinensis, Pacensis, Norbensis, which is named also
Cæsariana   To it are laid Castra Julia and Castra Cæcilia.
The fifth is Scalabis, called Præsidium Julium. The Municipium of Roman Citizens Olyssippo, named also Felicitas
Julia. Towns of the Old Latium, Ebora, which likewise was
called Liberalitas Julia : Myrtilis also, and Salatia, which we
have spoken of   Of Stipendiaries, which I am not loth to
name, beside the abovesaid, in the additions of Bætica,
Augustobrigenses, Ammienses, Aranditani, Axabricenses,
Balsenses, Cæsarobricenses, Capetenses, Caurenses, Colarni,
Cibilitani, Concordienses, the same as Bonori ; Interau-
senses, Lancienses, Mirobrigenses surnamed Celtici ; Medu-
bricenses, the same as Plumbarii ; Ocelenses, who also are
Lancienses ; Turtuli, named Barduli, and Tapori   *M. Agrippa*

---

[1] *Cæneus* is read in some editions, and *Cuneus* in others.

hath written, that Lusitania, with Asturia and Gallæcia, is in
Length 540 Miles, and in Breadth 526   But all the His-
paniæ (Spains), from the two Promontories of Pyrenæus along
the Seas, are supposed to take up in Circuit of the whole
Coast 2900 Miles, and by others, 2700.   Over against Celtiberia are very many Islands, called by the Greeks Cassiterides,
from the plenty of Lead.[1] and from the region of the Promontory of the Arrotrebæ, six named Deorum (*i. e* of the
Gods) which some have called Fortunatæ.   But in the very
Cape of Bætica, from the Mouth of the Strait 75 Miles,
lieth the Island Gades, 12 Miles long, as *Polybius* writeth,
and 3 Miles broad.   It is distant from the Continent, where
it is nearest, less than 700 Paces,[2] in other Parts above 7
Miles.   Its space containeth 15 Miles.   It hath a Town of
Roman Citizens, which is named Augusta, Urbs Julia
Gaditana.   On that side that looks toward Spain, within
about 100 Paces, is another Island, 3 Miles long, and a
Mile broad, wherein formerly was the Town of Gades.   The
Name of this Island, according to *Ephorus* and *Philistides*, is
Erythia: but according to *Timæus* and *Silenus*, Aphrodisias:
by the Native Inhabitants, of Juno.   The bigger, *Timæus*
saith, was by them called Cotinusa; our Countrymen name
it Tartessos, the Pœni Gadir,[3] which in the Punic Language signifieth[4] the number of seven.[5]   Erythia was
called, because the Tyri were reported to have had their
first beginning out of the (Red) Sea, Erythræum.   Some think
that *Geryon* here dwelt, whose Herds *Hercules* took away.
There are again some who think that it is another, over

[1] See p 36, c xvi.
[2] Less than three-quarters of a mile
[3] Or Gadiz
[4] *Septem*, or, as some read, *Septum* (*i. e.* a park or enclosure).
[5] From the Hebrew root signifying *to make a fence*, the Phœnicians
called any enclosed space *Gaddir*, and particularly gave this name to their
settlement on the south-western coast of Spain, which the Greeks from
them called *Gaderia*, the Romans *Gades*, and we *Cadiz*. See *Bochart*,
vol. i. 628–734. This name is very appropriately given to the island
mentioned by Pliny, but why it should be derived from a Punic word
signifying *seven* is not so apparent —*Wern. Club*

against Lusitania, and there sometime called by the same Name.

Chapter XXIII.

The Measure of all Europe.

HAVING finished the circuit of Europe, we must now yield the total Sum, that such as are desirous of Knowledge be not deficient in any thing. *Artemidorus* and *Isidorus* have set down the Length of it from Tanais to Gades 84,014 Miles. *Polybius* hath put down the Breadth of Europe, from Italy to the Ocean 1150 Miles, for then the largeness of it was not known. But the Breadth of Italy itself (as we have shewn) is 1220 Miles to the Alps: from whence by Lugdunum to the Port of the Morini in Britain, from which *Polybius* seemeth to take his Measure, is 1168 Miles. But the more certain Measure, and the longer, is directed from the said Alps to the extreme West and the Mouth of the Rhenus, through the Camps of the Legions of Germania, 1243 Miles. Now will we proceed to describe Africa and Asia.

IN THE FIFTH BOOK

ARE CONTAINED

REGIONS, NATIONS, SEAS, TOWNS, PORTS, HILLS, RIVERS, WITH
THEIR MEASURES, AND PEOPLE, EITHER AT THIS DAY
EXISTING, OR IN TIMES PAST, VIZ.:—

Herein you find Towns and Nations, principal Rivers, famous Mountains, Islands, 117. Towns also that are perished. Affairs, Histories and Observations.

LATIN AUTHORS ABSTRACTED:

Agrippa, Suetonius Paulinus, Varro Atacinus, Cornelius Nepos, Hyginus, L. Vetus, Mela, Domitius Corbulo, Licinius Mutianus, Claudius Cæsar, Aruntius, Livius the Son, *Sebosus,* the Records of the Triumphs.

FOREIGN WRITERS:

King *Juba, Hecatæus, Hellanicus, Damastes, Dicæarchus, Bion, Timosthenes, Philonides, Xenagoras, Astynomus, Staphylus, Aristotle, Dionysius, Aristocritus, Ephorus, Eratosthenes, Hipparchus, Panætius, Serapion Antiochenus, Callimachus, Agathocles, Polybius, Timæus* the Mathematician, *Herodotus, Myrsilus, Alexander Polyhistor, Metrodorus, Posidonius* who wrote Periplus or Periegesis, *Sotades, Periander, Aristarchus Sicyonius, Eudoxus, Antigenes, Callicrates, Xenophon Lampsacenus, Diodorus Syracusanus, Hanno, Himilco, Nymphodorus, Calliphon, Artemidorus, Megasthenes, Isidorus, Cleobulus, Aristocreon.*

THE FIFTH BOOK

OF THE

HISTORY OF NATURE.

WRITTEN BY

C. PLINIUS SECUNDUS.

The Description of Africa.

FRICA the Greeks have called Lybia; from which the Lybian Sea before it beginneth, and endeth in the Egyptian. No part of the Earth receiveth fewer Gulfs in that long compass of oblique Coasts from the West. The Names of its People and Towns are exceedingly hard to be Pronounced, unless by their own Tongues: and again, they for the most part dwell in Castles.

CHAPTER I.

Mauritania.

AT the beginning, the Lands of Mauritania, until the time of *C. Cæsar* (*i. e. Caligula*), son of *Germanicus*, were called Kingdoms: but by his Cruelty it was divided into two Provinces. The utmost Promontory of the Ocean is named by the Greeks Ampelusia. The Towns were Lissa and Cotes

beyond the Pillars of *Hercules*.   Now there is Tingi, formerly
built by *Antæus;* and afterwards by *Claudius Cæsar*, when he
made it a Colony, by whom it was called Traducta Julia.   It
is from Belonè, a Town in Bætica, by the nearest Passage, 30
Miles.   Five-and-Twenty Miles from it, in the Coast of the
Ocean, is a Colony of *Augustus*, now Julia Constantia, exempt
from the Jurisdiction of the Kings of Zilis : and commanded
to seek for Law to Bætica.   And 32 Miles from it is Lixos,
made a Colony by *Claudius Cæsar*, of which in old Time there
were related many Fabulous Tales.   There stood the Royal
Palace of *Antæus;* there was the combat with *Hercules;* there
also were the Gardens of the Hesperides.   Now there floweth
into it out of the Sea a Creek by a winding Channel, in
which Men now interpret that there were Dragons serving
as Guards.   It encloseth an Island within itself, which (notwithstanding the Tract near it is somewhat higher) is alone
not overflowed by the Tides of the Sea.   In it there standeth
an Altar of *Hercules;* and except wild Olives, nothing is to
be seen of that Grove, reported to bear Golden Apples
And indeed less may they wonder at the enormous lies of
Greece invented concerning these, and the River Lixus ;
who will think how of late our Countrymen have delivered
some Fables scarcely less monstrous, regarding the same
things : as, that this is a very strong City, bigger than great
Carthage.   moreover, that it is situated over against it, and
almost at an immense way from Tingi : and other such,
which *Cornelius Nepos* hath been very eager to believe.
From Lixus 40 Miles, in the Midland Parts, standeth Babba,
another Colony of *Augustus*, called Julia Campestris : also
a third 75 Miles off, called Banasa, but now Valentia.
35 Miles from it is the Town Volubilè, just in the midway
between both Seas.   But in the Coast, 50 Miles from Lixus,
there runneth Subur, a copious and navigable River, near to
the Colony Banasa.   As many Miles from it is the Town
Sala, standing upon a River of the same Name, near now to
the Wilderness, much infested with Herds of Elephants, but
much more with the Nation of the Autololes, through
which lieth the Way to Atlas, the most fabulous Mountain of

Africa. For Writers have given out that, rising out of the
very midst of the Sands, it mounteth to the Sky, rough and
ill-favoured on that side which lieth toward the Shore of the
Ocean, unto which it gave the Denomination : and the same
is shadowy, full of Woods, and watered with Sources of
spouting Springs, on the way which looketh to Africa, with
Fruits of all sorts, springing of their own accord, one under
another, in such a manner, that at no time is Fulness of Pleasure wanting. Moreover, that none of the Inhabitants are
seen by day : all is silent, like the Awe of Solitude : a secret
Devotion creepeth into the Hearts of those who approach
near to it, and besides this Awe they are lifted above the
Clouds, even close to the Circle of the Moon · that the same
(Mountain) shineth by Night with frequent Fires, and is
filled with the Lasciviousness of Ægipanes and Satyrs ; that it
resoundeth with the Melody of Flutes and Pipes; and
ringeth with the Sound of Drums and Cymbals. These are
the Reports of famous Writers, besides the Labours of
Hercules and *Perseus* there   The Way unto it is exceedingly
long, and not certainly known.   There were also Commentaries of *Hanno*, the General of the Carthaginians, who
in the time of the most flourishing state of Carthage had a
charge to explore the Circuit of Africa. Him, most of the
Greeks as well as our Countrymen following, among some
other fabulous Stories, have written that he also built many
Cities there : but neither any Memorial, nor Token of them
remain   When *Scipio Æmylianus* carried on War in Africa,
Polybius, the Writer of the Annals, received from him a Fleet;
and having sailed about for the purpose of searching into that
part of the World, he reported, That from the said Mountain
West, toward the Forests full of Wild Beasts, which Africa
breedeth, to the River Anatis, are 485 Miles ; and from
thence to Lixus, 205   *Agrippa* saith, That Lixus is distant
from the Straits of Gades 112 Miles.   Then, that there is a
Bay called Saguti; also a Town upon the Promontory,
Mutelacha.   Rivers, Subur and Sala.   That the Port
Rutubis is from Lixus 313 Miles.   Then the Promontory
of the Sun. The Port Risardir : the Gætulians, Autololes,

the River Cosenus, the Nation of the Scelatiti and Massati.
The Rivers Masatal and Darat, wherein Crocodiles are produced. Then a Bay of 516 Miles, enclosed within the Promontory of the Mountain Barcè, running out into the West, which
is called Surrentium. After it, the River Palsus, beyond which
are the Æthiopian Perorsi, and at their back are the Pharusi.
Upon whom join the inland People, the Gætuli Daræ. But
upon the Coast are the Æthiopian Daratitæ; the River
Bambotus full of Crocodiles and Hippopotami From which,
he saith, there is a Continuation of Mountains as far as to
that which we call Theon-Ochema (the Gods' Chariot).
Then, in sailing nine Days and Nights to the Promontory
Hesperium, he hath placed the Mountain Atlas in the midway, which by all other Writers is set down to be in the
utmost Borders of Mauritania. The Romans first warred in
Mauritania, in the time of *Claudius* the Prince· when
Ædæmon, the Freedman of King *Ptolemæus*, who was
slain by *C. Cæsar*, endeavoured to avenge his Death. For
as the Barbarians fled backward, the Romans came to the
Mountain Atlas. And not only to such Generals as had
been Consuls, and to such as were of the Senate, who at that
time managed affairs, but to Knights also, who from that
time had command there, was it a glory to have penetrated to the Atlas. *Five Roman Colonies, as we have
said, are in that Province, and by common fame it may seem
to be accessible. But this is found for the most part by
Experience very fallacious because Persons of high Rank,
when it is irksome to search out the Truth, find it not irksome through the shame of Ignorance, to give out Untruths·
and never are Men more credulous to be deceived than when
some grave Author fathereth the lie. And indeed I less
wonder, that things are not known, when they of the Equestrian Order, and those now also of the Senatorial Rank,
admire nothing but Luxury· which very powerful and prevailing Force is seen when Forests are searched for Ivory and
Citron-trees. and all the Rocks in Getulia for Murices and

* It seemeth that this clause is to be set in the beginning of the next
chapter.

Purpuræ. Nevertheless the natural Inhabitants report, That in the Sea-coast 150 Miles from Sala there is the River Asana, that receiveth Salt Water into it, but with a goodly Harbour: and not far from it a River, which they call Fut: from which to Dyris (for that is the Name in their Language of Atlas) are 200 Miles, with a River coming between, named Vior. And there, by report, are to be seen the certain tokens of a Soil formerly inhabited; the vestiges of Vineyards and Date-tree Groves. *Suetonius Paulinus* (a Consul in our time), who was the first Roman Leader that passed over Atlas for the space of some Miles, also hath reported regarding the height thereof and moreover, that the foot of it toward the bottom is full of thick and tall Woods, with Trees of an unknown kind, but the height of them is delightful to see, smooth and beautiful, the branches like Cypress; and, besides the strong smell, are covered over with a thin Down, of which (with some help of Art) fine Cloth may be made, such as the Silk-worm yieldeth that the top of it is covered with deep Snow, even in Summer, and that he reached up to it on the tenth day, and beyond to the River called Niger, through solitudes of black Dust, with sometimes conspicuous ragged Rocks, appearing as if burnt: places by reason of the Heat not habitable, although tried in the Winter Season. Those who dwelt in the next Forests were pestered with Elephants, wild Beasts, and Serpents of all sorts, and those People were called Canarii; because they and Animals feed together, and part among them the Bowels of wild Beasts. For it is sufficiently known that a Nation of Æthiopians, whom they call Peroresi, joineth to them. *Juba,* the Father of *Ptolemæus,* who formerly ruled over both Mauritaniæ, a Man more memorable for his illustrious Studies than for his Kingdom, hath written the like concerning Atlas; and (he saith) moreover, that there is an Herb growing there called Euphorbia, from his Physician's name that first found it: the Milky Juice of which he praiseth exceedingly much for clearing the Eyes and against Serpents and all Poisons, in a dedicated Book by itself. Thus much may suffice, if not too much, about Atlas.

Chapter II.

The Province Tingitania.

The Length of the Province Tingitania is 170 Miles. The Nations therein are these: The Mauri, which in times past was the principal, and of whom the Province took its Name. and those most Writers have called Marusii. Being by War weakened, they wasted to a few Families. Next to them were the Massæsuli, but in like manner they were extinguished. Now are the Nations inhabited by the Getulæ, Bannurri, and the Autololes, the most powerful of all: a part of whom were once the Vesuni. but being divided from them, they became a Nation by themselves, and were turned to the Æthiopians. This Province being full of Mountains eastward, affordeth Elephants. In the Mountain Abila, also, and in those which for their equal height they call the Seven Brethren · these are joined to Abila, which looketh over the arm of the Sea. From these beginneth the Coast of the Inward Sea. The River Tamuda navigable, and formerly a Town The River Laud, which also is able to receive Vessels The Town Rusaidir, and the Harbour The navigable River Malvana. The Town Siga, over against Malacha, situated in Hispania: the royal Seat of *Syphax*, and now the other Mauritania. For a long time they kept the names of the Kings, so that the furthest was called Bogadiana and likewise Bocchi, which now is Cæsariensis. Next to it is the Harbour for its space called Magnus, with a Town of Roman Citizens. The River Muluca, which is the limit of Bocchi and the Massæsuli. Quiza Xenitana, a Town of Strangers · Arsennaria, a Town of Latins, 3 Miles from the Sea · Carcenna, a Colony of *Augustus*, the Second Legion: Likewise another Colony of his, planted with the Pretorian Cohort: Gunugi and the Promontory of *Apollo*. And a most famous Town there, Cæsarea, usually in old time called Iol, the royal Seat of King *Juba* endowed by *Divus Claudius* with the Right of a Colony, by whose Appointment the old Soldiers were there bestowed. A new Town, Tipasa,

with the Liberties of Latium   Likewise Icosium, endowed
by *Vespasian* the Emperor with the same Gift.   The Colony
of *Augustus*, Rusconiæ: and Ruscurum, by *Claudius* honoured
as a City : Rusoezus, a Colony of *Augustus*.   Saldè, a Colony
of the same.   Igelgili also, and Turca, a Town seated upon
the Sea and the River Ampsaga.   Within Land, the Colony
Augusta, the same as Succubar; and likewise Tubrisuptus.
Cities, Timici, Tigavæ.   Rivers, Sardabala and Nabar.   The
Nation, Macurebi : the River Usar and the Nation of the
Nabades.   The River Ampsaga is from Cæsarea 233
Miles.   The Length of either Mauritania is 839 Miles, the
Breadth, 467.

Chapter III.

Numidia

Next to Ampsaga is Numidia, renowned for the Name of
Masanissa   called by the Greeks, the Land Metagonitis.
The Numidian Nomades (so named from changing their Pas-
ture), who carry their Huts, that is, their Houses, about with
them upon Waggons   Their Towns are Cullu and Rusicadè;
from which 48 Miles off, within the midland Parts is the
Colony Cirta, surnamed of the Sittiani; another also within
Cicca, and a free Town named Bulla Regia   But in the Coast,
Tacatua, Hippo Regius, and the River Armua.   The Town
Trabacha, of Roman Citizens : the River Tusca, which
boundeth Numidia : and besides the Numidian Marble, and
abundance of wild Beasts, nothing is there worth the
noting

Chapter IV.

Africa.

From Tusca forward is the Region Zeugitana, and the
Country properly called Africa.   Three Promontories : the
White; then that of *Apollo*, over against Sardinia. that of *Mercury* opposite to Sicily; which, running into the Sea, make
two Bays : the one Hipponensis, next to the Town which
they call Hipponis, named by the Greeks Diarrhyton, on

account of Brooks of Water · upon this bordereth Theudalis,
an exempt Town, but further from the Sea-side, then the
Promontory of *Apollo*. And in the other Bay, Utica, of
Roman Citizens, ennobled by the death of *Cato:* the River
Bagrada. A Place called Castra Cornelia . and the Colony
Carthago, among the Relics of great Carthage and the
Colony Maxulla Towns, Carpi, Misna, and the free Clupea,
upon the Promontory of *Mercury* Also, free Towns, Cu-
rubis and Neapolis. Soon is another distinction of Africa
itself. Libyphœnices are they called, who inhabit Byzacium;
for so is that Region named containing in Circuit 250 Miles,
exceedingly fertile, where the Ground sown yieldeth to the
Husbandman an hundred-fold Increase. In it are free Towns,
Leptis, Adrumetum, Ruspina, and Thapsus . then, Thenæ,
Macomades, Tacapè, Sabrata, reaching to the Lesser Syrtis:
unto which, the Length of Numidia and Africa from Am-
phaga is 580 Miles: the Breadth, of so much as is known,
200. This Part, which we have called Africa, is divided into
two Provinces, the old and the new, separated by a Fosse
brought as far as to Thenæ, within the African Gulf; which
Town is 217 Miles from Carthage The third Bay is separated into two; horrible Places for the Shallows and ebbing
and flowing of the Sea at the two Syrtes. From Carthage
to the nearer of them, which is the lesser, is 300 Miles, by
the Account of *Polybius* · who saith, also, that the said Passage of Syrtis is 100 Miles forward and 300 in Circuit By
Land also, the Way to it is by observation of the Stars, and
through the Desert over Sands and through Places full of
Serpents; you pass Forests filled with Numbers of wild
Beasts: and within, Solitudes of Elephants: and soon after,
vast Deserts, even beyond the Garamantes, who, from the
Augilæ, are distant twelve Days' Journey. Above them was
the Nation of the Psylli: and above them the Lake of *Lyco-
medes* environed with Deserts. The Augilæ themselves are
seated about the middle Way from Ethiopia; which bendeth
Westward, and from the Country lying between the two
Syrtes, with an equal Distance on each Side . but the Shore
between the two Syrtes is 250 Miles There standeth the

City Oeensis, the River Cinyps, and the Country.   Towns,
Neapolis, Taphra, Abrotonum, the other Leptis, called also
the Great   Then the Greater Syrtis, in Compass 625 Miles,
and in direct Passage 313   Then inhabit the Nation of Cisi-
pades   In the inmost Gulf was the Coast of the Lotophagi,
whom some have called Alachroas, as far as to the Altars of
the Philæni, and they are formed of Sand.   Next to them, not
far from the Continent, the vast Marsh admitteth into it the
River Triton, and taketh its Name from it   but *Callimachus*
calleth it Pallantias, and saith it is on this Side the lesser
Syrtes ; but many place it between both Syrtes   The Promontory that encloseth the greater is named Borion.   Beyond
is the Province Cyrenaica.   From the River Ampsaga to this
Bound, Africa containeth 26 separate People, who are subject
to the Roman Empire. among which are six Colonies, besides the above-named, Uthina and Tuburbis.   Towns of
Roman Citizens, 15 , of which those in the midland Parts to
be named are Azuritanum, Abutucensè, Aboriensè, Canopicum, Chilmanensè, Simittuensè, Thunusidensè, Tuburni-
censè, Tynidrumensè, Tribigensè, two Ucitana, the greater
and less; and Vagiensè   One Latin Town, Usalitanum.
One stipendiary Town near Castra Cornelia.   Free Towns,
30, of which are to be named, within, Acrolitanum, Achari-
tanum, Avinensè, Abziritanum, Canopitanum, Melzitanum,
Madaurensè, Salaphitanum, Tusdritanum, Tiricensè, Tiphi-
censè, Tunicensè, Theudensè, Tagestensè (Tigensè), Ulusi-
britanum, another Vagensè, Vigensè, and Zamensè.   The
rest it may be right to call not only Cities, but also for the
most Part, Nations; as the Natabudes, Capsitani, Misulani,
Sabarbares, Massili, Misives, Vamacures, Ethini, Massini,
Marchubii · and all Gætulia to the River Nigris, which
parteth Africa and Ethiopia.

Chapter V.

Cyrenè.

The Region Cyrenaica, called also Pentapolitana, is
illustrious for the Oracle of *Hammon*, which is from Cyrenæ

400 Miles, from the Fountain of the Sun; and principally
for five Cities, Berenicè, Arsinoè, Ptolemais, Apollonia, and
Cyrenè itself. Berenicè standeth upon the outermost Horn
of Syrtis, called formerly the City of the above-named Hesperides, according to the wandering Tales of Greece. And
before the Town, not far off, is the River Lethon, the sacred
Grove where the Gardens of the Hesperides are reported to
be. From Leptis it is 385 Miles. From it is Arsinoe, usually
named Teuchira, 43 Miles: and from thence 22 Miles,
Ptolemais, called in old time Barcè. And then 250 Miles
off, the Promontory Phycus runneth out through the Cretic
Sea, distant from Tænarus, a Promontory of Laconia, 350
Miles: but from Creta itself 125 Miles. And after it Cyrenè,
11 Miles from the Sea. From Phycus to Apollonia is 24
Miles: to Cherrhonesus, 88: and so to Catabathnus, 216
Miles. The Inhabitants there bordering are the Marmaridæ,
stretching out in Length almost from Parætonium to the
Greater Syrtis. After them the Ararauceles: and so in the
very Coast of Syrtis, the Nesamones, whom formerly the
Greeks called Mesammones, by reason of the Place, as
seated in the midst between the Sands. The Cyrenaic
Country, for the Space of 15 Miles from the Sea-shore, is
fruitful for Trees. and for the same Compass within the
Land, for Corn only: but then for 30 Miles in Breadth, and
250 in Length, for Laser [1] After the Nasamones live the
Hasbitæ and Masæ. Beyond them the Hammanientes, 11
Days' Journey from the Greater Syrtis to the West, and even
they also every Way are compassed about with Sands. but

---

[1] The plant that yielded the Cyrenaic juice called Laser, was the
Silphion of the Greeks, and the Laserpitium of the Romans (Thapsia
Silphion, *Vivani*), and agrees tolerably well with the rude figures struck
on the Cyrenean coins. It would appear, however, that the Cyrenaic
juice becoming scarce, the ancients employed some other substance of
similar, though inferior properties, as a substitute, and to both of them
they applied the term *Laser*. Pliny (lib xix. c 3) says, "For a long
time past the only Laser brought to us is that which is produced abundantly in Persia, &c., but it is inferior to the Cyrenaic." Now it is not at
all improbable that the Laser of Persia may have been our Asafœdita
(*Ferula Asafœdita*, Lin.)—*Wern. Club*

they find without much difficulty Wells almost in the Depth
of two Cubits, where the Waters of Mauritania settle. They
build themselves Houses of Salt, hewn out of their own
Mountains in the manner of Stone. From these to the Troglodites, in the South-west Coast, the Country is four Days'
Journey; with whom is a Traffic only for a precious Stone,
which we call a Carbuncle, brought out of Ethiopia. There
cometh between, the Country Phazania toward the Solitudes
of Africa, above the said Lesser Syrtis · where we subdued
the Nation of the Phazanii, with the Cities Alelè and Cillaba.
Also Cydamum, over against the region of Sabrata. Next to
these is a Mountain, reaching a great way from East to
West, called by our People Ater, as if burnt by Nature, or
scorched by the reflection of the Sun. Beyond that Mountain are the Deserts. also Matelgæ, a Town of the Garamantes, and likewise Debris, which casteth forth a Fountain,
the Waters boiling from Noon to Midnight, and for as many
Hours to Mid-day reducing again · also the very illustrious
Town Garama, the head of the Garamantes All which
Places the Roman Arms have conquered, and over them
Cornelius Balbus triumphed; the only Man of Foreigners
that was honoured with the (Triumphant) Chariot, and endowed with the Freedom of Roman Citizens; because being
born at Gades, he and his Uncle, *Balbus* the Elder, were
made free Denizens of Rome. And this wonder our Writers
have recorded, that besides the Towns above named by him
conquered, himself in his Triumph carried the Names and
Images, not of Cydamus and Garama only, but also of all
the other Nations and Cities; which went in this Order.
The Town Tabidium, the Nation Niteris, the Town Negligee-
mela, the Nation Bubeium; the Town Vel, the Nation Enipi;
the Town Thuben, the Mountain named Niger, the Towns
Nitibrum and Rapsa; the Nation Discera, the Town Debris,
the River Nathabur, the Town Tapsagum, the Nation Nan-
nagi, the Town Boin; the Town Pegè, the River Dasibari.
Presently these Towns lying continuously, Baracum, Buluba,
Alasi, Balsa, Galla, Maxala, and Zizama. The Mountain
Gyri, wherein *Titus* hath reported that precious Stones

were produced.[1]   Hitherto the Way to the Garamantes was
intricate, by reason of the Robbers of that Nation, who used
to dig Pits in the Way (which to them that know the Places
is no hard matter to do) and then cover them with Sand.
But in the last War which the Romans maintained against the
Oeenses, under the conduct of *Vespasian* the Emperor, there
was found a short Way of four Days' Journey · and this Way
is called *Præter caput Saxi* [beside the Rock's Head].   The
Frontier of Cyrenaica is called Catabathmos , which is a Town
and a Valley with a sudden Descent   To this Bound, from
the Lesser Syrtis, Cyrenaica Africa lieth in Length 1060
Miles, and in Breadth, for so much as is known, 800.

CHAPTER VI.

Libya Mareotis.

THE Country following is named Mareotis Libya, bounded
by Egypt; inhabited by the Marmaridæ, Adyrmachidæ, and
then the Mareotæ.   The Measure from Catabathmos to Pa-
retonium is 86 Miles.   In that Tract there lieth in the way
the Village Apis, a place noble for the Religion of Egypt.
From it to Paraetonium, 12 Miles.   From thence to Alexandria, 200 Miles · the Breadth is 169 Miles   *Eratosthenes*
hath delivered, That from Cyrenæ to Alexandria by Land the
Journey is 525 Miles.   *Agrippa* saith, that the Length of all
Africa from the Atlantic Sea, with the inferior part of Egypt,
containeth 3040 Miles.   *Polybius* and *Eratosthenes*, reputed
the most diligent, have set down from the Ocean to great
Carthage 600 Miles : from thence to Canopicum, the nearest
Mouth of Nilus, 1630 Miles   *Isidorus* reckoneth from Tingi
to Canopus 3599 Miles , and *Artemidorus*, 40 less than
Isiodorus.

---

[1] Some editions read *Titus prodidit,* while others have *titulus præcepit.*
     In the triumph of Vespasian and Titus, so minutely described by
Josephus ("Wars of the Jews," book vii. cap 5) a title was affixed to
the several images carried in procession, containing the names of the conquered nations and towns, with mention of their chief productions —
Wern. Club.

Chapter VII.

Islands about Africa, and over against Africa.

These Seas do not contain very many Islands. The fairest is Meninx, 35 Miles long and 25 broad, called by *Eratosthenes* Lotophagitis. It hath two Towns, Meninx on the side of Africa, and Thoar on the other. itself is situated from the right-hand Promontory of the Lesser Syrtis 200 Paces.[1] A hundred Miles from it against the left hand is Cercina, with a free Town of the same Name, in Length 25 Miles, and half as much in Breadth where it is most · but toward the end not above five Miles. To it there lieth a little one toward Carthage called Cercinitis, and it joineth by a Bridge. From these, almost 50 Miles, lieth Lopadusa, six Miles long. Then, Gaulos and Galata, the Earth of which killeth the Scorpion, a dangerous Creature of Africa. They say also that they will die in Clupea, over against which lieth Cosyra, with a Town. But against the Bay of Carthage are the two Æginori, more truly Rocks than Islands, lying for the most part between Sicily and Sardinia. Some write that these were inhabited, but sunk down.

Chapter VIII.

The Æthiopes.

But within the inner Compass of Africa, toward the South, and above the Gætuli, where the Deserts come between, the first People that inhabit are the Libii Ægyptii, and then the Leucæthiopes. Above them are the Æthiopian Nations. the Nigritæ, from whom the River was named : the Gymnetes, Pharusi, and those which now reach to the Ocean, whom we spake of in the border of Mauritania : the Perorsi. From all these are vast Solitudes eastward, to the Garamantes, Augylæ, and Troglodites, according to the truest opinion of them who place two Æthiopias above the Deserts of Africa : and especially of *Homer*, who saith, that the Ethiopians are divided two ways, towards the East and

[1] Or 1500 paces, *i e.* a mile and a half

West. The River Niger is of the same nature as Nilus,
producing the Reed and Papyrus, and the same living Creatures, and swelleth at the same Seasons. It springeth between the Tareleia Æthiopiæ, and the Oecalicæ. The Town
Mavin, belonging to this People, some have set upon the
deserts. near them the Atlantæ, the Ægipanæ, half beasts;
the Blemmyæ, the Gamphasantæ, Satyri, and Himantopodæ.
Those Atlantæ, if we will believe it, degenerate from Human
Manners: for neither call they one another by any Name:
and they look upon the Sun, rising and setting, with dreadful curses, as being pernicious to them and their Fields:
neither Dream they in their Sleep, as other Men. The
Troglodites dig Caverns, and these serve them for Houses:
they feed upon the Flesh of Serpents; they make a gnash-
ing Noise, not a Voice, so little exchange have they of Speech.
The Garamantes live out of Marriage, and converse with
their Women in common. The Augylæ only worship the
Infernal Gods The Gamphasantes are naked, and know no
Wars, and associate with no Foreigner. The Blemmyæ, by
report, have no Heads, but their Mouth and Eyes fixed in
their Breast The Satyri, besides their Shape, have nothing
of Human Manners. The Ægipanæ are shaped as you see
them commonly painted. The Himantopodæ are some of
them wry-legged, with which they naturally go creeping.
The Pharusi, formerly Persæ, are said to have been the
Companions of *Hercules*, as he went to the Hesperides.
More of Africa worth the noting does not occur.[1]

Chapter IX.

Of Asia.

Unto it joineth Asia, which from the Mouth of Canopus
unto the Mouth of Pontus, according to *Timosthenes*, is 2639
Miles. But from the Coast of Pontus to that of Mæotis,
Eratosthenes saith it is 1545 Miles. The whole, together with
Egypt unto Tanais, according to *Artemidorus* and *Isidorus*,
taketh 8800 Miles. Many Seas there are in it, taking their

---

[1] Notes on these alleged varieties of the human form will be found
b vii c 2, see also b vi c 30.—*Wern Club*

Names from the Borderers: and therefore they shall be
declared together. The next Country to Africa that is
inhabited is Egypt, receding withinward to the South, so
far as to the Æthiopians, who are stretched out on its Back.
The Nilus is on the lower part, and is divided on the Right
and Left; by its encircling it boundeth it with the Mouth
of Canopus from Africa, and with the Pelusiac from Asia,
with an interval of 170 Miles   For which cause, some have
reckoned Egypt among the Islands, considering that Nilus
doth so divide itself as to make a triangular figure of the
Land. And so, many have called Egypt by the Name of the
Greek letter Delta (Δ). The Measure of it from the Channel
where it is single, from whence it first parteth into sides, to
the Mouth of Canopus, is 146 Miles; and to the Pelusiac 256.
The upmost part bounding upon Æthiopia, is called Thebais.
It is divided into Townships, with separate Jurisdictions,
which they call Nomi. as Ombites, Phatunites, Apol-
lopolites, Hermonthites, Thinites, Phanturites, Captites,
Tentyrites, Diospalites, Antæopolites, Aphroditopolites, and
Lycopolites   The Country about Pelusium hath these Nomi:
Pharbœtites, Bubastites, Sethroites, and Tanites. But the
remainder, the Arabic, the Hammoniac which extendeth to
the Oracle of *Jupiter Hammon*, Oxyrinchites, Leontopolites,
Atarrhabites, Cynopolites, Hermopolites, Xoites, Mendesius,
Sebennites, Capastites, Latopolites, Heliopolites, Prosopites,
Panopolites, [Thermopolites, Saithes?] Busirites, Onuphites,
Sorites, Ptenethu, Pthemphu, Naucratites, Nitrites, Gynæ-
copolites, Menelaites, in the Country of Alexandria. In like
manner of Libya Mareotis. Heracleopolites is in an Island of
Nilus, 50 Miles long, wherein also is the place they call the
Town of *Hercules*. There are two Arsinoetes; they and
Memphites reach as far as to the Head of Delta. Upon it there
border, out of Africa, the two Ouasitæ. There are Writers
that change some of these Names, and substitute other Nomi:
as Heroopolites, and Crocodilopolites. Between Arsinoetes
and Memphites there was a Lake 250 Miles in Circuit; or,
as *Mutianus* saith, 450, and 50 Paces deep (i e. 150 Feet),
made by Hand; called the Lake Mœridis, from a King who

made it: 72 Miles from thence is Memphis, the Castle in
old time of the Egyptian Kings.   From which to the
Oracle of *Hammon* is 12 Days' Journey . and to the Division
of Nilus, which we have called Delta, 15 Miles.   The Nilus,
rising from unknown Springs, passeth through Deserts and
burning Countries: and going a vast way in Length, is
known by Fame only, without Arms, without Wars, which
have discovered all other Lands   It hath its beginning, so
far as King *Juba* was able to search, in a Mountain of the
lower Mauritania, not far from the Ocean, near to a stagnant Lake, which they call Nilides.   In it are found the
Fishes called Alabetæ,[1] Coracini, Siluri, and also the Cro-
codile.   Upon this argument the Nilus is thought to spring
from hence, for that it is seen dedicated by him at Cæsarea,
in Iseum, at this day.   Moreover, it is observed, that as the
Snow or Rain fills the Country in Mauritania, so the Nilus
increases.   When it is run out of this Lake, it scorneth
to pass through the sandy and unclean Places, and hideth
itself for some Days' Journey.   By and by out of another
greater Lake it breaketh forth in the Country of the Mas-
sæsyli, of Mauritania Cæsariensis ; and as if it looks about for
the Company of Men, with the same arguments of living
Creatures, again becomes received within the Sands, where
it is hidden a second time for 20 Days' Journey in the
Deserts, as far as to the next Æthiopæ: and so soon as it
hath again espied a Man, forth it leapeth (as it should seem)
out of that Spring, which they called Nigris   And then
dividing Africa from Æthiopia, being acquainted, if not presently with people, yet with the frequent company of wild and
savage Beasts, and creating the shade of Woods, it cutteth

---

[1] The first named, Alabes or Alabetæ, is a species of Lota of Cuvier,
or Burbot though perhaps not the same with the fish of that name that
inhabits the fresh waters of Europe   The name Coracinus has been
applied to more than one fish of a sooty colour but the species referred
to by Pliny is probably the *Perca Nilotica* of Linnæus the *Lates Nilo-
ticus* of Cuvier. The Silurus of Pliny is perhaps a species of Cuvier's
genus Schilbè, although true Siluri are found in the Nile   The Croco-
dile will be more particularly referred to in another place — *Wern. Club*

through the midst of the Æthiopians. there surnamed
Astapus, which in the Language of those Nations signifieth
a Water flowing out of Darkness. Thus dasheth it upon
such an innumerable Multitude of Islands, and some of them
so very great, that although it bear a swift Stream, yet is it
not able to pass beyond them in less space than five Days.
About the fairest of them, Meroe, the Channel going on the
Left is called Astabores, which is, the Branch of a Water
coming forth from Darkness but that on the Right is
Astusapes, which adds the signification of Lying hid. And
it never taketh the Name of Nilus, until its Waters meet
again and accord together   And even so was it formerly
named Siris for many Miles : and by *Homer* altogether
Ægyptus by others, Triton here and there hitting upon
Islands, and stirred with so many Provocations : and at the
last enclosed within Mountains : and in no place is it more a
Torrent, while the Water that it beareth hasteneth to a
Place of the Æthiopii called Catadupi, where in the last
Cataract among the opposing Rocks it is supposed not to
run, but to rush down with a mighty Noise. But afterwards
it becometh gentle, as the Stream is broken and the violence
subdued and partly wearied with his long way and so,
though with many Mouths, it dischargeth itself into the
Egyptian Sea. Nevertheless, on certain Days it swelleth
to a great height : and when it hath travelled through all
Egypt, it overfloweth the Land, to its great Fertility. Different causes of this Increase have been given. but those
which carry the most probability are either the rebounding
of the Water driven back by the Etesian Winds, at that time
blowing against it, and driving the Sea upon the Mouths of
the River or the Summer Rain in Æthiopia, by reason
that the same Etesian Winds bring Clouds thither from
other parts of the ·World. *Timæus* the Mathematician
alleged an hidden reason for it, which is, that the Fountain of the Nilus is named Phiala, and the River itself is
hidden within Trenches under the Ground, breathing forth
in a Vapour out of reeking Rocks, where it lieth concealed.
But so soon as the Sun during those Days cometh near, it is

drawn up by the force of Heat, and while it hangeth aloft it
overfloweth · and then, lest it should be devoured, it hideth
again   And this happeneth from the rising of the Dog
through the Sun's entrance into Leo, while the Star standeth
perpendicularly over the Fountain . when in that Tract there
are no Shadows to be seen.   Many again were of a different
Opinion : that a River floweth more abundantly when the
Sun is departed toward the North Pole, which happeneth in
Cancer and Leo, and therefore at that time it is not so easily
dried : but when it is returned again toward Capricorn and
the South Pole, it is drunk up, and therefore floweth more
sparily.   But if, according to *Timæus*, it would be thought
possible that the Water should be drawn up, the want of
Shadows during those Days, and in those Places, continueth ·
still without end.   For the River beginneth to increase at
the New Moon, that is after the Solstice, by little and little
gently, so long as the Sun passeth through Cancer, but most
abundantly when he is in Leo.   And when he is entered
into Virgo it falleth in the same measure as it rose before.
And it is altogether brought within its banks in Libra, as
Herodotus thinketh, by the hundredth day.   While it riseth
it hath been thought unlawful for Kings or Governors to sail
upon it.   Its increasings are measured by Marks in certain
Pits.   The ordinary Height is sixteen Cubits.   The Waters
short of this do not overflow all ; when more than that they
are a hinderance, by reason that they retire more slowly   By
these the Seed Time is consumed, by the Earth being too
Wet, by the other there is none, because the Ground is
Thirsty.   The Province taketh reckoning of both.   For
in 12 Cubits it findeth Famine : at 13 it feeleth Hunger ; 14
Cubits comfort their Hearts ; 15 bring Safety, and 16
Dainties.   The greatest Increase that ever was known until
these Days was 18 Cubits, in the time of Prince *Claudius :*
and the least, in the Pharsalian War : as if the River by
that Prodigy turned away with horror from the Slaughter of
that great Man.[1]   When the Waters have stood, they are

---

[1] Pompey the Great, slain by treachery in Egypt.—*Wern Club*

admitted by opening the Flood-gates   And so soon as any
part of the Land is freed from the Water it is sowed.   This
is the only River, of all others, that breatheth out no Air.
The Dominion of Egypt beginneth at Syenè, from the Frontier
of Æthiopia, for that is the Name of a Peninsula a hundred
Miles in Compass, wherein are the Cerastæ upon the side of
Arabia and over against it the four Islands Philæ, 600
Miles from the Division of Nilus, where it began to be called
Delta, as we have said   This space of Ground hath *Artemidorus* published , and that within it were 250 Towns.
Juba setteth down 400 Miles.   *Aristocreon* saith, That from
Elephantis to the Sea is 750 Miles. The Island Elephantis
is Inhabited beneath the lowest Cataract three Miles, and
above Syenè 16 : and is the utmost Point that the Egyptians sail unto. It is 586 Miles from Alexandria. So far
the Authors above written have erred : there the Æthiopian
Ships assemble ; for they are made to fold up together, and
are carried upon Shoulders, so often as they come to those
Cataracts.   Egypt, above the other glory of Antiquity,
pretends that in the Reign of King *Amasis* there were inhabited in it 20,000 Cities   And even at this Day it is full
of them, though of base account.   Nevertheless, that of
Apollo is renowned ; and near to it that of Leucothea, and
Diospolis[1] the Great, the same as Thebes, noble for the
Fame of its Hundred Gates. Also, Captos, a great commer-
cial Town very near to Nilus, frequented for Merchandise of
India and Arabia   Near is the Town of *Venus*, and another
of *Jupiter ;* and Tentyris, beneath which standeth Abydus,
the royal Seat of *Memnon ,* and renowned for the Temple of
Osiris, seven Miles and a half distant from the River, toward
Lybia.   Then Ptolemais, Panopolis, and another of *Venus.*
Also in the Lybian Coast, Lycon, where Mountains bound
Thebais.   After these, the Towns of *Mercury,* Alabastron,
Canum, and that of *Hercules* spoken of before.   After these,
Arsinoè, and the abovesaid Memphis, between which and
the Nomos Arsinoctes, in the Lybian Coast, are the Towns
called Pyramids ; the Labyrinth built up out of the Lake

[1] The city of Jupiter

Mœris without any Timber to it, and the Town Crialon. One besides, standing within and bounding upon Arabia, called the Town of the Sun . of great importance.

Chapter X.

Alexandria.[1]

But justly worthy of praise is Alexandria, standing upon the Coast of the Egyptian Sea, built by *Alexander* the Great on the Part of Africa, 12 Miles from the Mouth of Canopus, near to the Lake Mareotis : which Lake was formerly called Arapotes.[2]　*Dinochares*, the Architect, renowned for his remarkable Ability in many ways, laid out the Plan with the great Extent of the Circuit of 15 Miles, according to the Shape of a Macedonian Cloak , full of Plaits, with the Circuit waved on to the right Hand and on the left with an angular Extension; and yet, even then, he assigned one-fifth Part of this Space for the King's Palace.　The Lake Mareotis[3] from the South Side of the City, meeteth with an Arm of the River Nilus, brought from out of the Mouth of the said River called Canopicus, for the more commodious Commerce out of the inland Continent.　This Lake containeth within it sundry Islands, and, according to *Claudius Cæsar*, it is 30

[1] Alexandria is connected with much that is interesting in the estimation of the Christian and philosopher. It was built b c 331, and became the capital of Egypt under the Ptolemies, at a subsequent period, its library was the most renowned in the world; its school rose into high repute during the second and third centuries, it long continued a flourishing bishopric of the early Christian Church (having been planted by St Mark), and was the scene of many Christian persecutions in common with the rest of the empire. Of the ancient city little remains, the only monuments of its extent and grandeur being, as Dr Robinson relates, "a few cisterns still in use, the catacombs on the shore, the granite obelisk of Thothmes III , with its fallen brother, brought hither from Heliopolis, and usually called 'Cleopatra's Needle ,' and the column of Dioclesian, commonly called ' Pompey's Pillar '"—*Wern. Club*

[2] Or, Rachobes.

[3] (*Various reading*)—"The Lake Mareotis, from the south part of the city, by an arm of the sea, is sent through the mouth of Canopus for inland traffic; it also embraces many islands, and is 30 miles in breadth, and 150 in circuit, as *Claudius Cæsar* says." — *Wern. Club.*

Miles over. Others say, that it lieth in Length 40 Schœni; and as every Schœnus is 30 Stadia, it cometh to be 150 Miles long, and as many broad. There are many Towns of importance standing upon the Course of the River Nilus, and those especially which have given Names to the Mouths, not to all those (for there are 11 of them, besides 4 more, which they themselves call false Mouths), but to the most celebrated 7: as, to that of Canopus, next to Alexandria; then Bolbitinum, Sebenniticum, Phatniticum, Mendesicum, Taniticum, and last, Pelusiacum; besides, Buros, Pharbœtos, Leontopolis, Athribis, the Town of Isis, Busiris, Cynopolis, Aphrodites, Sais, Naucratis, whence some name the Mouth Naucraticum, which others call Heracleoticum, preferring it before Canopicum, next to which it standeth.

Chapter XI.

Arabia.

Beyond the Pelusiac Mouth is Arabia, bordering on the Red Sea. and that Arabia, so rich and odoriferous, and renowned with the Surname of Happy. This Desert Arabia is possessed by the Catabanes, Esbonitæ, and Scenite Arabians: barren, except where it toucheth the Confines of Syria, and, setting aside the Mountain Casius, nothing memorable. This Region is joined to the Arabians, Canchlei on the East Side, and to the Cedræi Southward; and they both are joined afterwards with the Nabathæi Moreover, two Bays there be, one Bay is called that of Heroopoliticus, and the other, Elaniticus: in the Red Sea, bordering on Egypt, 150 Miles distant, between two Towns, Elana and Gaza, which is in our [Mediterranean] Sea. *Agrippa* counteth from Pelusium to Arsinoe, a Town upon the Red Sea, through the Deserts, an hundred and five-and-twenty Miles So small a Way lieth between things of such Difference in Nature.

Chapter XII.

Syria, Palæstina, Phœnicè.

Near the Coast is Syria, a Region which in Times past was the chiefest of Lands, and distinguished by many Names.

For where it toucheth upon the Arabians, it was called Palæstina,[1] Judæa, Cœle (Syria); and afterward, Phœnicè: and where it passes inward, Damascena. Still further southwards, it is named Babylonia And the same between the Rivers Euphrates and Tigris is called Mesopotamia, and when it passeth the Mountain Taurus, it is Sophenè · but on this Side Comagenè, and beyond Armenia, is Adiabenè, formerly named Assyria; and where it meets Cilicia, it is known by the Name of Antiochia. The whole Length of Syria between Cilicia and Arabia is 470 Miles: the Breadth from Seleucia Pieria to Zeugma, a Town seated upon the Euphrates, is 175 Miles. They that minutely divide it would have Phœnicè to be environed with Syria; and that it is the Sea-coast of Syria, a Part of which compriseth Idumæa and Judæa: then Phœnicè, and then Syria. And that Sea which lieth along that Coast beareth the Name of the Phœnician Sea. This Nation of the Phœnicians hath had great Glory for the Invention of Letters, and for the Arts of the Stars, Navigation, and Skill in War. Beyond Pelusium is Chabriæ Castra, the Mountain Casius, the Temple of *Jupiter Casius*, the Tomb of *Pompeius Magnus*, and Ostracinè. From Pelusium to the Frontiers of Arabia are 65 Miles.

CHAPTER XIII.

Idumæa,[2] Syria, Palæstina, Samaria.

Soon after beginneth Idumæa and Palestina, from the Rising up of the Lake Sirbon, which some have reported to

---

[1] The following division of Palestine under the Romans will throw light upon the comments which follow :—

Palestina Prima, Kingdom of Judah (Judæa) and Samaria
Palestina Secunda, Galilee and Trachonitis.
Palestina Tertia, Peræa and Idumæa Proper.

Wern. Club

[2] Idumæa comprised the country in the southern extremity of Judæa, and embraced also *a part of Arabia*, which, from having been left nearly depopulated during the Babylonian captivity, was seized upon by the Idumæans, and continued to be called Idumæa in common with Idumæa

possess a circuit of 150 Miles. *Herodotus* saith it lies close by the Mountain Casius; but now it is a small Lake. The Towns are Rhinocolura, and within the Land, Raphæa also Gaza, and within, Anthedon, and the Mountain Angoris. Samaria, the Region through the Coast; the free Town 'Ascalon, and Azotus: the two Jamnes, whereof one is within the Land; and Joppè, in Phœnicia, which, by report, is more ancient than the Deluge over the Earth [1] It is situated upon a Hill, with a Rock before it, in which they shew the Remains of the Chains of *Andromeda.*   There the fabulous *Derceto* is worshipped.   Then is Apollonia; the Town of Strato, called also Cæsarea, founded by King *Herod:* it beareth now the Name of Prima Flavia, a Colony derived from *Vespasian* the Emperor.   The Bounds of Palæstina are 180 Miles from the Confines of Arabia: and there entereth Phœnicè. But within-land are the Towns of Samaria, and Neapolis, which formerly was named Mamortha [or Maxbota].   Also Sebastè upon the Mountain, and Gamala, which yet standeth higher than it.

Proper, to a later period than the date of our author.   The bounds of Palestine, in the time of the Romans, embraced Judæa, Samaria, Galilee, and Trachonitis; and Peræa and Idumæa — *Wern Club*

[1] Mandeville, who travelled through these countries about the year 1323, and collected all the information that fell in his way, without discrimination, says· "And whoso wil go longe tyme on the See, and come nerrer to Jerusalem, he schal go fro Cipre, be see, to the Port Jaff.   For that is the nexte Havene to Jerusalem.   For fro that Havene is not but o Day Journeye and an half to Jerusalem. And the Town is called Jaff· for on of the Sones of Noe, that highte Japhet, founded it, and now it is clept Joppe.   And zee schulle undrestonde, that it is on of the oldest Townes of the World· for it was founded before Noes Flode.   And zitt there schewethe in the Roche ther, as the Irene cheynes were festned, that Andromade, a great Geaunt, was bounden with, and put in Presoun before Noes Flode of the whiche Geaunt, is a rib of his Syde, that his 40 Fote longe" In the Ethiopics of Heliodorus, book x , the Ethiopic kings are said to derive their pedigree from Perseus and Andromeda; whose history is by Pliny treated as something more than a fable But the mistake of Mandeville, in confounding Andromeda with the monster that was to have devoured her, is perfectly consistent with other errors in regard to the Scriptures and classical learning, which occur in his narrative — *Wern. Club*

CHAPTER XIV.[1]

Judæa and Galilæa.

ABOVE Idumæa and Samaria, Judæa spreadeth out far in Length and Breadth. That part of it which joineth to Syria, is called Galilæa : but that which is next to Syria and Egypt is named Peræa [*i. e* beyond Jordan]: full of rough Mountains dispersed here and there : and separated from the other Parts of Judæa by the River Jordan. The rest of Judæa is divided into ten Toparchies, which we will speak of in order of Hiericho, planted with Date-trees ; Emmaus, well watered with Fountains ; Lydda, Joppica, Accrabatena, Gophnitica, Thamnitica, Betholenè, Tephenè, and Oriuè, wherein stood Hierosolyma, by far the most illustrious of the Cities of the East, and not of Judæa only. In it also is the Toparchy Herodium, with a famous Town of the same Name.

CHAPTER XV.

The River Jordan.[2]

THE River Jordanis springeth from the Fountain Paneades, which gave the Surname to Cæsarea, whereof we will

[1] This chapter should properly have been embodied with the preceding, which treats of Palestine, that name having been applied by the Greeks to the whole country on account of the number of the Philistines always within its bounds, both before and after the final conquest of that people by David and Solomon. "Judæa," in its real signification, implies the whole of the country inhabited by the Jews, in fact, the whole "Land of Promise," from Dan to Beersheba in length, and including the region allotted to the two tribes and a half on the other side Jordan, the term was originally synonymous with "the land of Judah," but on the separation of the ten tribes, the latter term was applied to the territories of Judah and Benjamin, then formed into a separate kingdom, and hence "Judæa" also came to be applied to that district in particular. Pliny is also in error in speaking of Judæa as "spreading out far in length *above* Idumæa and *Samaria*," inasmuch as Samaria occupies the central portion of Judæa itself, and there is, therefore, an evident contradiction in the description — *Wern. Club.*

[2] This river rises at Cæsarea Philippi, its length is 100 miles or there-

speak.   It is a pleasant River, and so far as the Situation of the Country will permit, spacious, offering itself to the neighbouring Inhabitants; and reluctantly, as it were, it passeth to the Lake Asphaltites, cursed by Nature: by which it is swallowed up; it loseth its own esteemed Waters, by their becoming mixed with those of the Pestilential Lake. And therefore upon the first opportunity of any Valleys, it poureth itself into a Lake, which many call Genesara, which is 16 Miles Long and 6 Broad.   This is environed with beautiful Towns: on the East side with Julias and Hippo; on the South with Tarichea, by which Name the Lake is by some called; and on the West with Tiberias, an healthful Place on account of the Hot Waters.

Chapter XVI.

Asphaltites.

Asphaltites[1] produceth nothing besides Bitumen, from whence the name.   No Body of any Creature doth it receive: Bulls and Camels float upon it.   And hence ariseth the

abouts, and its *embouchure* is into the Dead Sea; its inner banks, to within a few miles of this place, are covered with willows, oleanders, reeds, &c &c whilst its periodical overflowings have formed a wider channel, defined by a second or outer bank on either side.— *Wern Club.*

[1] *Asphaltites*, in other words the bituminous lake, from the abundance of asphalt (bitumen) which occurs in it.   Dr. Shaw estimated its length at 72 English miles, and its breadth 19 miles.   Dr. Robinson, however, estimates its length at only 50, and its average breadth 10 or 12 miles.   The constituents of the water of the Dead Sea are as follows :—

Muriate of lime	3·920	grains.
Muriate of magnesia	10·246	"
Muriate of soda	19·360	"
Sulphate of lime	0·054	"

34·580 grains in each 100

Several analyses have been made by Marat, Gay-Lussac, Gmelin, &c., with nearly the same result.   The origin of this lake accounts for the above facts, and the phenomena by which it is surrounded equally evidence its truth—sterility in land, water, and air, are its saddening characters.   It is reputed to be very shallow, which seems to be a mistake. It also bore the name of the "Sea of the Plain."   The history of this lake is best seen in the Bible.— *Wern Club.*

Report that nothing will sink in it. This Lake in Length exceedeth 100 Miles, in Breadth 25 Miles where broadest, and 6 where narrowest. On the East, Arabia of the Nomades confronteth it, and on the South, Machærus, in Time past the second Fortress of Judæa, next to Hierosolyma. On the same side is a Fountain of Hot Waters, useful in Medicine, named Callirhoe; a Name that expresseth the Glory of the Waters.

Chapter XVII.

The Race of the Esseni.

Along the West Coast retire the Esseni:[1] a Nation living alone, and beyond all others throughout the World wonderful: without any Women, casting off the whole of Venus: without Money, keeping company only with Date-trees. Yet the Country is ever well peopled, because daily numbers of Strangers resort thither from other Parts: and such as are weary of Life are by the Waves of Fortune driven thither to their manner of Living. Thus for thousands of Ages (beyond belief to say), the Race is eternal in which no one is Born: so prolific to them is the Repentance of Life of other Men. Beneath them stood the Town Engadda, for Fertility (of Soil) and Groves of Date-trees the next City to Hierosolyma, now a Place for the Dead. Beyond it is Massada, a Castle upon a Rock, and not far from Asphaltites. And thus much concerning Judæa.

[1] The Essenes were a Jewish sect, divided into two classes. First, the *practical*, who lived in society, and applied themselves to husbandry and other harmless occupations; and second, the *contemplative*, who were also called *therapeutæ*, or physicians, from their application principally to the cure of the diseases of the soul, these last devoted themselves wholly to meditation, and avoided living in great towns, as unfavourable to a contemplative life. Both classes were exceedingly abstemious and highly exemplary in their moral deportment. Although our Saviour censured all the other sects of the Jews for their vices, yet He never spoke of the Essenes, neither are they mentioned by name in any part of the New Testament. Pliny's object in the account he has thought fit to give of them appears to have been to say something that might excite wonder and ridicule.— *Wern Club.*

Chapter XVIII.

Decapolis.

There is joined to it on the side of Syria the Region Decapolis,[1] so called from the number of Towns, in which all Men observe not the same. Nevertheless most Men speak of Damascus and Opotos, watered by the River Chrysorrhoa, and also of the fruitful Philadelphia and Raphana, all lying within Arabia. Moreover, of Scythopolis, so named from the Scythians there planted: and formerly Mysa, so named of Father *Liber*, because his Nurse was buried there. Gadara, with the River Hieromiax running before it, and the before-named Hippos Dios. Pella, enriched with Waters, Galaza and Canatha. The Tetrarchies lie between and about these Cities; every one resembling a Region: and they are reduced into several Kingdoms: Trachonitis, Panias, wherein standeth Cæsarea, with the Fountain abovesaid; Abila, Arca, Ampeloessa, and Gabè.

Chapter XIX.

Tyrus[2] and Sidon.

We must return to the Sea-coast of Phœnicè, where a River runneth called Crocodilon, on which stood a Town bearing the same Name. Also there are the Memorials of the Cities, Dorum, Sycaminon, the Promontory Carmelum; and a Town on the Mountain so named, but in old Time called Ecbatana. Near this is Getta and Jebba: the River Pagida or Belus, mixing on its little Shore the Sands fertile in Glass. This River floweth out of the stagnant pond Ceudevia, from the foot of Carmel. Near it is the City Ptole-

---

[1] Josephus mentions the following cities as contained within this region.—Pella, Gerasa, Gadara, Hippos Dios, Damascus, Philadelphia, Otopos, Raphana, and Scythopolis —*Wern Club*

[2] There were two cities of this name, one on the Syrian coast of the Continent (*vide* Bishop Newton), and the other on an adjacent island, which, in our author, are both spoken of *together*. Tyre has been called the daughter of Sidon, because "The merchants of Sidon replenished it"—(*Isaiah*, xxiii 2)—*Wern Club*

mais, a Colony of *Claudius Cæsar,* formerly called Acè. The Town Ecdippa; the Promontory Album; Tyrus, in old Time an Island, lying almost three quarters of a Mile within the Deep Sea: but now, by the Besieging Works of *Alexander,* joined to the firm Land: renowned for having produced Cities of ancient Name, Leptis, Utica, and that Carthage, the Rival of the Empire of Rome for the Dominion of the whole World: yea and Gades, founded beyond the Bounds of the Earth. But now all the Glory thereof standeth upon the (Shell-fishes) Chylium and Purpura.[1] The Circumference of it is 19 Miles, comprised within Palætyrus. The Town itself taketh up 22 Stadia. Near it are the Towns Lynhydra, Sarepta, and Ornithon: also Sidon, where Glass is made, and which is the Parent of Thebes in Bœotia.

Chapter XX.

The Mountain Libanus.

Behind it beginneth Mount Libanus,[2] and for 1500 Stadia it reacheth as far as to Smyrna, where it is named Cœlè-Syria. Another Mountain equal to it, and lying opposite to it, is called Antilibanus; with a Valley lying between, which in old Time was joined (to the other Libanus) by a Wall. Being past this, there is the Region Decapolis; and the above-named Tetrarchies with it, and the whole expanse of Palestina. But in that Coast still along the Foot of Libanus, is the River Magoras, and the Colony Berytus, called also Fœlix Julia. The Town Leontos; the River Lycos; Palæbyblos; the River Adonis; the Towns Byblos, Botrys, Gigarta, Trieris, Calamos; and Tripolis, subject to the Tyrians, Sidonians, and Aradians. Orthosia and the River Eleutheros. The Towns Simyra, Marathos, and over against Aradus, Antaradus, a Town of seven Stadia; and an

---

[1] See b. ix. c 36, &c.

[2] *Libanus* (Lebanon) is a chain of limestone mountains; the cedars for which they were formerly famed still grow there, though in reduced numbers, forming a small grove, in a small hollow at the foot of the highest peak. *Anti-Libanus* is the more lofty ridge of the two.—*Wern. Club*

Island less than a quarter of a Mile from the Continent.
The Country where the said Mountains end, and in the Plains
lying between, beginneth Mount Bargylis: and thence
Phœnicè endeth, and Syria beginneth again.   The Towns
Carnè, Balanea, Paltos, Gabalè, the Promontory wherein is
the Free (City) Laodicea, with Diospolis, Heraclea, Cha-
radius, Posidium.

Chapter XXI.

Syria Antiochena.

Thenceforward is the Promontory of Syria Antiochena,
within is the Free City itself, Antiochena, surnamed Epi-
daphnè; through the midst runneth the River Orontes.
But in the Promontory is the Free (City) Seleucia, named
also Pieria

Chapter XXII.

The Mountain Casius.

Above (the City) Seleucia, there is another Mountain
named Casius, as well as the other.   This is of that Height,
that if a Man be upon the Top of it in the Night, at the
Fourth Watch, he may behold the Sun rising.   So that
with a little turning of his Body, he may at one Time see
both Day and Night.   The Passage round to the Top is 19
Miles; but directly up, it is only Four Miles.   In the Borders runneth the River Orontes, which riseth between Libanus and Antilibanus, near to Heliopolis.   Then, the Town
Rhosos: and behind, the Passages between the Mountains
Rhosii and Taurus, which are called Portæ Syriæ.   In the
Coast, the Town Myriandros, the Mountain Amanus,
where is the Town Bomitæ. This separateth Cilicia from
the Syrians.

Chapter XXIII.

Cæle-Syria.[1]

Now, to speak of the Midland parts.   Cœlè hath Apamia, separated from the Nazerines' Tetrarchy by the River

[1] *Cælo-Syria* (or Lower Syria) signifying "Syria in the Hollow."
It may be considered, says Strabo, "either in a proper and restrained

Marsia: Bambycè, otherwise called Hierapolis; but of the Syrians, Magog. There is worshipped the monstrous Idol Atargatis,[1] called by the Greeks Derceto. Also Chalcis, surnamed Upon Belus: from which, the Region Chalcidenè, the most fertile of all Syria, taketh its Name. Then the Region Cyrrhistica, Cirrhus, Gazatæ, Gindareni, and Gabeni. Two Tetrarchies, called Granucomatæ. The Hemiseni, Hylatæ, the Nation of the Ituræ, and those of them

sense, as comprehending only the tract of land between Libanus and Anti-Libanus; or in a larger signification, and then it will comprehend all the country in obedience to the king of Syria, from Seleucia or Arabia and Egypt.—*Wern Club.*

[1] The Syrian idol Atargatis is the same as the Astarte or Ashtaroth, so often mentioned in Holy Scripture; it is also the Derceto of the Greeks, who represent her to be the daughter of Venus, or, as some say, Venus herself. The upper half of this monster had the form of a woman, while the lower was that of a fish. Atargatis is fabled to have thrown herself into a lake near Ascalon in Syria, through vexation at the loss of her chastity, after having given birth to a daughter named Semiramis. From this circumstance the Syrians abstained from eating the fish of that lake, deified Atargatis, and built a temple to her memory on the borders of the lake. Her daughter, Semiramis, was left exposed in a desert; but her life was preserved by doves for one whole year, till a shepherd of Ninus found her and brought her up as his own child. She afterwards married Menones, the governor of Nineveh, and at length became the celebrated Queen of Assyria. After her death she was changed into a dove, and received immortal honours in Assyria. Ovid alludes to both mother and daughter in the commencement of his 4th Book of the Metamorphoses.

> "But she awhile profoundly seemed to muse,
> Perplex'd amid variety to choose;
> And knew not whether she should first relate
> The poor Dercetis, and her wondrous fate,
> (The Palestines believe it to a man,
> And shew the lake in which her scales began.)
> Or, if she rather should the daughter sing,
> Who in the hoary verge of life took wing,
> Who soar'd from earth, and dwelt in towers on high,
> And now a dove, she flits along the sky."
>
> Eusden's *Translation*

It may be doubted whether she is not identical with Dagon, the first goddess of the Phœnicians.—*Wern Club*

who are named Betarrani, and the Mariammitani. The
Tetrarchy named Mammisea Paradisus, Pagræ, Pinaritæ,
and two Seleuciæ, besides the abovenamed ; one called Upon
Euphrates, and the other, Upon Belus: the Carditenses.
The rest of Syria hath besides these which shall be spoken
of with the Euphrates, the Arethusi, Beræenses, and Epi-
phanenses. Eastward, the Laodiceni, which are entituled,
Upon Libanus: the Leucadii, and Larissæi : besides 17
Tetrarchies reduced into Kingdoms under Barbaric Names.

CHAPTER XXIV.

Euphrates.[1]

THIS is the fittest Place to speak of the Euphrates. Its
Source, by the Report of them who have seen it most closely,
is in Caranitis, a Province of Armenia the Greater. These
are *Domitius Corbulo*, who says, that it riseth in the Mountain Aba; and *Licinius Mutianus*, who affirmeth, that it
issueth from the Foot of the Mountain which they call
Capotes, 12 Miles higher than Simyra: and that in the
beginning it was called Pyxirates. It runneth first to Der-
xene, and then to Ana also, shutting out the Regions of Armenia from Cappadocia. The Dastusæ from Simyra is 75
Miles. From thence it is navigable to Pastona, Fifty Miles:
from it to Melitenè in Cappadocia, 74 Miles. To Elegia in
Armenia, Ten Miles: where it receiveth the Rivers, Lycus,
Arsania, and Arsanus. Near Elegia it meeteth the Moun-

---

[1] *Euphrates* rises in Armenia, near Mount Aba, and after flowing by
Syria, Mesopotamia, and the site of Babylon, empties itself into the Persian Gulf. It overflows its banks at certain seasons, and in consequence
its banks are very fertile

The Euphrates is universally allowed to take its rise in Armenia
Major; but in what particular spot, or in what direction it afterwards
shapes its course, is still a matter of the greatest disagreement. Pliny's
account entirely differs from those of Strabo and Mela The best com-
pendium of the discoveries of modern geographers and travellers on
this subject will be found in the *Penny Cyclopædia* articles " Asia" and
" Euphrates." See also Macdonnald Kinneir's large map.—*Wern. Club.*

tain Taurus : yet stayeth it not, but prevaileth, although it
be in Breadth Twelve Miles. Where it breaketh through
they call it Omiras : and so soon as it hath cut through it is
named Euphrates · full of Rocks and very violent. There
it separateth Arabia on the Left Hand, called the Region of
the Meri, by the Measure of Three Schœnæ, and on the
Right, Comagenè. Nevertheless, even there where it conquereth Taurus, it suffers a Bridge. At Claudiopolis in Cappadocia, it taketh its Course westward And here the
Taurus, although resisted at first, hindereth him of his Course:
and notwithstanding it was overcome and dismembered, it
conquereth in another way, and drives it thus broken into
the South. Thus Nature matcheth these Forces: The one
proceeding whither it chooseth, and the other not suffering
it to run which way it will. From the Cataracts it is Navigable, and Forty Miles from that place standeth Samosata,
the Head of all Comagenè. Arabia aforesaid hath the Towns
Edessa, sometime called Antiochea ; Callirrhoe, taking its
Name from the Fountain; and Carræ, famous for the
slaughter of *Crassus*. Here joineth the Prefecture of Mesopotamia, which taketh its beginning from the Assyrians, in
which stand the Towns Anthemusa and Nicephorium. Presently the Arabians, called Rhetavi, whose Capital is Sin-
gara. But from Samosatæ, on the side of Syria, the River
Marsyas runneth into Euphrates. Gingla limiteth Comagenè, and the City of the Meri beginneth it. The Towns
Epiphania and Antiochia have the River running close to
them, and they are called Euphrates. Zeugma likewise,
72 Miles from Samosatæ, is ennobled by the Passage over
Euphrates . for it is joined to Apamia, over against it, by a
Bridge, built by *Seleucus* the Founder of both. The People
that join to Mesopotamia are called Rhoali. But the Towns
of Syria are Europum ; Thapsacum, formerly, now Amphipolis ; Arabian Scœnitæ. Thus it passeth as far as to the
Place Ura, in which turning to the East, it leaveth the
Deserts of Palmyra in Syria, which reach to the City Petra
and the Country of Arabia called the Happy.

Chapter XXV.

Palmyra [1]

THE City Palmyra, noble for its situation, the Riches of its Soil, and its pleasant Streams, encloseth its Fields with a vast compass of Sand. And as if shut out by Nature from all other Lands, it is by a peculiar lot between two mighty Empires, the Romans and the Parthians; wherein Discord is ever the first object on both Sides. It is distant from Seleucia of the Parthians, which is called, on the Tigris, 537 Miles· and from the nearest Coast of Syria, 252· and from Damascus, 27 nearer.

Chapter XXVI.

Hierapolis

BENEATH the Solitudes of Palmyra, lieth the Country Stelendena,[2] wherein are the Cities named at this Day Hierapolis, Berœa, and Chalcis. Beyond Palmyra also, Hemesa taketh up some part of those Deserts: and likewise Elutium, nearer to Petra by one-half than is Damascus. And next to Astura standeth Philiscum, a Town of the Parthians, on Euphrates From which by Water it is a Journey

[1] We are at a loss to account for the praise bestowed on the site of Palmyra, situated as it is on the borders of a vast wilderness, it can only be from comparison with the surrounding sterility, and the supply of water obtained here, which is so rare a blessing in the sandy plains of the East The country does not appear to have undergone any change from the period of the foundation of this ancient city, until now; Tadmor (its original name) was built by king Solomon, probably for the purpose of cutting off all commerce between the Syrians and Mesopotamians, and it rose into note in consequence In later times it was also much frequented by the caravans of Persia and the countries beyond — *Wern Club*

[2] Stelendena does not appear to be mentioned by any other writer than Pliny. Hierapolis has been just before spoken of under the name of Bambycè or Magog, as the Syrians call it. It is the Magog of Holy Scripture (Ezekiel, xxxviii) concerning the situation of which great diversity of opinion has been entertained — *Wern Club*

of Ten Days to Seleucia, and about as many to Babylon
Euphrates is divided Fourscore and Three Miles from Zeugma, about the Village Massicè, and on the Left Side it
passeth into Mesopotamia, through Seleucia, it being poured
into the River Tigris as it runneth by: but on the right
Channel it passeth toward Babylon, formerly the Chief City
of Chaldæa; and passing through the midst of it, as also of
another which they call Otris, it is drawn off into Marshes
It riseth at certain Times after the manner of the Nilus,
but with a little difference; for it overfloweth Mesopotamia
when the Sun is the 20th degree of *Cancer*, and beginneth
again to diminish when the Sun is past *Leo*, and is entered
into *Virgo* · so that in the 29th degree of *Virgo*, it is reduced
again.

Chapter XXVII.

*Cilicia, and the Nations adjoining, Isauricæ, Homonades,
Pisidia, Lycaonia, Pamphylia: the Mountain Taurus,
and Lycia*

But we will return to the Coasts of Syria, to which
Cilicia is the nearest. The River Diaphanes, the Mountain
Crocodilus, Passages of the Mount Amanus: Rivers, Andri-
con, Pinarus, and Lycus, the Gulf Issicus. The Town Issa,
then the River Chlorus, the Free Town Ægè, the River Pyra-
mus, and the Passages of Cilicia. The Towns Mallos and
Magarsos; and within Tarsos, the Plains, Aleii; the Towns,
Cassipolis and Mopsum, which is free, and standeth upon the
River Pyramus, Thynos, Zephyrium, and Anchialæ. The
Rivers Saros and Sydnus, which runneth through Tarsus, a
free City, far from the Sea: the Country Celenderitis, with
the Town. The Place called Nymphæum, and Solœ Cilicii,
now Pompeiopolis, Adana, Cibira, Pinara, Pedalie, Halix,
Arsinoe, Tabæ, and Doron: and near the Sea ye shall find a
Town, an Harbour, and a Cave, all named Corycos. Soon
after, the River Calycadnus. The Promontory Sarpedon,
the Towns Olmè and Mylæ, the Promontory and Town of
Venus, nearest to which is the Isle of Cyprus. But in the
Mainland are the Towns Myanda, Anemurium, Corace-

sium : and the River Melas, the ancient Bound of Cilicia
Within are to be spoken of, the Anazarbeni, at this Day
named Cæsar-Augustani ; Castabla ; Epiphania, formerly
Eniandos, Eleusa, and Iconium.   Seleucia upon the River
Calicadmus, surnamed also Trachiotis, removed backward
from the Sea, where it was called Hormia.   Furthermore,
within the Country, the Rivers Liparis, Bombos, and Paradisus   The Mountain Jubarus.   All Authors have joined
Pamphylia to Cilicia, and never regarded the Nation Isau-
rica.   The Towns within it are, Isaura, Clibanus, Lalassis ;
and it shooteth down to the Sea-side of the Country Anemurium abovesaid.   In like sort, as many as have set forth
Descriptions of these Matters, had no Knowledge of the
neighbouring Nation, the Homonades, which have a Town
within their Country called Homona.   Other Fortresses, to
the number of 44, lie hidden among the rugged Valleys.
The Pisidæ, formerly called Solymis, are placed on the top ;
a Colony of which is Cæsarea, the same as Antiochia.   The
Towns are Oroanda and Sagalessos.   This Nation is enclosed
within Lycaonia, lying within the Jurisdiction of Asia : with
which are joined the Philomelienses, Tymbrians, Leucolithi,
Pelteni, and Hyrienses.   There is given a Tetrarchy out of
Lycaonia, on that side that bordereth upon Galatia : to
which belong 14 Cities, whereof the most celebrated is Iconium.   In Lycaonia itself, those of celebrity are Tembasa
upon Taurus, Sinda in the Confines of Galatia and Cappadocia.   But on the Side thereof above Pamphylia, the Myliæ,
descended in old Time from Thrace, whose Town is Aricanda.
Pamphylia was in ancient Time called Mopsopia.   The Pamphylian Sea joineth to the Cilician.   Its Towns are Sidè, As-
pendus on the Mountain, Platanistus, and Perga.   Also the
Promontory Leucolla, the Mountain Sardemisus, the River
Eurymedon running near Aspendum.   Cataractes, near which
stand Lyrnessus and Olbia ; and the furthest of that Coast,
Phaselis.   Joined to it is the Lycian Sea, and the Nation of
the Lycians, where is a great Gulf.   The Mountain Taurus,
coming from the Eastern Shores, fixeth the limit by the
Promontory Chelidonium.   This (Taurus) is a mighty Moun-

tain, and is an overlooker to a very great Number of Nations.
So soon as it is risen from the Indian Sea, it parteth . and the
right Hand passeth Northward, the left Southward, bending
toward the West : dividing Asia through the midst : and
(but that it meeteth the Seas) ready to oppress the whole
Earth   It retireth, therefore, toward the North, fetching a
great Circuit, and so making way, as if the Industry of
Nature continually opposed the Seas against it ; on one side
the Phœnician Sea, on another the Sea of Pontus ; here the
Caspian and Hyrcanian Seas, and full against him the Lake
Mœotis.   And notwithstanding these Bars, within which it
is pent and entwined, yet at last Conqueror ; it winds away
and passeth on until it encounters its kindred Riphæan
Mountains : and wherever it goeth, it is distinguished by a
Number of new Names.   For in the Beginning of its Course
it is called Imaus : a little forward Emodus, Paropamisus,
Circius, Camibades, Parphariades, Choatras, Oreges, Oro-
andes, Niphates, Taurus ; and where it is predominant, Caucasus ; where it stretcheth forth its Arms, as if now and then
endeavouring toward the Seas, it taketh the Name Sarpedon,
Coracesius, and Cragus ; and then again Taurus, even where
it gapeth, and opening itself to the People   And yet it
claimeth its Unity still, and (these Passages are called) by
the Names of Gates ; as in one Place Armeniæ, in another
Caspiæ, and again Ciliciæ.   And besides being broken into
Parcels, and escaped far from the Sea, it taketh here and
there many Names of Nations ; as, on the right Hand Hyr-
canus and Caspius ; on the left, Pariedrus, Moschicus,
Amazonicus, Coraxicus, and Scythicus   And throughout all
Greece, Ceraunius.

To return to Lycia, beyond its Promontory, is the Town
Simena, the Mountain Chimæra, emitting Flames by Night ;
the City Hephæstium, where the Hills likewise oftentimes
are known to burn.   Formerly the City Olympus stood there ;
but now the Mountain Towns, Gagè, Corydalla, and Rhodio-
polis.   Near the Sea, Lymira with a River, into which
Arycandus runneth : also the Mountain Massyrites, the
Cities Andriarca and Myra.   These Towns, Apyrè and Anti-

phellos, which formerly was called Habessus, and in a corner, Phellus. Then Pyrrha, and also Xanthus, 15 Miles from the Sea, and a River of the same Name Soon after Patara, formerly named Sataros; and Sydinia on a Hill; the Promontory Ciagus Beyond which is a Gulf equal to the former. There is Pinara; and Telmessus, that boundeth Lycia In ancient Time Lycia possessed threescore Towns, but now 36; of which the most celebrated, besides the above-named, are Canæ, Candyba, where the Wood Oenium is praised;. Podalia, Choma upon the River Adesa, Cyanè, Ascandalis, Amelas, Noscopium, Tlos, and Telanorus. It containeth in the midland Parts Chabalia, with three Towns thereto belonging: Oenonda, Balbura, and Bubon.

Beyond Telmessus is the Asiatic Sea, otherwise called Carpathium, and the Country which is properly called Asia. *Agrippa* hath divided it into two Parts, of which the one by his Description boundeth Phrygia and Lycaonia, eastward: but on the West Side it is limited by the Ægean Sea. Southward it boundeth upon Egypt: and in the North upon Paphlagonia. The Length thereof by his Computation is 470 Miles, the Breadth 300. The other he hath limited Eastward from Armenia the Less: Westward by Phrygia, Lycaonia, and Pamphylia; on the North by the Province of Pontus; and on the South by the Pamphylian Sea: it containeth 575 Miles in Length, and 325 in Breadth The next Coast bordering upon it is Caria: and near it, Ionia; beyond that, Æolis. For Caria encloseth Doris in the midst, environing it round on every Side to the Sea. In it is the Promontory Pedalium, and the River Glaucus, charged with (the River) Telmessus. The Towns, Dædala and Crya, peopled with Fugitives; the River Axon, and the Town Calydua.

CHAPTER XXVIII.

The River Indus

THE River Indus, rising in the craggy Mountains of the Cybiratæ, receiveth threescore regularly running Rivers, but of Torrents above an hundred The Free Town Caunos, and

a little off, Pyrnos. The Port Cressa, from which the Island
Rhodus is distant 20 Miles   The Place Loryma; the Towns
Tysanusa, Taridion, Larymna; the Bay Thymnias, and the
Promontory Aphrodisias; the Town Hyda, the Bay Schœnus.
The Country Bubassus; where stood the Town Acanthus,
otherwise called Dulopolis.   On the Promontory is the Free
(Town) Gnidos, Triopia, then Pegusa, called likewise Stadia
Beyond which Doris beginneth.   But first it is convenient to
have pointed out the midland Jurisdictions and the Parts
which lie behind : one is named Cibiratica.   The Town itself
is in Phrygia, and to it are joined 25 Cities.

Chapter XXIX.

Laodicea, Apamia, Ionia, Ephesus.

The most celebrated City is Laodicea [1]   It is seated on
the River Lycus, Asopus and Caper washing its Sides. This
City was first called Diospolis, and afterwards Rhoas.   The
other Nations belonging to that Jurisdiction worth the Naming are the Hydrelitæ, Themisones, and Hierapolitæ. Another
Jurisdiction taketh its Name from Synnada : and to it repair
the Licaones, Appiani, Eucarpeni, Dorylæi, Midæi, Julienses,
and fifteen other ignoble People   A third (Jurisdiction)
goeth to Apamia, which in old Time was called Celænæ, and
afterwards Ciboton.   It is situated at the Foot of the Moun-

[1] Laodicea, so named in honour of Laodicè, wife of Antiochus II., by
whom the city was enlarged   From all accounts it appears to have been
built on a volcanic hill, and boasted, in its prosperity, many public buildings of note, of which the remains of an aqueduct and amphitheatre are
still to be seen.

Ephesus was the capital of Proconsular Asia, and was situated in Ionia
(now Natolia), about five miles from the Ægean Sea, on the sides and
at the foot of a range of mountains overlooking a fine plain watered and
fertilised by the river Cayster. The city was celebrated for the Temple
of Diana, a most magnificent edifice, erected at the common expense
of the inhabitants of Asia Proper, and described by Pliny, b. xxxvi. c. 14,
but of which the site is now unknown   Ephesus was finally overthrown
in the fourteenth century, after continued struggles   There are numerous
traces of its magnificence still extant, though the neighbouring country
bears all the marks of desolation and decay —*Wern. Club.*

tain Signia, environed with the Rivers Marsyas, Obrima, and Orga, which fall into the Mæander. The River Marsyas, which a little from his Spring is hidden under Ground, where *Marsyas* contended with *Apollo* in playing on the flute, sheweth itself again in Aulocrenæ, for so is the Valley called, ten Miles from Apamia, as Men travel to Phrygia. Under this Jurisdiction we should do well to Name the Metropolitæ, Dionysopolitæ, Euphorbeni, Acmoneses, Pelteni, and Silbiani. There are besides 60 ignoble Towns. Within the Bay of Doris, Leucopolis, Amaxitos, Elæus, and Euthenè Then Towns of Caria, Pitaium, Eutaniæ, and Halicarnassus. To this (City) were annexed by *Alexander* the Great, six Towns: Theangela, Sibdè, Medmossa, Euranium, Pedasium, and Telmessum. It is inhabited between the two Gulfs, Ceramicus and Jasius. From thence Myndus, and where formerly stood Palæmyndus, Neapolis, Nariandus, Carianda, the Free City Termera, Bergyla, and the Town Jasus, which gave Name to the Gulf Jasius. But Caria is most renowned for the Places of Name within it, for therein are these Cities: Mylasa Free, and Antiochia, where sometime were the Towns Seminethos and Cianaos. and it is now environed about with the Mæander and Mossinus. In the same Tract also stood Mæandropolis. There is Eumenia close by the River Cludrus; the River Glaucus; the Town Lysias and Orthasia. The Tract of Berecinthus, Nysa, Trallis, which also is named Euanthia, and Seleucia, and Antiochia. It is washed by the River Eudonè, and Thebanis passeth through it. Some report that the Pigmæi[1]

[1] The Pygmæi were a fabulous nation inhabiting Thrace and other regions, who brought forth young at five years of age, and were old at eight Homer has celebrated their memorable defeats by cranes.—*Iliad, 3d Book.*

> "———— When inclement winters vex the plain
> With piercing frosts, or thick descending rain,
> To warmer seas the cranes embodied fly,
> With noise, and order, through the mid-way sky:
> To pigmy nations wounds and death they bring,
> And all the war descends upon the wing "—*Pope.*

Pliny has described these tiny creatures in Lib. vi c 22 and 35, and

formerly there dwelt. Besides, there are Thydonos, Pyrrha, Euromè, Heraclea, Amyzon, and the Free Alabanda, from which that Jurisdiction took its Name. The Free Stratonicea, Hynidos, Ceramus, Trœzenè, and Phorontis. There are Nations farther remote that resort to that Court the Othromenses, Halydienses or Hyppini, Xystiani, Hydissenses, Apolloniates, Trapezopolitæ, and the Free Aphrodisienses. Besides these, there are Cossinus and Harpasa, close by the River Harpasus, which also ran under Trallicon, when such a Town existed. Lydia is watered by the windings of the River Mæander: and it reacheth above Ionia: being near upon Phrygia in the East, upon Mysia in the North, and in the South side enclosing Caria; and was formerly named Mœonia It is celebrated chiefly for Sardis, seated upon the side of the Mountain Tmolus, formerly called Timolus, planted with Vineyards; and from it flows Pactolus, called likewise Chrysorrhoa as also the Fountain Tarnes This City was commonly by the Mœoniæ called Hydè, and was famous for the Lake of Gyges. That Jurisdiction is at this Day called Sardiana. Thither resort besides the abovenamed, the Macedonian Caducnes, the Loreni,

---

again in lib. vii c. 2. See also Aristotle's *Hist. Anim* lib viii, and *Mela,* lib iii. There can be no question but that the ancient fictions of pygmies, satyrs, cynocephali, cynoprosopi, &c, and other supposed tribes of human monsters, originated in vague accounts of different species of simiæ, though the Bushmen of South Africa are supposed also to have been referred to as a nation of pigmies. The earliest unquestionable reference to any of the true apes is found in the *Periplus* of Hanno, circ 500 B.c

"For three days," says the Carthaginian admiral, "we passed along a burning coast, and at length reached a bay called the Southern Horn In the bottom of this bay we found an island similar to that already mentioned, this island contained a lake, that in its turn contained another island, which was inhabited by wild men The greater number of those we saw were females, they were covered with hair, and our interpreters called them Gorilloi We were unable to secure any of the men as they fled to the mountains, and defended themselves with stones. As to the women, we caught three of them, but they so bit and scratched us that we found it impossible to bring them along; we therefore killed and flayed them, and carried their hides to Carthage."—*Wern. Club*

Philadelpheni, and those Mœonians inhabiting on the
River Cogamus, at the Foot of Tmolus; and the Tripoli-
tani, who, together with the Antoniopolitæ, are washed by
the River Mæander; also, the Apollonos-Hieritæ, Myso-
tmolites, and others of mean Reputation.

Ionia beginneth at the Bay of Jasius, and all its Coast is
full of Indentations. The first Bay in it is Basilicus; the
Promontory Posideum, and the Town called the Oracle of
the Branchidæ, but at this Day, of Apollo Didymæus, 20
Stadia from the Sea-side. And beyond this 180 Stadia,
standeth Milletus, the Head (City) of Ionia, named in Time
past Lelegeis; Pityusa, also named Anactoria. From which,
as from a Mother, are descended more than eighty others,
built along the Sea-coast. Neither is this City to be de-
frauded of the Citizen *Cadmus*, who taught first to declaim
in Prose. The River Mæander issueth out of a Lake in the
Mountain Aulocrenè; and passing by many Towns, and
filled with Abundance of Rivers, it fetcheth such windings
to and fro, that oftentimes it is thought to run backward
again. The first Country it passeth through is Apamia: and
presently Eumenitica, and so through the Plains Bargyl-
letici. Last of all, it cometh gently into Caria, and watering
all that Land with a very fruitful Mud, about ten Stadia
from Miletus it glideth into the Sea. Near (to that River) is
the Mountain Latmus: the Town Heraclea, surnamed
Caryca, from a Hill of that Name; also Myus, which,
as the Report goeth, was first founded by the Iones after
their proceeding from Athens; Naulochum, and Pyrenè.
Upon the Sea-coast the (Town) called Trogilia; the River
Gessus. This Region is sacred to all the Ionians, and therefore it is named Panionia. Near it was Phygela, built for
Fugitives, as appeareth by the Name: and the Town Maia-
thesium: and above it Magnesia, designated with the surname On-Mæander, sprung from the Thessalian Magnesia.
From Ephesus it is distant 15 Miles; and from Tralleis it is
three Miles farther. Formerly it was called Thessalocè and
Androlitia: and being situated upon the Shore, it took away
with it from the Sea other Islands called Derasides. Within-

land Thyatira (in old Time called Pelopia and Euhippa) is washed by the Lycus. But upon the Sea-coast is Manteium; and Ephesus, a Work of the Amazons. But many Names it had gone through before; for in the Time of the Trojan War it was called Alopes: soon after, Ortygia and Morges: and it took the Name of Smyrna, with addition of Trachæa (*i e.* Rough), Samornium, and Ptelea. It is mounted on the Hill Pionè, and is washed by the Caystrus, which springeth out of the Cilbian Hills, and bringeth down with it many other Rivers, and the Lake Pegaseum, which dischargeth itself by the River Phyrites. From these Rivers proceedeth a large quantity of Mud, which increaseth the Land · so that it hath thrown good way within the Land the Island Syrie. There is a Fountain within the City called Callipia: and two (Rivers) Selinuces, coming from different Countries, encircle the Temple of *Diana.* From Ephesus you come to another Manteium, inhabited by the Colophonii: and within, the Country Colophon itself, with the (River) Halesus flowing by it. Then the Sacred Place (Fane) of *Apollo Clarius,* and Lebedos And there formerly was the Town Notium. The Promontory Coryceon: the Mountain Mimas, which reacheth out 250 Miles, and endeth at length in the Plains within the Continent. This is the place where *Alexander* the Great commanded the Plain to be cut through for seven Miles and a half in Length, to join the two Gulfs, and to bring Erythræ and Mimas together, to be environed around therewith. Near this Erythræ were the Towns, Pteleon, Helos, and Dorion: now, there is the River Aleon, and Corineum: upon the Mount Mimas, Clazomenè, Partheniæ; and Hippi, called Chytophoria, when they were Islands: the same *Alexander* united them to the Continent for the Space of two Stadia. There have perished within, Daphnus, Hermesia, and Sipylum, called formerly Tantalis, the chief City of Mœonia, where now is the Lake Salè. And for that cause Archæopolis succeeded to Sipylus, and after it Colpè, and to it Lebadè. Returning thence twelve Miles off is Smyrna, on the Coast, built by an Amazon, but restored by *Alexander* the Great;

made pleasant by the River Meles, which hath its Source
not far off.   The most celebrated Mountains in Asia, for the
most part, spread themselves at large in this Tract, as Mastusia, on the Back of Smyrna; and Termetis that meeteth
close to the Foot of Olympus   This (Olympus) endeth in
Draco, and Draco in Tmolus; Tmolus at Cadmus; and Cadmus in Taurus.   Beyond Smyrna are Plains, formed by the
River Hermus, and therefore adopting its Name.   This
(River) hath its Beginning near Doryleus, a City of Phrygia,
and collecteth into it many Rivers; among which is Phrygè,
which giveth Name to the whole Nation and divideth Phrygia and Caria asunder.   Moreover, Lyllus and Crios, which
are well filled by the other Rivers of Phrygia, Mysia, and
Lydia.   In the Mouth of this River stood the Town Temnos .
now in the further portion of the Gulf are the Rocks Myr-
meces.   Also the Town Leucè upon the Promontory, which
was an Island: and Phocæa, which boundeth Ionia.   A large
part of Æolia, of which we will speak by and by, repaireth
commonly to the Convention of Smyrna · and likewise the
Macedonians, surnamed Hyrcani , and the Magnetes from
Sipylum.   But to Ephesus, which is another Light of Asia,
resort those that dwell farther off · the Cæsarienses, Metropolitæ, Cylbiani, the Myso-Macedones, as well the Higher
as the Lower, the Mastaurenses, Brullitæ, Hyppœpeni, and
Dios-Hieritæ.

CHAPTER XXX.

Æolis, Troas, and Pergamus.

ÆOLIS, in old Time called Mysia,[1] is nearest (to Ionia)
and so is Troas, which boundeth upon the Hellespontus.

[1] The people of Mysia, according to Cicero, "were despicable and base
to a proverb." Their country was bounded on the west by Troas, in
which region was situated the city of that name, of which numerous
vestiges remain, attesting its former splendour. "Indeed," says Mr.
Fellowes, who visited the spot in 1838, "for many miles round the soil is
rendered useless for agriculture, by the multitude of broken marbles,
stones, and arches, which lie under the surface in every direction "
Pergamus was the ancient capital of Mysia, and, as its ruins also attest,
was a magnificent city.—*Wern. Club.*

Being past Phocæa, there is the Port Ascanius : and then
the Place where Larissa stood : and now Cymè, and Myrina,
which calleth itself Sebastopolis.   Within the Land, Ægæ,
Attalia, Posidea, Neon-tichos, and Temnos.   Upon the Coast,
the River Titanus, and a City taking its Name from it.   There
was also Grynia, now only a Port of the Ground ; the Island
being taken into it.   The Town Elæa, and the River Caïcus
coming out of Mysia.   The Town Pytanè, the River Canaius.
There are perished, Canæ, Lysimachia, Atarnea, Carenæ,
Cisthenè, Cilla, Cocillum, Thebæ, Astyrè, Chrysa, Palœ-
stepsis, Gergithos, and Neandros   At this Day, there is the
City Perperenè, the Tract Heracleotes ; the Town Coryphas,
the River Chryliosolius, the Country called Aphrodisias,
which formerly was Politicèorgas, the Country Scepsis ;
the River Evenus, upon the Bank of which have perished
Lyrnessos and Miletos.   In this Tract is the Mountain Ida.
And in the Sea-Coast Adramytteos, formerly called Pedasus,
where the Bay and Convention are named Adramytteos
Rivers, Astron, Cormalos, Eryannos, Alabastros, and Hieros
out of Ida.   Within, Mount Gargara, and a Town of the
same Name.   And then again on the Sea-side, Antandros,
formerly called Edonis : then, Cymeris, and Assos, which
also is Apollonia.   Also there was a Town called Palame-
dium.   The Promontory Lecton, dividing Æolus and Troas.
There also was the City Polymedia, and Cryssa, with another
Larissa   The Temple Smintheum remaineth still.   Within,
the Town Colonè is destroyed, and the Business removed
to Adramytteum.   The Apolloniatæ, from the River Rhyn-
dicus : the Eresii, Miletopolites, Pœmaneni, Macedones,
Aschilacæ, Polychnæi, Pionitæ, Cilices, and Mandagandeni.
In Mysia, the Abrettini, and those called Hellespontii ; besides others of base account.   The first place in Troas is
Amaxitus : then, Cebrenia, and Troas itself, named Antigonia, now Alexandria, a Roman Colony.   The Town Nee :
the navigable River Scamander ; and on the Promontory,
formerly, the Town Sigæum.   Then the Port of the Greeks,
(Portus Achæorum,) into which Xanthus and Simöeis run
together ; as also Palæ-Scamander, but first it maketh a

Lake. The remainder celebrated by *Homer* as Rhæsus, Heptaporus, Caresus, and Rhodius, have no Vestiges remaining. The Granicus floweth by a different Tract into the Propontis. Yet there is at this Day a little City called Scamandria, and one Mile and a half from the Port, the Free City Ilium, from which proceedeth all that great Name. Outside of this Gulf lieth the Coast Rhœtea, inhabited with the Towns upon it, of Rhœteum, Dardanium, and Arisbè. There was also Acheleum, a Town near the Tomb of *Achilles*, founded by the Mitylenei, and afterwards re-edified by the Athenians, on the Bay Sigæum, where his Fleet rode. There also was Acantium, built by the Rhodians, in another Horn, where *Ajax* was interred, thirty Stadia distant from Sigæum, and the very Station of his Fleet. Above Æolis and a part of Troas, within the Continent, is the (Town) called Teuthrania, which the Mysi in old Time held. There springeth Caicus, the River abovesaid. A large Country this is of itself, and especially when it was united to Mysia, and also so called · containing in it Pioniæ, Andera, Calè, Stabulum, Conisium, Tegium, Balcea, Tiarè, Teuthrania, Sarnaca, Haliseinè, Lycidè, Parthenium, Thymbrè, Oxyopum, Lygdanum, Apollonia · and Pergamus, the most illustrious City of Asia by many Degrees; through it passeth the River Selinus, and Cætius runneth by it, issuing out of the Mountain Pindasus. Not far from thence is Elea, which, as we have said, standeth on the Shore. The Jurisdiction of this Tract is named Pergamena. To it resort the Thyatyreni, Mygdones, Mossini, Bregmenteni, Hieracomitæ, Perpereni, Tyareni, Hierapolenses, Harmatapolitæ, Attalenses, Pantaenses, Apollonidenses, and other Cities of little Honour. Dardanium, a small Town, is threescore and ten Stadia distant from Rhœteum. Eighteen Miles from thence is the Promontory Trapeza, where first the Hellespont rusheth along roughly. *Eratosthenes* saith, That the Nations of the Solymi, Leleges, Bebrices, Colycantii, and Trepsedores, are utterly perished from Asia. *Isidorus* reporteth the same of the Arymei and Capretæ, where Apamia was built by King *Seleucus*, between Cilicia, Cappadocia, Cataonia, and Armenia.

And because he had vanquished most Fierce Nations, at the first he named it Damea.

Chapter XXXI.

The Islands before Asia, the Pamphylian Sea; Rhodus, Samus, and Chios.

The first of the Islands before Asia is in the Canopic Mouth of the Nilus, so called, as they say, from *Canopus*, the Pilot of King *Menelaus*.[1]   The second is Pharus, which is joined to Alexandria by a Bridge.   In old Time it was a Day's Sailing from Egypt : and now by Fires from a Watch-Tower, Sailors are directed in the Night.   It is a Colony of *Cæsar* the Dictator.   Alexandria is encompassed with deceitful Shallows, and there are but three Channels from the Sea ; Tegamum, Posideum, and Taurus.   Next to that Isle, in the Phœnician Sea before Joppa, lieth Paria, an Island not larger than the Town, in which they report that *Andromeda* was exposed to the Beast[2]   Also Arados beforenamed, between which and the Continent, as *Mutianus* says, there is a Fountain in the Sea, where it is fifty Cubits deep, out of which Fresh Water is drawn from the very Bottom of the Sea, through Pipes made of Leather.   The Pamphylian Sea hath some Islands of little Importance.   In the Cilician Sea is Cyprus, one of the Five greatest, and it lieth east and west, opposite Cilicia and Syria ; in Times past the Seat of Nine Kingdoms.   *Timosthenes* saith, that it contained in Circuit four hundred and nineteen Miles and a half ; but *Isidorus* is of opinion, that it is but three hundred and seventy-five Miles in Compass.   Its Length between .the two Promontories, Dinaretas and Acamas, which is westward, *Artemidorus* reporteth to be 160½ Miles : and

[1] Jacob Bryant, in his "Analysis of Ancient Mythology," (vol. ii p. 4,) says, " that the priests of Egypt laughed at this account of the pilot of Menelaus, as an idle story ; affirming that the place was much more ancient than the people of Greece ; and the name not of Grecian original " Also Stephanus of Byzantium calls the pilot Pharos, and not Canopus — *Wern Club.*

[2] See p. 67 of this vol.

Timosthenes 200, who saith besides, that formerly it was called Acamantis · according to *Philonides*, Cerastis : after *Xenagoras*, Aspelia, Amathusia, and Macatia : *Astynomus* calleth it Cryptos and Colinia.   Towns in it, 15 · Paphos, Palæpaphos, Curias, Citium, Corineum, Salamis, Amathus, Lapethos, Solœ, Tamaseus, Epidarum, Chytri, Arsinoe, Carpasium, and Golgi.   There were in it besides, Cinirya, Marium, and Idalium.   And from Anemurium in Cilicia, is 50 Miles.   The Sea which is stretched between they call Aulon Cilicium.   In this Tract is the Island Elæusa : and four others before the Promontory named Clides, over-against Syria.   Likewise one more, named Stiria, at the other Cape. Over-against Neampaphos, Hierocepia.   Over-against Salamis, Salaminæ.   But in the Lycian Sea, Illyris, Telendos, Attelebussa, and three Cypriæ, all barren : also Dionysia, formerly called Caretha.   Then over-against the Promontory of Taurus, the Chelidoniæ, dangerous to Sailors : and as many more, together with the Town Leucola Pactiæ, Lasia, Nymphais, Macris, Megista, the City of which is gone.   Then many of no Importance.   But over-against Chimera, Dolichistè, Chirogylium, Crambussa, Rhodè, Enagora, eight Miles.   Dædaleon, two : Cryeon, three : and Strongylè, over-against Sidynia of *Antiochus :* and toward the River Glaucus Lagusa, Macris, Didymæ, Helbo, Scopè, Aspis, and Telandria ; in which the Town is gone . and, near to Caunus, Rhodussa.   But the fairest of all is the Free (Isle) Rhodos ; in Compass 130 Miles ; or if we rather give Credit to *Isidorus*, 103.   Cities in it well peopled, Lindus, Camirus, and Ialysus, now called Rhodus.   By the Account of *Isidorus*, it is from Alexandria in Egypt, 578 Miles : but according to *Eratosthenes*, 569 : according to *Mutianus*, 500 ; and from Cyprus, 416.   In Times past it was called Ophyusa, Asteria, Æthræa, Trinacria, Corymbia, Pœessa, Atabyria from the King(*Atabyris*) . and finally, Macaria, and Oloessa.   Islands of the Rhodians, Carpathus, which gave name to the Sea (Carpathium) ; Casos, formerly Achmè : and Nisyros, distant from Gnidos twelve Miles and a half ; which heretofore had been called Porphyris.   And in the same Range, Symè,

between Rhodus and Gnidus ; it is in Circuit six-and-thirty
Miles and a half.   It is blessed with eight Harbours.   Besides these, there lie about Rhodus, Cyclopis, Teganon, Cor-
dylusa, four under the Name of Diabetè · Hymos, Chalcis,
with a Town : Seutlusa, Narthecusa, Dimastos, and Prognè.
Beyond Gnidos, Cicerussa, Therionarcè, Calydnè with three
Towns, Notium, Nisyius, Mendeterus and in Arconesus,
the Town Ceramus.   Upon the Coast of Caria, the Islands,
twenty in number, called Argiæ : and Hyetussa, Lepsia, and
Leros.   But the most noble in that Bay is Cos, which is distant from Halicarnassus 15 Miles ; and in Compass 100, as
many judge ; called Meropè, as *Staphylus* saith : but accord-
ing to *Dionysius*, Cos Meropis : and afterwards Nymphæa.
There is the Mountain Prion · and as they think, Nysiris
broken off ; formerly named Porphyris.   Beyond this,
Carianda, with a Town : and not far from Halicarnassus,
Pidosus.   Moreover, in the Gulf Ceramicus, Priaponnesus,
Hipponesus, Psyra, Mya, Lampsemandus, Passala, Crusa,
Pyrrhè, Sepiussa, Melano ; and within a short Distance of
the Continent, another called Cinedopolis, from the shameful
Persons that King *Alexander* left there.   The Coast of Ionia
hath (the Islands) Ægeæ and Corseæ, besides Icaros, spoken
of before.   Also Ladè, formerly called Latæ and among
some others of no worth, the two Camelides near to Miletus.
Mycalenum, Trogyliæ, Trepsilion, Argennon, Sardalion :
and the free Samos, which in Circuit is fourscore and seven
Miles , or as *Isidorus* thinketh, 100. *Aristotle* writeth,
that at first it was called Parrhania, afterwards Dryusa, and
then Anthemusa. *Aristocritus* giveth it other Names, as
Melamphyllus, and afterward Cyparissia : others term it
Partheno-arusa, and Stephanè.   Rivers in it, Imbrasus,
Chesius, and Ibettes · Fountains, Gigarto and Leucothea :
the Mountain Cercetius.   There lie adjoining to it the
Islands Rhypara, Nymphæa, and Achillea.   Fourscore and
thirteen Miles from it, is Chios, free, with a Town ; which
Island is as renowned as Samos   *Ephorus* by the ancient
Name calleth it Æthalia : *Metrodorus* and *Cleobulus*, Chia,
from the Nymph *Chio*.   Others suppose it was so called

from Chion, *i. e.* Snow : and some would have it to be Macris and Pityusa.   It has a Mountain called Pellenæus, the
Marble called Chium.   Ancient Geographers have written,
that it is 125 Miles in Circuit ; and *Isidorus* addeth nine
more.   It is situated between Samos and Lesbos, for the most
part opposite to Erythræ.   Near it lieth Thallusa, which some
write Dapnusa, Œnussa, Elaphites, Euryanassa, Arginussa
with a Town.   Now all these are about Ephesus, as also
those called *of Pisistratus*. and the Anthinæ, Myonnesus, and
Diareusa.   In both these the Towns are lost.   Poroselenæ
with a Town, Cerciæ, Halonè, Commonè, Illetia, Lepria,
and Rhespheria, Procusæ, Bolbulæ, Phanæ, Priapos, Sycè,
Melanè, Ænarè, Sidusa, Pela, Drymusa, Anydros, Scopelos,
Sycussa, Marathussa, Psilè, Perirheusa, and many others of
no Importance.   But among the illustrious is Teos, in the
deep Sea, with a Town : distant from Chios fourscore and
one Miles, and as much from Erythræ   Near Smyrna are
the Peristerides, Carteria, Alopecè, Elæussa, Bachina, Pys-
tira, Crommyonnesus, and Megalè.   Before Troas, the Asca-
niæ, and three Plateæ.   Then the Lamiæ, and two Plitaniæ ;
Platè, Scopelos, Getonè, Artheidon, Celæ, Lagussæ, and
Didymæ.   But the most illustrious is Lesbos, which is from
Chios threescore and five Miles.   It was called Hemerte, and
Lasia, Pelasgia, Ægira, Æthyope, and Macaria · famous for
eight Towns ; of which Pyrrha is swallowed up by the Sea :
and Arisbè is overthrown by an Earthquake.   Methymna
was peopled from Antissa, which was united to it, and in it
were eight Cities, and it is about seven-and-thirty Miles from
Asia.[1]   Also Agamedè and Hiera have perished.   There
remain Eresos, Pyrrha, and the free Mitylenæ, which hath
continued powerful for 500 Years.   *Isidorus* saith, that this
Island is in Circuit 173 Miles : but the old Geographers, 195.
In it are these Mountains, Lepethymus, Ordymnus, Macistus,
Creon, and Olympus.   It is distant eight Miles and a half from
the Continent, where it lieth nearest.   Islands near it, Sauda-
lion, and the five Leucæ.   Of these, Cydonea hath a Foun-

----

[1] Natolia

tain of hot Water. The Argenussæ are distant from Ægæ
four Miles. Then Phellusa and Pedua. Outside the Hellespont, over-against the Sigean Coast, lieth the Isle Tenedus,
called sometimes Leucophrys, Phœnicè, and Lyrnessos.
From Lesbos it is six-and-fifty Miles, and from Sigæum
twelve Miles and a half.

Chapter XXXII.

Hellespontus, Mysia, Phrygia, Galatia, Bithynia, Bosporus.

The Hellespont then assumeth its Violence and over-
cometh the Sea, digging a Way with its Eddies, until it hath
torn away Asia from Europe. That Promontory we have
named Trapeza, ten Miles beyond which standeth the Town
Abydum, where the Straits are seven Stadia over. Beyond it is the Town Percotè, and Lampsacum, called formerly Pityusa · the Colony Parium, which *Homer* called
Adrastia   The Town Priapos, the River Æsepus, Zelia,
Propontus; as the Place is called where the Sea enlargeth
itself. The River Granicum, the Harbour Artacè, where
once stood a Town. Beyond it is an Island, which *Alexander*
joined to the Continent, in which standeth the Town Cyzi-
cum, founded by the Milesians, called heretofore Arconne-
sos; Dolionis, and Dindymis, near the Top of which is the
Mountain Dindymus   Presently the Towns Placia, Aviacos,
Scylacè: and behind them, the Mountain Olympus, called
Mæsius. The City Olympena. The Rivers Horisius and
Rhyndacus, formerly named Lycus. This River taketh its
Beginning in the Lake Artynia, near to Miletopolis   It
receiveth the Marestos and many others; and separateth
Asia from Bithynia. This Region was called Cronia. after-
ward Thessalis, then Malianda and Strymonis. These (Na-
tions) *Homer* named Halizones, because they are environed
with the Sea. There was a very great City named Attusa.
At this Day there are fifteen Cities, among which is Gordiu-
comè, now called Juliopolis; and on the Coasts Dascylos.
Then the River Gebes: and within-land, the Town Helgas,

the same as Germanicopolis, known also by another Name
Booscœtè, as also Apamea, now called Myrtea of the Colo-
phonians.   The River Etheleum, the ancient limit of Troas,
and where Mysia beginneth.   Afterwards the Gulf into
which runneth the River Ascanium, the Town Bryllion.
The Rivers Hylas and Cios, with a Town of that Name:
which was a Place of Trade, not far off from the Inhabitants
of Phrygia, and built by the Milesians in a Place called Ascania of Phrygia.   And therefore we cannot do better than
here to speak of that Country.   Phrygia spreadeth out above
Troas and the Nations before named, from the Promontory
Lectus unto the River Etheleus.   It bordereth on the
North upon part of Galatia, southward it boundeth on Lycaonia, Pisidia, and Mygdonia; and on the east it reacheth
to Cappadocia   The most celebrated Towns besides those
before spoken of, are Ancyra, Andria, Celænæ, Colossæ, Ca-
rina, Cotiaion, Ceranæ, Iconium, and Midaion.   Certain
Authors write, that out of Europe have passed over the
Mysi, Bryges, and Thyni, from whom are named the Mysi,
Phryges, and Bithyni

At the same time I think it good to write also of Galatia,
which lying higher than Phrygia, possesseth a greater part of
its plain Country, and the former Capital of it, called Gordium.
They who inhabited that Quarter were sprung from the Gauls,
and were called Tolistobogi, Voturi, and Ambitui: but they
that occupied the Country of Mæonia and Paphlagonia were
named Trocmi.   Cappadocia is spread along from the North
and East; and the most plenteous Tract thereof the Tectosages and Teutobodiaci kept in their Possession.   And thus
much for these Nations.   The People and Tetrarchies are in
all a hundred and ninety and five   The Towns: of the
Tectosages, Ancyra: of the Trocmi, Tavium: of the Tolisto-
bogians, Pesinus.   Besides these, there are celebrated the
Attalenses, Arasenses, Comenses, Dios-Hieronitæ, Lystreni,
Neapolitani, Oeandenses, Seleucenses, Sebasteni, Timmonia-
censes, and Tebaseni.   Galatia extendeth to Gabalia and
Milyæ in Pamphylia; which are situated about Baris: also
Cyllanticum and Oroandicum, a Tract of Pisidia: likewise

Obigenè, a part of Lycaonia.   Rivers there are in it, beside
those beforenamed, Sangarium and Gallus, from which the
Priests of the Mother of the Gods were named.   Now to
speak of what remains on the Sea-coast: inward from Cios
is Prusa within Bithynia; founded by *Annibal* beneath
Olympus.   From Prusa to Nicæa, five-and-twenty Miles;
the Lake Ascanius lying between.   Then Nicæa, in the out-
most part of the Gulf Ascanium, which before was called
Olbia: also to another Prusa, under the Mountain Hippius.
There were Pythopolis, Parthenopolis, and Choryphanta.
Now there are upon the Sea-side the Rivers, Æsius, Bryazon,
Plataneus, Areus, Siros, Gendos, named also Chrysorrhoas.
The Promontory on which stood the Town Megaricum.   Then
the Gulf which was called Craspedites; because that Town
stood as it were in a Fold of it.   There was also the Town
Astacum, from which the Bay took the Name of Astacenus
There was also the Town Libyssa, where now remaineth
nothing but the Tomb of *Annibal.*   In the inmost part of
the Gulf is the very handsome Town of Bithynia, called
Nicomedia.   The Promontory Leucatas which encloseth the
Bay of Astarenus, is from Nicomedia forty-two Miles and
a half.   Being past this Bay, the opposite Shores approaching together, the Straits reach as far as to the Thracian Bosphorus.   Upon these Straits standeth the Free (City) Chalcedon, seventy-two Miles and a half from Nicomedia.   Formerly
it was called Procerastis · then, Compusa : afterwards, the
City of the Blind; because they who founded it were so
ignorant as not to give a preference to a Place seven Stadia
from Byzantium, so much more favourable in every respect.
But within-land, in Bithynia, is the Colony Apamena: also,
the Agrippenses, Juliopolitæ, and they of Bithynium   The
Rivers, Syrium, Lapsias, Pharmicas, Alces, Crynis, Lylæus,
Scopius, Hieras, which parteth Bithynia from Galatia.   Beyond Chalcedon, stood Chrysopolis   then, Nicopolis, of
which the Gulf still retaineth the Name · wherein is the
Port of Amycus · the Promontory Naulochum · Estia,
wherein is the Temple of *Neptune;* and the Bosphorus,
half-a-mile over, which now again parteth Asia from Europe.

From Chalcedon, it is twelve Miles and a half. There begin
the narrow Straits, where it is eight Miles and a quarter
over: where stood the Town Philopolis.   All the Coasts
are inhabited by the Thyni, but the Inland Parts by
the Bithyni.   This is the end of Asia, and of 282 Nations,
which are reckoned from the Gulf of Lycia to this place
The Space of the Hellespont and Propontis to the Thracian
Bosphorus containeth in Length 188 Miles, as we have
before said.   From Chalcedon to Sigeum, by the computation of *Isidorus,* it is 372 Miles and a half.   Islands lying in
Propontis before Cyzicum are these, Elaphonnesus, from
whence cometh the Cyzicen Marble; and the same Isle was
called Neuris, and Proconnesus.   Then follow Ophiusa,
Acanthus, Phœbè, Scopelos, Porphyrionè, and Halonè, with
a Town.   Delphacia, Polydora: Artacæon, with the Town.
And over-against Nicomedia, is Demonnesos. likewise, beyond Heraclea, over-against Bithynia, is Thynnias, which
the Barbarians call Bithynia.   There is also Antiochia: and
opposite to the narrow Straits of Rhyndacus, Besbicos,
eighteen Miles in Circuit.   Also there is Elæa, two Rho-
dussæ, Erebinthus, Magalè, Chalcitis, and Pityodes.

IN THE SIXTH BOOK

ARE CONTAINED

REGIONS, NATIONS, SEAS, CITIES, PORTS, RIVERS, WITH THEIR DIMENSIONS; AND PEOPLE THAT ARE OR HAVE BEEN :—

Towns of name, 195. Nations of account, 566. Famous Rivers, 180. Notable Mountains, 38. Principal Islands, 108. Cities and Nations perished, 195. In sum, there are rehearsed in this Book, of other Things, Histories and Observations, 2214.

LATIN AUTHORS ABSTRACTED:

M. Agrippa, Varro Atacinus, Cornelius Nepos, Hyginus, Lu. Vetus, Mela Pomponius, Domitius Corbulo, Licinius Mutianus, Claudius Cæsar, Aruntius Sebosus, Fabricius Thuscus, T. Livius, Seneca, Nigidius.

FOREIGN WRITERS:

King *Juba, Polybius, Hecatæus, Hellanicus, Damastes, Eudoxus, Dicæarchus, Beto, Timosthenes, Patrocles, Demodamas, Clitarchus, Eratosthenes, Alexander* the Great, *Ephorus, Hipparchus, Panætius, Callimachus, Artemidorus, Apollodorus, Agathocles, Polybius, Eumachus Siculus, Alexander Polyhistor, Amometus, Metrodorus, Posidonius, Onesicritus, Nearchus, Megasthenes, Diognetus, Aristocreon, Bion, Dialdon, Simonides* the Younger, *Basiles,* and *Xenophon Lampsacenus.*

THE SIXTH BOOK

OF THE

HISTORY OF NATURE.

WRITTEN BY

C. PLINIUS SECUNDUS.

Chapter I.

Pontus Euxinus.

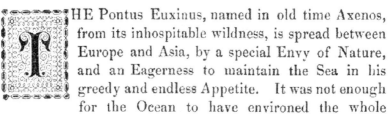 HE Pontus Euxinus, named in old time Axenos, from its inhospitable wildness, is spread between Europe and Asia, by a special Envy of Nature, and an Eagerness to maintain the Sea in his greedy and endless Appetite. It was not enough for the Ocean to have environed the whole Earth, and to have taken away a great part of it, with exceeding Rage; it sufficed not, to have broken through the shattered Mountains, and also having torn Calpe[1] from Africa, to have swallowed up a much larger space than it left behind: nor to have poured out Propontis through the Hellespont,[2] so again devouring the Land: from the Bosphorus also it is spread abroad into a large Space without

[1] Mouth of Gibraltar.

[2] The ideas of the ancients appear to have been confounded in the wide

being satisfied, until they are very wide, and the Lake Mœotis joineth its ruin to them. And that this hath happened in spite of the Earth, appeareth by so many Straits and such narrow Passages of opposing nature, considering that at the Hellespont the Breadth is not above 875 Paces · and at the two Bosphori even Oxen easily pass over : and hereupon they both took their Name : and in this disunion appeareth an agreement of relationship. For Cocks may be heard to crow, and Dogs to bark from one Side to the other : and by the interchange of Human Speech Men out of these two Worlds may talk one to another in continued discourse, if the Winds do not carry away the Sound.

Some have made the Measure of Pontus from the Bosphorus to the Lake Mœotis to be 1438 Miles. But *Eratosthenes* reckoneth it less by one hundred. *Agrippa* saith, that from Chalcedon to Phasis is a thousand Miles, and onward to Bosphorus Cimmerius, 360 Miles. We will set down in general the Distances of Places collected in our own Days, when our Armies have carried on War even in the very Mouth of the Cimmerian Strait.

Beyond the Straits of the Bosphorus is the River Rhebas, which some have called Rhœsus. and beyond it, Psillis : the Port of Calpas ; and Sangarius, one of the principal Rivers : it ariseth in Phrygia, receiveth large Rivers into it, and amongst the rest Tembrogius and Gallus. The same Sangarius is by many called Coralius, from which begin the Gulfs Mariandin and the Town Heraclea, situated upon the River Lycus. It is from the Mouth of Pontus 200 Miles There is the Port Aconè, cursed with the poisonous Aconitum ; and the Cave Acherusia. The Rivers Pedopiles, Callichorum, and Sonantes. Towns, Tium, eight-and-thirty Miles from Heraclea : the River Bilis.

expanse of the ocean · in consequence, probably, of the creeping manner of their navigation Homer speaks of—

"All wide Hellespont's unmeasured main"—*Iliad*, b 24

Chapter II

The Nation of the Paphlagonians, and Cappadocians.

Beyond this River Bilis is the Nation of Paphlagonia, which some have named Pylæmenia, and it is enclosed with Galatia behind it. The Town Mastya of the Milesians: and next to it Cromna. In this quarter the Heneti inhabit, as *Cornelius Nepos* saith, from whom the Veneti in Italy, who bear their Name, are descended, as he would have us believe. The Town Sesamum, which is now called Amastris. The Mountain Cytorus, 64 Miles from Tium The Towns Cimolus and Stephanè, the River Parthenius; the Promontory Corambis, which reacheth a mighty way into the Sea; and it is from the Mouth of the Pontus 315 Miles, or as others think, 350 It is also as far from the (Strait) Cimmerius, or as some would rather have it, 312 Miles and a half A Town there was also of that Name: and another beyond it called Armmum. but now there is the Colony Sinopè, 164 Miles from Citorum. The River Varetum; the People of the Cappadoces, the Town Gaziura, and Gazelum, the River Halys, which, issuing out of the foot of Taurus, passeth through Cataonia and Cappadocia. The Towns, Grangrè, Carissa; the Free City Amisum, distant from Sinopè 130 Miles. A Gulf, bearing the Name of this Town, runneth so far within the Land that it seemeth to make Asia almost an Island: for from thence through the Continent to the Gulf Issicus in Cilicia, is not above 200 Miles. In all which Tract there are no more than three Nations which justly may be called Greeks: which are the Dorians, Ionians, and Æolians: for all the rest are Barbarians. To Amisum there was joined the Town Eupatoria, founded by *Mithridates* and when he was vanquished, both together took the Name of Pompeiopolis [1]

[1] From Pompey the Great, who conquered him.—*Wern Club*

Chapter III.

Cappadocia.

In the interior of Cappadocia is a Colony founded by *Claudius Cæsar*, called Archelais, situated upon the River Halys. The Town Comana, by which the (River) Sarus runneth: Neo-Cæsarea, washed by the Lycus: and Amasia, on the River Iris, in the Country Gazacena. In Colopena, also, are Sebastia and Sebastopolis: little Towns, but equal with those aboresaid. In the other part (of Cappadocia) is the City Melita, built by Queen *Semiramis*, not far from the Euphrates: also, Dio-Cæsarea, Tyana, Castabala, Magnopolis, Zela: and under the Mountain Argæus, Mazaca, which now is named Cæsarea. That part of Cappadocia which lieth before Armenia the Greater, is called Melitenè: that which bordereth upon Comagenè, Cataonia: upon Phrygia, Garsauritis: upon Sargaurasana, Cammanenè: and upon Galatia, Morimenè. And there the River Cappadox separateth the one from the other. From this River the Cappadocians took their Name, having formerly been called Leucosyri. The River Lycus divideth the above-named new Armenia from Neo-Cæsarea. Within the Country there runneth also the famous Ceraunus. But on the Coast beyond Amysum is the Town Lycastum, and the River Chadisia: and still further the Country Themiscyra. The River Iris, bringing down the Lycus. In the midland Parts the City Ziela, ennobled by the slaughter of *Triarius*,[1] and the Victory of *C. Cæsar*. In the Coast the River Thermodon, which issueth from before a Castle named Phanarœa, and passeth

---

[1] Triarius, a Roman general under Lucullus in the Mithridatic war, was defeated by the enemy, at the battle of Ziela, with the loss of 7000 of his men. And at the same place, some years afterwards, Julius Cæsar gained an important victory over Pharnaces, the son of Mithridates, deprived him of the kingdom of Pontus, and entirely ruined his army. It was on this occasion that Cæsar, when describing the rapidity and despatch he had employed in the victory, made use of the well-known sentence, " Veni, vidi, vici," I came, I saw, I conquered.—*Wern. Club.*

by the foot of the Mountain Amazonius. There was a Town of the same Name, and five others, namely, Phamizonium, Themiscyra, Sotira, Amasia, Comana, now called Manteium.

Chapter IV.

The Nations of the Region Themiscyrenè.

The Nations of the Genetæ and Chalybes; a Town of the Cotyi. Nations called Tibareni; and Mossyni, who mark their Bodies with Figures.[1] The Nation of the Macrocephali, the Town Cerasus, the Port Cordulæ. The Nations Bechires; Buzeti; the River Melas. The Nation Macrones, Sideni, and the River Sydenum, upon which is situated the Town Polemonium, distant from Amisum 120 Miles: beyond this the Rivers Jasonius and Melanthius: also 80 Miles from Amisum, the Town Pharnacea: the Castle and River of Tripolis. Also, Philocalia, and Liviopolis without a River: also, the Free City Trapezus, environed with a high Mountain, 100 Miles from Pharnacea. Beyond Trapezus is the Nation of the Armenochalybes, and Armenia the Greater: which are 30 Miles asunder. On the Coast is the River Pyxites that runneth before Trapezus: and beyond it the Nation of the Sanni Heniochi. The River Absarus, with a Castle likewise so named in its Mouth; from Trapezus is 150 Miles. Behind the Mountains of that quarter is Iberia: but in the Coast of the same are the Heniochi, Ampreutæ, and Lazi. The Rivers Campseonysis, Nogrus, Bathys. The Nations of the Colchians; the Town Matium, the River Heracleum, and a Promontory of the same Name; and the most renowned (River) of Pontus, called Phasis. This River riseth out of the Moschian Mountains, and for 38 Miles and a half is Navigable for great Vessels. And then for a great way it carrieth smaller Vessels; having

---

[1] The practice of tattooing is general through the islands of the Southern Ocean; the inhabitants of which, however, were not known to Pliny. But it is also practised, even in our day, by the people of Burma, and perhaps in other nations of the East. The same practice is again referred to in b. vii. c. 11.—*Wern. Club.*

over it 120 Bridges   It had many Towns upon its Banks;
the most celebrated being Tyritacen, Cygnus, and Phasis,
situated at its very Mouth.   But the most illustrious was
Æa, fifteen Miles from the Sea : where Hippos and Cyanos,
two very great Rivers, coming from different Parts, flow into
it   Now it possesseth Surium only, which taketh its Name
from the River Surium, that runneth into it.   And thus far
we said that Phasis was capable of being navigated by great
Ships.   And it receiveth other Rivers, remarkable for size
and number, among which is the River Glaucus.   In the
Mouth of this River (Phasis) there are Islands without a
Name.   It is distant from Bsarus 75 Miles.   Being past
Phasis, there is another River called Charien ; the Nation of
the Salæ, named in old Time Phthirophagi and Suani ; the
River Cobus, which issueth out of Caucasus, and runneth
through the Country of the Suani.   Then Rhoas, the region
Ecrecticè : the Rivers Sigania, Tersos, Atelpos, Chrysorrhoas,
and the Nation Absilæ : the Castle Sebastopolis, a hundred
Miles from Phasis ; the Nation of the Sanigares, the Town
Cygnus, the River and Town called Pityus.   And last of all,
the Nations of the Heniochæ, which have many Names.

CHAPTER V.

The Region of Colchis, the Achæi, and other Nations in that Tract.

NEXT followeth the region of Colchis, which is likewise
in Pontus : wherein the craggy Summits of the Caucasus
wind and turn toward the Rhiphæan Mountains, as hath been
hinted ; on the one side bending down toward the Euxinus
and Mœotis ; and on the other inclining to the Caspian and
Hircanian Seas.   The remainder of the Coasts are occupied by
savage Nations, as the Melanchlæni, the Choruxi ; Dioscurias,
a City of the Colchi, near the River Anthemus, now lying
waste, although it was so renowned in Time past, that by the
report of *Timosthenes* there were settled therein 300 Nations
which used distinct Languages.   And afterwards our Romans were forced to provide 130 Interpreters for the Traffic

with this People. Some think that it was first founded by *Amphitus* and *Telchius*, who had the charge of the Chariots of *Castor* and *Pollux* [1] for certain it is, that the fierce Nation of the Heniochi are from them descended. Being past Dioscurias, there is the Town Heraclium, which from Sebastopolis is 80 Miles distant. The Achæi, Mardi, and Carcetæ after them the Serri, and Cephalotomi. Far within that Tract stood the very wealthy Town Pitius, which by the Heniochians was plundered On the back part thereof inhabit the Epageritæ, a People of the Sarmatæ, upon the tops of the Caucasus · after which the Sauromatæ Hither had fled King *Mithridates* in the time of Prince *Claudius*, and he made report that the Thali dwell thereby, and border Eastward upon the very opening of the Caspian Sea: which becometh Dry when the Sea ebbeth. But on the Coast near to the Cercetæ is the River Icarusa, with a Town and River called Hierum, 136 Miles from Heracleum. Then come ye to the Promontory Cronea, in the steep Ridge of which the Toretæ inhabit. The City Sindica, 67 Miles from Hierum: the River Sceaceriges.

CHAPTER VI

Mœotis and the Bosphorus Cimmerius.

FROM the above-said River to the Entrance of the Cimmerian Bosphorus is 88 Miles and a half But the Length of the Peninsula itself, which stretcheth out between the Lakes Pontus and Mœotis is not above 87 Miles, and the Breadth in no place less than two Acres of Land They call it Eionè The very Coasts of the Bosphorus, both of Asia and Europe, are curved towards the Mœotis The Towns in

---

[1] There is frequently occasion to remark, that Pliny speaks of the deities of his country, as if it was an acknowledged fact that they were once living men. Æolus, Hercules, and even Jupiter, are so regarded, and as he speaks of the impiety of this opinion, b. vii c 47, when applied to some particular cases, we are at liberty to believe that his regard for the established heathenism of his country was exceedingly slight — *Wern. Club*

the very first Passage of Bosphorus are Hermonassa and then Cepi, founded by the Milesians. Close by is Stratiha (or Stratoclea), Phanagoria, and Apaturos, which is almost unpeopled. and last of all, in the mouth, Cimmerius, formerly called Cerberian.

CHAPTER VII.

Nations about Mæotis.

BEYOND Cimmerium is the Lake Mœotis, spoken of before in Europe. Beyond Cimmerium inhabit the Mœotici, Vati, Serbi, Archi, Zingi, and Psesii. After this you come to the River Tanais, which runneth with two Mouths: and on the sides of it dwell the Sarmatæ, descended, as they say, from the Medi: but themselves divided into many Races. And first the Sauromatæ, surnamed Gynæcocratumeni, from whence the Amazons are provided with Husbands. Next to them are the Euazæ, Cottæ, Cicimeni, Messeniani, Costobocci, Choatræ, Zigæ, Dandari, Thussageæ, and Turcæ, even as far as the Wilderness, rough with woody Valleys. Beyond them are the Arimphæi, who live upon the Riphæan Mountains. The Tanais itself the Scythians call Silys; and Mœotis they name Temerinda,[1] that is to say, the Mother of the Sea. There stood also a Town at the mouth of Tanais. The Lares first inhabited the Borders. afterwards the Clazomenii and Mœones: and in process of time the Panticapenses. Some Authors write, that about Mœotis toward the higher Mountains Ceraunii, the following Nations inhabit on the Coast, the Napææ and above them the Essedones, joining on the Colchi, and the tops of the Mountains. After them the Carmacæ, the Orani, Antacæ, Mazacæ, Ascantici, Acapeatæ, Agagammatæ, Phycari, Rhimosoli, and Asco-

---

[1] It is easy to discern that many of the names of nations mentioned by Pliny are not those which the people themselves would have recognised; but Greek descriptive designations But the word " Temerinda " is believed to have been " Scythian," and to be rightly interpreted by the author. Daleschamp supposes the true expression to be " Themers-end," or, in modern terms, " Dess-mærs-end "—*Wern Club.*

marci ; and on the Tops of Caucasus, the Icatalæ, Imaduchi, Rani, Anclacæ, Tydii, Charastasci, and Asuciandæ Along the River Lagous, issuing out of the Mountains Cathei, and into which Opharus runneth, are these Nations : the Caucadæ and the Opharitæ· the River Menotharus, and Imitues divided from the Mountains Cissii, which passeth among the Agedi, Carnapæ, Gardei, Accisi, Gabri, and Gregaii : and about the source of this River Imitues, the Imitui and Apartheni. Others say that the Suitæ, Auchetæ, Satarnei, and Asampatæ, overflowed this Part ; the Tanaitæ and Nepheonitæ were slain by them to a Man. Some write, that the River Opharius runneth through the Canteci and the Sapæi and that the River Tanais traversed through the Phatarei, Herticei, Spondolici, Synthietæ, Amassi, Issi, Catazeti, Tagori, Catoni, Neripi, Agandei, Mandarei, Saturchei, and Spalei.

CHAPTER VIII.

Cappadocia.

WE have gone through the Nations and Inhabitants of the Coasts of the Mediterranean Sea. Now are we to speak of the People inhabiting the Inland Parts· wherein I shall advance many things different from the ancient Geographers : because I have made diligent Search into the state of those Regions, especially by enquiry of *Domitius Corbulo*, in regard of the things done by himself, and also of the Kings who came from thence as Petitioners, and of those King's Sons that were Hostages. And we will begin with the Nation of the Cappadocians. This is a Country that of all which bound upon Pontus, reacheth farthest within the Land : for on the left Hand it passeth by the Greater and Less Armenia, and Comagenè : and on the right, all those Nations in Asia before-named : being overflowed with a Multitude of People : and with great Might climbing up Eastward to the Tops of Taurus, it passeth Lycaonia, Pisidia, and Cilicia : and with that quarter which is called Cataonia, it pierceth above the Tract of Antiochia, and reacheth as far as to its Region Cyrrhestica.   And therefore the Length of Asia there may contain 1250 Miles, and the Breadth 640

Chapter IX.

Armenia, the Greater and Less.

The Greater Armenia, beginning at the Mountains Pariedri, is divided from Cappadocia by the River Euphrates, as hath been said before. and where the River Euphrates turneth, from Mesopotamia by the River Tigris, scarcely less renowned than the other. It poureth forth both these Rivers, and constitutes the beginning of Mesopotamia, which is situated between them both.   The Land which lieth between is possessed by the Arabs Orei.   In this manner it extendeth its Border to Adiabenè.   Beyond this, being hemmed in with Mountains that stand across it, it spreadeth its Breadth on the left Hand to the River Cyrus: and then across to the River Araxes: but it carrieth its Length to the Lesser Armenia, being separated from it by the River Absarus, which falleth into the Pontus: and by the Mountains Pariedri, from which the River Absarus issueth.   The River Cyrus springeth in the Mountains Heniochii, which some have called Coraxici.   The Araxes issueth out of the same Mountain from whence Euphrates cometh, and there is not above the Space of six Miles between them.   This River Araxes is augmented with the River Musis; and then itself loseth its Name, and, as most have thought, is carried by the River Cyrus into the Caspian Sea.   These Towns are famous in the Lesser (Armenia); Cæsarea, Aza, and Nicopolis.   In the Greater is Arsamotè, near the River Euphrates, and Carcathiocerta, upon the Tigris.   In the higher Country is Tigranocerta, but in the Plain, near the Araxes, Artaxata.   *Aufidius* saith, that both the Armeniæ contain in all 500 Miles.   *Claudius Cæsar* reporteth, that in Length from Dascusa to the Confines of the Caspian Sea is 1300 Miles, and in Breadth half as much, from Tigranocerta to Iberia   This is well known, that it is divided into Præfectures, which they call Strategiæ; and some of them in old time were as large as Kingdoms · the

Number being 120, with barbarous Names. It is enclosed
Eastward with Mountains, but neither the Ceraunii, nor the
Region Adiabenè, do immediately border on it. The Country
of the Sopheni lieth between next are the Mountains Ce-
raunii; and beyond them dwell the Adiabeni. But through
the flat Valleys the next Neighbours to Armenia are the
Menobardi and Moscheni. The River Tigris and steep
Mountains encompass Adiabenè. On the left Hand its
Region is of the Medians, and the Prospect of the Caspian
Sea. This is poured in from the Ocean (as we shall shew in
its place), and is enclosed wholly within the Mountains of
Caucasus. We will now speak of the Inhabitants of these,
through the Confine of Armenia.

CHAPTER X

Albania and Iberia.

THE Nation of the Albani inhabit all the plain Country
from the River Cyrus. Beyond it is the Region of the Iberes,
who are separated from the Albani by the River Alazon,
which runneth down from the Caucasian Mountains into the
Cyrus   The strong Towns of Albania: Cabalaca; of Iberia,
Harmastis, near the River Neoris: the Region Thasiè, and
Triarè, as far as to the Mountains Partedori.   Beyond them
are the Deserts of Colchis: and on the side of them which
lieth toward the Ceraunii the Armenochalybes inhabit: and
the Tract of the Moschi to the River Iberus, that floweth into
the Cyrus. Beneath them, inhabit the Sacassani, and beyond
them the Macrones, who reach to the River Absarus.   Thus
the Plain and the hanging of the Hills are inhabited. Again,
from the Frontiers of Albania, in all the front of the Mountains are the savage Nations of the Sylvi; and beneath them,
of the Lubieni, and so forward the Diduri, and Sodii.

CHAPTER XI.

The Gates of the Caucasus.

BEYOND the Sodii are the Gates of Caucasus, which many
have very erroneously called Caspiæ Portæ, or the Caspian

Gates: a mighty Piece of Nature's Work, by suddenly cleaving asunder those Mountains, where the Gates were barred up with iron Bars, whilst under the midst thereof, the River Dyriodorus runneth: and on this Side of it standeth a formidable Castle called Cumania, situated upon a Rock, able to arrest the Passage of a very numerous Army, so that in this Place, by means of these Gates, one Part of the World is excluded from the other · and chiefly over-against Harmastis, a Town of the Iberi. Beyond the Gates of Caucasus, through the Mountains Gordyei, the Valli and Suarni, uncivilised Nations, are employed only in the Mines of Gold. Beyond them as far as to the Pontic Sea, are many Races of the Heniochi; and soon after, of the Achæi. And thus much concerning this Tract of the Lands among the most renowned. Some have set down, that between Pontus and the Caspian Sea, it is not above 375 Miles. *Cornelius Nepos* saith it is but 150; into such Straits is Asia driven again. *Claudius Cæsar* hath reported, that from the Cimmerian Bosphorus to the Caspian Sea, is 150 Miles; and that *Seleucus Nicator* purposed to cut the Land through, at the Time when he was slain by *Ptolomæus Ceraunus*. It is almost certain, that from the Gates of Caucasus to Pontius is 200 Miles.

CHAPTER XII.

Islands in the Pontus.

In Pontus lie the Islands Planctæ, otherwise Cyaneæ or Symplegades. Then Apollonia, named also Thynnias, for Distinction sake from that other so named in Europe it is from the Continent one Mile, and in Circuit three. And over-against Pharnacea is Chalceritis, which the Greeks called Aria, sacred to *Mars*, wherein are Birds which fight with a Blow of their Wings against others that come thither.

CHAPTER XIII.

Nations on the Scythian Ocean

HAVING thus discoursed of all the Countries in the interior of Asia, let us now determine to pass over the Rhiphæan

Mountains, and discover the Coasts of the Ocean which lie
on the right hand   Asia is washed by this Ocean on three
Sides: on the North Side is the Scythian   on the East it is
called Eous: and from the South they name it the Indian.
And according to the various Gulfs, and the Inhabitants, it is
divided into many Names.   But a great part of Asia toward
the North hath in it extensive Wildernesses, by reason of the
violence of its frozen Star.   From the extreme North to the
North-east are the Scythians   Beyond whom, and the very
point of the North Pole, some have placed the Hyperborei;
of whom we have spoken at large in the Treatise of Europe.
The first Promontory that you meet with in the Country
Celtica is named Lytarmis: and then the River Carambucis,
where, by the forcible influence of the Stars, the Mountains
Rhiphæi are deprived of their ragged Tops.   And there we
have heard that there are a People named Arimphæi: a
Nation not much unlike the Hyperborei.   They have their
Habitations in Forests; their Food is Berries, both Women
and Men count it a shame to have Hair; mild in their manners; and therefore, by report, they are held to be sacred,
and to be inviolable even by those wild People that dwell
near them; neither do they respect them only, but also those
who fly to them.   At some distance beyond them are the
Scythians,[1] as well the Cimmerii, Cicianthi, and Georgi;
and the Nation of the Amazons.   These reach to the Caspian
and Hircanian Sea: for it breaketh forth from the Scythian
Ocean,[2] toward the back parts of Asia, and is called many
Names by the neighbouring Inhabitants, but especially by
two of the most celebrated, the Caspian and Hircanian.
Clitarchus is of opinion that this Sea is full as great as the

---

[1] At this day, the Moschovites, white and black Russians, Georgians,
Amazonians, and the less Tartary —*Wern Club.*

[2] Strabo (lib xi.) entertains the same erroneous opinions respecting
the Caspian Sea   That both these intelligent writers, as well as other
ancient geographers, should have been so mistaken is the more extraordinary, as Herodotus (lib i 203) had given a just description of it long
before   "The Caspian Sea," he says, "is a sea of itself, which does not
mingle with any other."—*Wern. Club.*

Pontus Euxinus. And *Eratosthenes* setteth down the measure of it as being from East to South, along the Coast of Cadusia and Albania, 5400 Stadia: from thence by the Aratiatici, Amarbi, and Hircanii, to the mouth of the River Zonus, 4800 Stadia: from it to the mouth of the Jaxartes, 2400 Stadia: which being put together amount to 1575 Miles. *Artemidorus* counteth less by 25 Miles *Agrippa*, in limiting the Circuit of the Caspian Sea, and the Nations around it, and Armenia with them, from the East with the Ocean of the Seres, Westward with the Mountains of Caucasus, on the South side with the Mountain Taurus, and on the North with the Scythian Ocean, hath written, That the whole, so far as is known, may contain in Length 590 Miles, and 290 in Breadth. There want not others who say, That the whole Circuit of that Sea, from the Strait is 2500 Miles. This throat is very narrow where it bursts forth, but exceedingly long · but where it beginneth to enlarge it fetcheth a Compass with lunated Horns, and after the manner of a Scythian Bow, as *M. Varro* saith, it windeth along from its Mouth toward the Lake Mœotis. The first Gulf is called Scythicus, for the Scythians inhabit on both Sides, and by means of the narrow Straits between have business one with another: for on one side are the Nomades and Sauromatæ, with many Names: and on the other, the Abzoæ, who have no fewer denominations. At the entry of this Sea on the right hand, the Udini, a People of the Scythians, dwell upon the very point of these Straits. and then along the Coast, the Albani, descended (as they say) from *Jason;* where the Sea that lieth before them is called Albanum. This Nation is spread also upon the Mountains of Caucasus to the River Cyrus, and descendeth, as hath been said, to the border of Armenia and Iberia. Above the Maritime Coasts of Albania and the Nation of the Udini, the Sarmatæ, called Utidorsi, and Atoderes, are planted. and behind them the Sauromatides, Amazons, already pointed out. The Rivers of Albania, which fall into the Sea, are Cassios and Albanos: and then Cambises, which hath its Head in the Caucasian Mountains : and soon after Cyrus, which ariseth out of the

Mountains Corax, as is before said. *Agrippa* writeth that this whole Coast, from the lofty and inaccessible Mountains of Caucasus, containeth 425 Miles. Beyond the Cyrus, the Caspian Sea beginneth to take that Name; and the Caspii dwell there. And here the error of many is to be corrected, even of those who were lately with *Corbulo* in Armenia with the Army: for they called those Gates of Caucasus, of which we spoke before, the Caspian Gates of Iberia: and the Maps and Descriptions which are painted and sent from thence, have that Name written on them. Likewise the threatening of Prince *Nero*, when he sought to gain those Gates, which through Iberia lead into Sarmatia, made mention of the Gates Caspiæ, which had scarcely any Passage by reason of the Mountains so closely approaching each other. There are other Gates near the Caspian Sea, that join upon the Caspian Nations, which could not have been distinguished from the other but by the relation of those that accompanied *Alexander* the Great in his Expeditions. For the Kingdoms of the Persians, which at this day we take to be those of the Parthians, are elevated between the Persian and Hircanian Seas upon the Mountains of Caucasus; in the Descent of which on both sides bordering upon Armenia the Greater, and on that part of the front which vergeth to Comagenè, it joineth (as we have said) with Sephenæ: and upon it bordereth Adiabenè, the beginning of the Assyrians: Arbelitis, which is nearest to Syria, is a part of this. where *Alexander* vanquished *Darius* All this Tract the Macedonians surnamed Mygdonia,[1] from its resemblance. The Towns Alexandria; and Antiochia, which they call Nisibis: from Artaxata it is 750 Miles. There was also Ninus,[2] seated upon the Tigris, looking towards the West, and in Times past highly renowned. But on the other Side, where it lieth toward the Caspian Sea, the Region Atropatenè, separated by the River Araxes from Otenè in Armenia: its City, Gazæ, is 450 Miles

---

[1] From its resemblance to a part of Greece of that name, with which they were well acquainted.—*Wern Club*

[2] The ancient Nineveh.—*Wern. Club.*

from Artaxata · and as many from Ecbatana of the Medes, some part of which the Atropateni hold.

Chapter XIV.

Media, and the Gates Caspiæ.

Ecbatana, the head of Media, was founded by King *Seleucus:* and it is from Seleucia the Great 750 Miles: and from the Caspian Gates 20. The other Towns of the Medes are Phausia, Agamzua, and Apamia, named also Rhaphanè. The Straits there, (called the Caspian Gates,) have the same reason for being so named as the other (by Caucasus); because the Mountains are broken through with so narrow a Passage, that hardly a single line of Carts is able to pass it for the Length of Eight Miles. and all done by the hand of Man. The Cliffs that hang over on the right Side and on the left are as if they were scorched · through a silent Tract of 38 Miles; for all the Moisture running together out of those Cliffs, and pouring through the Straits, obstructs the Passage. Besides, the Multitude of Serpents prevents Travelling except in Winter.

Chapter XV.

Nations about the Hircanian Sea.

Unto Adiabenè are joined the Carduchi, so called in Times past, and now Cordueni; along which the Tigris runneth, and on them the Pratitæ border, called also Paredoni, who hold the Caspian Gates. On the other side of whom you meet with the Deserts of Parthia, and the Mountains of Cithenus: and beyond these is the most pleasant Tract of the same Parthia, called Choara. There stand two Cities of the Parthians, formerly opposed against the Medians: namely, Calliopè; and Issatis, situated in times past upon another Rock. The Capital of Parthia itself, Hecatompylos, is from the (Caspian) Gates 133 Miles. Thus the Kingdoms of the Parthians are shut up by Doors. When passed out of these Gates, presently we enter on the Caspian Nation, which reacheth as far as the Sea-shore, and gave the Name to the Gates and the Sea. The left hand is full of Mountains: and from this Nation backward to the River Cyrus, is by report 220 Miles. From that River, if you would go higher up to the Gates, it is 700 Miles. And from this starting-place began *Alexander* to reckon his Journeys: making from those Gates to the Entrance of India, 15,680 Stadia: from thence to the Town of Bactra, which they call Zariaspa, 3700, and thence to the River Jaxartes five Miles.

CHAPTER XVI.

Other Nations also.

FROM the Caspian Country eastward, lieth the Region called Zapanortenè,[1] and in it Daricum, a place celebrated for Fertility. Then come the Nations of the Tapyri, Anariaci, Stauri, and Hircani, at whose Coasts the same Sea beginneth to take the Name Hircanum, from the River Syderis About it are the Rivers Mazeras and Stratos, all issuing out of Caucasus. Then follows the Region Margiana, famous for its warm Sunshine, and the only place in all that quarter which yieldeth Vines. It is environed with pleasant Mountains, for the compass of 1500 Stadia: difficult of approach by reason of the Sandy Deserts for the space of 120 Miles; and it is situated over against the Tract of Parthia, wherein *Alexander* had built Alexandria; which being destroyed by the Barbarians, *Antiochus* the Son of *Seleucus* rebuilt it in the same place, upon the River Margus, which runneth through it, together with another River Zotalè, and it was called Syriana.[2] But he desired rather that it should be named Antiochia. This City containeth in Circuit 70 Stadia · and into it *Orodes*, after the Slaughter of *Crassus* and his Army, brought his Roman Prisoners. Being past the high Country (Margiana), you come to the Nation of the Mardi,

[1] Some copies read Zapauortenè and Apauortenè.—*Wern. Club.*
[2] Or rather Seleucia.

a Fierce People, subject to none; they inhabit the Rocky Summits of Caucasus, which reach as far as to the Bactrians. Beyond that Tract are the Nations Ochani, Chomari, Berdrigei, Hermatotrophi, Bomarci, Commani, Marucæi, Mandrueni and Iatii The Rivers Mandrus and Gridinus. Beyond, inhabit the Chorasmii, Gandari, Attasini, Paricani, Sarangæ, Parrasini, Maratiani, Nasotiani, Aorsi, Gelæ, whom the Greeks called Cadusii, and the Matiani. The Town Heraclea, built by *Alexander*, which afterwards was over-thrown: but when it was repaired again by *Antiochus*, he named it Achais. The Derbices, through the midst of whose Borders runneth the River Oxus, which hath its Beginning from the Lake Oxus: the Syrmatæ, Oxii, Tagæ, Hemiochi, Bateni, Saraparæ, and the Bactri, with their Town Zariaspè, called afterwards Bactrum, from the River (Bactra); this Nation inhabiteth the back parts of the Mountain Paropa-misus, over against the Source of the River Indus; and it is inclosed by the River Ochus. Beyond are the Sogdiani; the Town Panda , and in the utmost Borders of their Terri-tory is Alexandria, built by *Alexander* the Great There are the Altars erected by *Hercules* and *Liber Pater*, also by *Cyrus*, *Semiramis*, and *Alexander* : the very end of all their Voyages in that part of the World being included within the River Jaxartes, which the Scythians call Silys· *Alexander* and his Soldiers thought it had been the Tanais. *Demonax*, a General of the Kings *Seleucus* and *Antiochus*, passed over that River, and set up Altars to *Apollo Didymæus*. And this *Demonax* for the most part we follow.

CHAPTER XVII.

The Scythian Nation.

BEYOND (the Realm Sogdiana) inhabit the People of the Scythians. The Persians called them in general Sacas, from a People adjoining, and the Ancients Aramei The Scythians for their part called the Persians, Chorsari : and the Mountain Caucasus, they called Graucasus, that is to say, White with Snow.[1] The People are exceedingly numerous: as much so as the Parthians. The principal People of Scythia are the Sacæ, Massagetæ, Dahæ, Essedones, Ariacæ, Rhymnici, Pesici, Amordi, Histi, Edones, Camæ, Camacæ, Euchatæ, Corieri, Antariani, Pialæ, Arimaspi, formerly called Cacidiri, Asæi, and Oetei The Napæi and Apellæi who dwelt there, are said to have perished. The noble Rivers of those People are Mandagræus and Caspasius. And surely there is not a Region wherein Geographers vary as they do in this: and I believe this to proceed from the very great number of those Nations, and their wandering to and fro. *Alexander* the Great reporteth that the Water of the Scythian Sea is fresh and potable; and *M. Varro* saith that *Pompey* had such Water brought to him when he carried on the War in that Neighbourhood against *Mithridates*: by reason, no doubt, of the great Rivers that fall into it, which overcome the Saltness of the Water. *Varro* saith also, that during this Expedition of *Pompey* to the Bactri it was known that it is but seven Days' Journey from India to the River Icarus, which runneth into the Oxus: and that the Merchandise of India, transported by the Caspian Sea, and so to the River Cyrus, may be brought in not more than five Days by Land as far as to Phasis in Pontus. Many Islands lie all over that Sea: but one above the rest is Tazata; for thither all the Shipping from the Caspian Sea and the Scythian Ocean bend their Course, the Sea-coasts being all turned to the East. The first part of this is uninhabitable, from the Scythian Promontory, by reason of the Snow: and the next Regions to this are left uncultivated because of the Fierceness of those Nations that border upon it. The Anthropophagi are in Scythia, who live on Man's flesh.[2] This is the cause why there are nothing there but vast Deserts,

[1] The Emodus or Imaus of Pliny (a word which in the language of the inhabitants signifies snowy,) derived its origin immediately from the Himaleh of the Hindoos; which really signifies in their language "snowy," or more strictly speaking, "the seat of snow."—*Quarterly Review*, vol. xxiv p. 103 —*Wern Club*

[2] We find a further account of this people, whom the ancients regarded with horror, in the 7th Book, c 2. The nation referred to was probably

with a multitude of Wild Beasts, lying in wait for Men as savage as themselves. Then again the Scythians; and again a Wilderness full of Wild Beasts, as far as to the craggy Mountain overlooking the Sea, called Tabis. Almost one-half of the length of that Coast, which looketh toward the East, is uninhabited. The first of the People that are known are the Seres,[1] famous for the fine Silk that their Woods yield. They collect from the Leaves of the Trees their hoary Down, and when it is steeped in Water they card it; wherein our Women have a double Labour, both of undoing and again of weaving this kind of Thread: with so much Labour and so far away is it sought after, that our Matrons when they go abroad in the street may shine with Transparency   The Seres are a mild People, but they resemble Beasts, in that they fly the Company of other People[2] when they desire inter-

the Samoieds, in the north of Russia · their name signifying people who eat each other, but the word has long survived the practice it described. Ovid speaks of such a people seated near the place of his exile on the Euxine

"Illi quos audis hominum gaudere cruore"
TRIST. l 4, explained by AGELL. ix. 4.—*Wern Club*

[1] There can be no question that the people here referred to are the Chinese, who are again mentioned in the 22d chapter. It was a pardonable error to suppose that silk was the produce of a tree, instead of being the production of a creature which fed on it, but it appears that the Romans were at great pains in disentangling the woven texture, that it might again be formed into garments which better suited their taste or habits   Martial speaks of this material under the name of Bombycina (Apophoreta, 24), and from his account it was of very fine texture, and probably expensive   When it was worn, the hair was bound up into a knot and fastened with a gold pin, in order that it might not soil so exquisite a dress. It permitted the beauty of form and colour to be seen through its substance.

"Fœmineum lucet sic per bombycina corpus·"
So female beauty shines through woven silk
Epig B 8. 68

See book ii. c. xxii. where Pliny corrects the errors of this chapter.—*Wern Club.*

[2] Even at this day they set abroad their wares with the prices, upon the shore, and go their ways then the foreign merchants come and lay down the money, and have away the merchandise; and so depart without any communication at all.

course with them.   The first River known among them is
Psitaras. the next Carabı. the third Lanos: beyond which
the Pıomontoıy, the Gulf Chrȳsè, the River Cymaba, the
Bay Attanos, and the Nation of the Attaci, a kind of People
secluded from all noisome Wind by pleasant Hills, with the
same Temperatuıe that the Hyperboreans live in.   Of this
People, *Amonetus* hath specially written a Book; as *Hera-
tæus* hath done of the Hyperboreans.   Beyond the Attacores
are the Thyri and Tochari, and then the Casiri, who now
belong to the Indıans.   But they withinland, that lie toward
the Scythıans, feed on Man's Flesh.   The Nomades of
India likewise wander to and fro.   Some write that they
border upon the very Cıconians and Brysanians on the North
Side.   But there (as all agree) the Mountains Emodi arise,
and the Nation of the Indians begınneth, lying not only by
that Sea, but also on the Southern, which we have named
the Indian Sea.   And this part opposite the East, stretcheth
straightforward to that place where it beginneth to bend
toward the Indian Sea; and it containeth 1875 Miles.
Then that Tract which ıs bent towards the South taketh
2475 Miles (as *Eratosthenes* hath set down), even to the
River Indus, which is the utmost limit of Indıa Westward.
But many others have set down the whole Length of India
in this manner, that it requıreth 40 Days and Nights' Saıl-
ıng; and also, that from the North to the South is 2750
Mıles. *Agrippa* saith that ıt is 3003 Miles Long, and
2003 Broad. *Posidonius* hath measured it from the North-
east to the South-east; and by this means fixeth it dırectly
opposıte to Gaul, which he likewise measured along the
West Coast, from the North-west poınt where the Sun goeth
down at Mıdsummer, to the South-west, where it setteth
ın the midst of Winter.   He teacheth also, by very good
Reasons, that thıs West Wind, which from opposite bloweth
upon India, is very healthful for that Country.   The Indians
have a dıfferent Aspect of the Sky from us.   Other Stars rise
in their Hemisphere.   They have two Summers ın the Year;
two Harvests: and their Winter between hath the Etesian
Wınds blowıng ınstead of the Northern Blasts wıth us.   The

Winds are mild with them, the Sea navigable, the Nations and the Cities innumerable, if any one would take in Hand to reckon them all. For India hath been discovered, not only by the Arms of *Alexander* the Great, and of other Kings his Successors (for *Seleucus* and *Antiochus,* and their Admiral *Patrocles,* sailed about it, even to the Hircan and Caspian Seas): but also other Greek Authors, who abode with the Kings of India (as *Megasthenes,* and *Dionysius,* who was sent thither for this purpose by *Philadelphus*) have made relation of the Forces of those Nations. And further Diligence is to be employed, considering they wrote of Things so various and incredible. They who accompanied *Alexander* the Great in his Indian Voyage have written, that in that Quarter of India which he conquered, there were 5000 Towns, not one of them less than (the City) Cos: and nine Nations. Also that India is a third Part of the whole Earth.[1] that the People in it were innumerable. And this they delivered with good Appearance of Reason: for the Indians were almost the only Men of all others that never went out of their own Country. They collect that from the Time of Father *Liber* to *Alexander* the Great, there reigned over them 154 Kings, for the Space of 5402 Years and three Months. The Rivers are of wonderful bigness. It is reported that *Alexander* sailed every Day at least 600 Stadia upon the River Indus, and yet it took him five Months and some few Days to reach the end of that River, although it is allowed to be less than the Ganges. Also, *Seneca,* one of ourselves, who laboured to write Commentaries on India, hath made Report of 60 Rivers therein, and of Nations, 118. It would be as great a Labour to reckon up the Mountains. Imaus, Emodus, Paropamisus, parts of Caucasus, join together; from which the whole passes into a very extensive Plain, like to Egypt. But to shew the Continent, we will follow the Steps of *Alexander* the Great. *Diognetus* and *Beton,* the Measurers of the Journeys of that Prince, have written, that from

---

[1] " India, a third part of the whole earth ," which is near the truth, although it contradicts what Pliny says in the 33d chapter of this Book — *Wern Club.*

the Caspian Ports to Hecatompylos of the Parthians, there are as many Miles as we have set down already. From thence to Alexandria Arion, which City the same King founded, 562 Miles: from whence to Prophthasia of the Drangæ, 199 Miles: and so forward to the Town of the Arachosi, 515 Miles. From thence to Orthospanum, 250 Miles· thence to the Town of Alexandria in Opianum, 50 Miles. In some Copies these Numbers are found to differ: this City is situated at the very Foot of Caucasus From which to the River Chepta, and Pencolaitis, a Town of the Indians, are 227 Miles. From thence to the River Indus and the Town Taxila, 60 Miles: to the noble River Hydaspes, 120 Miles: to Hypasis, a River of no less account, 4900, or 3900,[1] which was the End of *Alexander's* Voyage: but he passed over the River, and on the opposite Bank he dedicated Altars. The Letters also of the King himself agree to this. The other Parts of the Country were surveyed by *Seleucus Nicator:* to Hesidrus, 168 Miles: to the River Joames as much; and some Copies add five Miles more: from thence to the Ganges, 112 Miles: to Rhodapha, 119; and some say, that between them it is 325 Miles. From it to the Town Calimpaxa 167 Miles and a half, others say 265. Thence the Junction of the Rivers Jomanes and Ganges 625 Miles, and many put thereto 13 Miles more· from thence to the Town Palibotra 625 Miles. To the Mouth of the Ganges 638 Miles The Nations which it is not irksome to name, from the Mountains Emodi, of which the Promontory is called Imaus, which signifieth in the Language of the Inhabitants, Snowy.[2] there are the Isari, Cosyri, Izgi, and upon the very Mountains, the Ghisiotosagi· also the Brachmanæ,[3] a Name common to many Nations, among whom are the Maccocalingæ. Rivers, Pumas and Cainas,

---

[1] " Ad Hypasin non ignobiliorem xxix mill. cccxc. Hoc est novem et viginti milliaria cum trecentis et xc pass."—*Note in the Regent Edition* —*Wern Club*

[2] See p. 117

[3] If these were a sect of the Gymnosophists, they are referred to by Plutarch in his life of Alexander, but Pliny seems to be of opinion that

the latter of which runneth into the Ganges, and both are navigable. The Nations called Calingæ are close upon the Sea; but the Mandei and Malli, among whom is the Mountain Mallus, are above them; and then is the Ganges, the farthest Bound of all that Tract.

Chapter XVIII.

The River Ganges.

Some have said that the Fountains of the Ganges are uncertain, like those of the Nilus; and that it overfloweth the neighbouring Countries in the same manner. Others have said that it issueth out of the Mountains of Scythia. There run into it nineteen Rivers: of which, besides those before-named, there are navigable, Canucha, Vama, Erranoboa, Cosaogus, and Sonus. Some report that the Ganges presently breaketh out to a great Magnitude from its own Sources with great Violence, falling down over steep and craggy Rocks: and when it is arrived in the flat and even Country, that it taketh Shelter in a certain Lake; and out of it carrieth a gentle Stream, 8 Miles broad where it is narrowest: and 100 Stadia over for the most part, but 160 where it largest · but in no Place under 20 Paces deep.

Chapter XIX.

The Nations of India.

The first Nation is that of the Gandaridæ, the Region of the Calingæ is called Parthalis. The King hath in readiness for his Wars 80,000 foot, 1000 Horsemen, and 700 Elephants. The other Nations of the Indians are of different Conditions and milder Habits Some apply themselves to Tillage: others are devoted to War: one Sort export their

several separate people are so denominated They are probably the same as those mentioned in the 19th chapter, as being always prepared for a voluntary death. — *Wern. Club.*

own Commodities to other Countries, and bring foreign
Merchandise into their own. Those that are the richest and
most worthy manage the affairs of the State, distribute Justice, or sit in Council with the Kings. A fifth Kind there is
besides, in great repute, and given wholly to the Study of
Wisdom and Religion; and these make profession of being
always ready for a voluntary Death: and they end their
Days on a great funeral Fire, which they have prepared
beforehand. Besides all these, one Thing there is amongst
them half Savage, and full of exceeding Toil, and yet by
which all the Estates abovesaid are maintained; which is the
practice of hunting and taming Elephants. It is with them
they plough their Ground, upon them they ride: these are
the best Cattle they know. with them they go to War, and
contend in defence of their Frontiers. In the choice of them
for War they consider their Strength, their Age, and Bigness
of Body. There is an Island in the Ganges of great size,
containing one Nation, named Modogalica. Beyond it are
seated the Modubæ, Molindæ, where standeth the fruitful
and stately City Molinda, the Galmodroesi, Preti, Calissæ,
Sasuri, Fassalæ, Colubæ, Orxulæ, Abali, and Taluctæ. The
King of these Countries hath in Arms 50,000 Foot, 3000
Horsemen, and 400 Elephants. Then comes the stronger
Nation of the Andaræ, with many Villages, and with 30
Towns, fortified with Walls and Towers. These maintain
ready to serve the King 100,000 Foot, 2000 Horsemen,
and 1000 Elephants. The Dardæ are the richest in Gold;
and the Setæ, in Silver. But above all the Nations of India
throughout, and not of this Tract only, the Prasii far exceed
in Power and Reputation; and the largest and richest City,
Palibotra, from whence some have named this Nation, yea,
and all the Country generally beyond Ganges, Palibotros.
Their King keepeth continually in pay 600,000 Footmen,
30,000 Horsemen, and 9000 Elephants, every Day. Whereby
you may guess the mighty Wealth of this Prince. Beyond,
more within, inhabit the Monedes and Suari, who possess
the Mountain Maleus: in which, for six Months, the Shadows in Winter fall northward, and in Summer, south-

ward.[1]   The Polar Stars in all that Tract are seen but once
in the Year, and that only for 15 Days ; as *Beton* maketh
report : but *Megasthenes* writeth, that this is usual in other
Parts of India also.   The South Pole is called by the Indians
Dramasa   The River Jomanes runneth into the Ganges
through Palibotros, between the Towns Methora and Cyriso-
borca   Beyond the River Ganges, in that quarter which lieth
southward, the People are coloured by the Sun · but though
tinted, yet not so burnt as the Ethiopians.   And the nearer they
approach to the Indus, the deeper coloured they are with the
Sun : for closely beyond the Nation of the Prasii is the Indus : among whose Mountains the Pigmæi are reported to
inhabit.   *Artemidorus* writeth, that between these two Rivers
there is a Distance of 21 Miles.

Chapter XX

The River Indus.

THE Indus, which the People of that Country call Sandus,
issueth out of that top of the Mountain Caucasus, which is
called Paropamisus . it taketh its Course against the Sun-
rising, and receiveth 19 Rivers   Among these the principal
are Hydaspes, which bringeth with it four more : and Can-
tabra, conveying three.   Moreover, of such as are of themselves navigable, Accsines and Hypasis : and yet so modest
is the Course of its Waters, that in no place is it either above
50 Stadia over, or deeper than 15 Paces.[2]   This River
encloseth a very great Island named Prasianè, and another
that is less, which they call Patalè.   They that have written
it with the least, say that it is navigable for 1240 Miles ;
and turning with the Course of the Sun, it keepeth him company westward, until it is discharged into the Ocean.   The
Measure of the Coast to it I will set down generally as I find
it written : although there is no Agreement among Writers

---

[1] The reader is referred to the concluding chapter of this Book for a
more particular account of the climates and the direction of the shadows
—*Wern Club*

[2] That is, seventy-five feet —*Wern. Club.*

concerning it.   From the Mouth of the Ganges to the Cape Calingon, and the Town Dandagula, are 725 Miles : from thence to Tropina, 1225 Miles.   Then to the Promontory of Perimula, where is the chief Town of Merchandise in all India, 750 Miles · from which to the abovesaid Town Patalè, within the Island, 620 Miles.   The Mountain Nations between it and Jomanes are the Cesi and the savage Catreboni : next to them the Megallæ, whose King hath 500 Elephants ; and of Foot and Horsemen an uncertain number.   The Chrysci, Parasangæ, and Asangæ, are full of Tigers : they arm 30,000 Foot, 800 Horsemen, and 300 Elephants.   The Indus shuts them in, and they are enclosed with a crown of Mountains and Wildernesses for 625 Miles.   Beneath these Deserts are the Dari and Suræ ; and then again Deserts for 188 Miles, compassed about for the most part with Banks of Sands, like Islands in the Sea.   Under these Deserts are the Maltecoræ, Singæ, Marobæ, Rarungæ, Moruntes, Masuæ, and Pagungæ.   Now for those who inhabit the Mountains, which in a continual range without interruption stand upon the Coasts of the Ocean, they are free and subject to no Kings, and many Cities they hold among these Mountains. Then come the Naræe, enclosed within the highest Mountain of all the Indian Hills, Capitalia.   On the other side of this the Inhabitants dig extensively in Gold and Silver Mines. Then you enter upon Oratura, whose King hath indeed but 10 Elephants, but a great abundance of Footmen ; and the Varctatæ, who under their King keep no Elephants, trusting to their Horsemen and Footmen   The Odomboeræ and Salabastræ, the beautiful City Horata, fortified with Fosses and Marshes : through which the Crocodiles, on account of their greedy Appetite for Men's Bodies, will suffer none to pass into the Town, but over the Bridge.   Another Town there is among them, of great Name : Automela, standing on the Sea-side : a noble resort of Merchants, by reason of five great Rivers which meet all there in one confluence. Their King possesseth 1600 Elephants, 150,000 Footmen, and 5000 Horsemen.   The King of the Charmæ is poor ; he possesseth 60 Elephants, and his Power is otherwise small. Beyond them are the Pandæ, the only Nation of the Indians

which is governed by Women. One of this Sex, they say,
was begotten by *Hercules,* in which regard she was the better
accepted, and was appointed over the greatest Kingdom.
Those who draw their Origin from her have Dominion
over 300 Towns, and the Command of 150,000 Foot, and
500 Elephants. Beyond this Realm are the Syrieni, containing 300 Cities; the Derangæ, Posingæ, Buzæ, Gogyarei,
Umbræ, Nereæ, Prancosi, Nobundæ, Cocondæ, Nesei, Peda-
tritæ, Solobriasæ, and Olostræ, touching on the Island[1]
Patalè: from the utmost Shore of which Island unto the
Gates Caspiæ, are reckoned 18,025 Miles. Again, on this
side the River Indus, over against them, as appeareth by
evident Demonstration, there dwell the Amatæ, Bolingæ,
Gallitalutæ, Dimuri, Megari, Ordabæ, and Mesæ. Beyond
them, the Uri and Sileni; and then Deserts for 250 Miles;
which being passed over, there are the Organages, the
Abaortæ, Sibaræ, and the Suertæ: and beyond these a Wilderness as great as the former. Again, the Sarophages,
Sorgæ, Baraomatæ, and the Gumbritæ; of whom there are
thirteen Nations, and each one hath two Cities. The Aseni
inhabit three Cities: their capital City is Bucephala, built in
the very Place where King *Alexander's* horse, called Bucephalus, was buried. Above them are the Mountaineers
below the Caucacus, named Soleadæ and Sondræ and having passed the Indus, going along its Banks are the Sama-
rabriæ, the Sambruceni, the Brisabritæ, Osii, Antixeni, and
Taxillæ, with a famous City called Amandra: from which all
that Tract now lying plain within the Country is named
Amandra. Four Nations there are: the Peucolaitæ, Arsa-
galitæ, Geretæ, and Asoi: for many set not down the River
Indus as the limit westward; but add four Provinces
(Satrapæ) Gedrosi, Arachotæ, Arii, and Paropamisadæ.

CHAPTER XXI.

The Arii and the Nations adjoining

OTHER Writers prefer the opinion, that the utmost limit
is the River Cophetes, all which quarters are within the Ter-

[1] Babul.

iitory of the Arii: and most of them affirm that the City Nysa, as also the Mountain Merus consecrated to Father *Liber*, belong to India. This is that Mountain from which arose the Fable, that he sprung from the Seed of *Jupiter*. Likewise (they assign to India) the Country of the Aspagonæ, so plentiful in Vines, Laurels, and Box, and generally all sorts of Fruits that grow in Greece. Many wonderful, and in a manner fabulous things, they report of the Fertility of that Land, of the sorts of Fruits, of Trees bearing Cotton, of Wild Beasts, of Birds, and other Creatures: which I will reserve for their proper places in another part of this Work. Those four Satrapies, which I mentioned before, I will speak of presently: for now I hasten to the Island Taprobanè. But there are other Isles first, as Patalæ, which we have noted to lie in the very Mouth of the River Indus, of a Triangular figure, 220 Miles in Breadth. Without the Mouth of the Indus, two other Islands, Chrysè and Agyrè, abounding, as I suppose, in Gold and Silver Mines; for I cannot easily believe, that the Soil there is all Gold and Silver, as some have reported. Twenty Miles from them is Crocala: and twelve Miles further Bibaga, abundant in Oysters and other Shell-fishes. Then, nine Miles beyond it, Toralliba sheweth itself, and many other petty Islands.

CHAPTER XXII.

The Island Taprobanè.[1]

IT hath been for a long time thought that Taprobanè was another World under the appellation of the Antichthones. But from the time of *Alexander* the Great, and the intercourse in those parts, it was discovered to be an Island. *Onesicratus*, the Admiral of his Fleet, hath written, that the Elephants bred in this Island are bigger and better fitted for War than those of India. *Megasthenes* saith, that there is a River which divideth it, and that the Inhabitants are called

---

[1] This is now generally concluded to be the island of Ceylon, in the East Indies, now subject to British dominion.—*Wern. Club.*

Palæogoni: that it affordeth more Gold and bigger Pearls than the Indian. *Eratosthenes* also took the Measure of it, in length 7000 Stadia, and in breadth 5000: that there are no Cities, but Villages to the number of 700 It beginneth at the Sea Eoos, from which it extendeth between the East and West of India: and in times past was believed to lie out into the Sea from the Prasian Nation twenty Days' Sailing But afterwards, because the Vessels and Rigging used upon this Sea in the Passage thither were made of Paper Reeds, like those of the River Nile, the Voyage was estimated, by comparison with our Ships, at about seven Days All the Sea lying between is full of Shallows, no more than five Fathoms Deep, but in certain Channels it is so deep that no Anchors will reach the Bottom: and so narrow are these Channels, that a Ship cannot turn within them; and therefore, to avoid the necessity of turning, the Ships have Prows at both ends. In Sailing, there is no Observation of the Stars. The North Pole is never seen: but they carry with them Birds, which they send off at intervals and follow their Course, as they fly to Land: neither used they go to Sea for more than three Months in the Year; and for one hundred Days from the Solstice they take most heed; for at that time it is Winter with them. And thus much we know by relation of ancient Writers. But we obtain better Intelligence, and more accurate Information, by Ambassadors who came out of that Island, in the reign of *Claudius,* which happened after this manner. A Freed-man of Annius Plocamus, who had Farmed from the Exchequer the Customs of the Red Sea, as he sailed about the Coasts of Arabia, was driven with the North Winds beyond the Realm of Carmania, and in the Space of 15 Days he reached an Harbour of that Country, called Hippuros He found the King of that Country so courteous, as to afford him Entertainment for six Months. And as he used to discourse with him about the Romans and Cæsar, he recounted to him at large of all things But among many other Reports that he heard, he wondered most at their Justice, because their Denarii of the Money which was taken were always of the same Weight, although the different Images shewed that they were made by different Persons. And hereupon especially was he moved to seek for the Friendship of Rome; and so despatched four Ambassadors, of whom *Rachias* was the chief. From them it became known that there were five hundred Towns in it, and that there was a Harbour facing the South, lying conveniently near the Town Palesimundum, the principal City of all that Realm, and the King's Seat; that there were 200,000 common Citizens: that within this Island there was a Lake called Magisba, 270 Miles in Circuit, containing in it some Islands fruitful in nothing but Pasturage. Out of this Lake issued two Rivers; the one, Palesimundas, passing near to the City of the same Name, and running into the Harbour with three Streams; of which the Narrowest was five Stadia Broad, and the largest fifteen; the other Northward towards India, by Name Cydara: also that the next Cape of this Country to India is called Colaicum, from which to the nearest Port (of India) is counted four Days' Sailing: in the midst of which Passage, there lieth the Island of the Sun. They said, moreover, that the Water of this Sea was of a deep green Colour, and, what is still more extraordinary, full of Trees growing within it [1] so that the Pilots with their Helms broke off the Crests of those Trees They wondered to see the Stars about the North Pole (Septentriones) and Vergiliæ, as if it had been a new Heaven. They confessed also they never saw, with them, the Moon above the Earth before it was eight Days old,[2] nor after the sixteenth Day That the Canopus, a great and bright Star, used to shine all Night with them. But the thing that they were most surprised at was, that they observed the Shadow of their own

[1] Branched corals, beyond a doubt.—*Wern. Club*

[2] It is surprising to find an author so intelligent as Pliny relating such extraordinary circumstances as these ambassadors from Ceylon reported without any animadversion, and particularly that he takes no notice of what they said concerning the appearance of the moon, as such a phenomenon could not take place in any region of the earth.—*Wern. Club*

Bodies to fall toward our Hemisphere, and not to theirs;
and that the Sun rose on their Left Hand and set on their
Right, rather than contrarywise.   Furthermore they related,
that the Front of that Island which looked toward India
contained 10,000 Stadia, and reached from the South-east
beyond the Mountains Emodi.   Also, that the Seres were
within their Sight, with whom they had Acquaintance by
Merchandise: and that the Father of *Rachias* used many
times to travel thither: affirming, moreover, that if any
Strangers came thither, they were assailed by Wild Beasts ·
and that the Inhabitants themselves exceeded the ordinary
Stature of Men, having red Hair, blue Eyes, their Voice
harsh, their Speech not fitted for any Commerce.   In all
things else their Practice is the same as that of our Merchants.   On the farther side of the River, when Commodities are laid down near the Things for Sale, if the Exchange
please them they take them away, and leave the other Merchandise in lieu thereof: with a juster Hatred of Luxury
than if the mind shall consider what and whence it is sought
for, and to what end.   But even this Island Taprobanè,
seeming, as it were, to be separated by Nature from all the
World, is not without the Vices with which we are tainted.
For Gold and Silver are even there also highly esteemed:
and Marble, especially if it be fashioned like a Tortoise-shell.
Gems and Pearls also, of the better sort, are in great honour:
and the Abundance of our Luxury.   These Ambassadors said
that their Riches were greater, but that we had more use of
them.   They affirmed, that no Man with them had any
Slaves; neither slept they after Day-light, nor in the Day-
time: that the Manner of Building their Houses is low, that
the Price of Victuals did not fluctuate; and there were no
Courts, or going to Law.   *Hercules* is worshipped.   Their
King is chosen by the People, if he is aged, merciful, and
childless; but if he should have Children afterward, then he
is deposed, in order that the Kingdom may not become here-
ditary.   He hath thirty Governors assigned to him by the
People. and no Person can be condemned to Death unless
by the Majority of them: and even then he may appeal to

the People. Seventy Judges are deputed to sit upon his
Cause; and if it happen that they acquit him, then the
thirty who condemned him are ever displaced from their
Dignity, with a very severe Rebuke   The King is adorned
like *Liber Pater* but others in the habit of Arabians. If
the King offend in any thing, Death is his Punishment: but
no Man doeth Execution. All Men turn away from him,
and deny him any Intercourse, of even a Word. They are
destroyed during a solemn Hunting, which, it appears, is
exceedingly agreeable to the Tigers and Elephants. They
cultivate their Ground diligently. They do not use Vines,
but all sorts of Fruits they have in Abundance. They also
take Pleasure in Fishing, and especially in taking Tortoises
and so great are they found there, that one of their Shells
serves to cover a House. They count a hundred Years no
long Life. Thus much we have learned concerning Taprobanè It remaineth now to say somewhat of those four
Satrapies, which we put off to this Place.

CHAPTER XXIII.

Capissenè, Carmania

BEYOND those Nations which border nearest on the River
Indus, the Mountain Portions of Capissænè possess the City
Capissa, which *Cyrus* destroyed. Arachosia, with a City,
and a River also of that Name; which City some have called
Cophè, founded by Queen *Semiramis* The River Her-
mandus, which runneth by Abestè, of the Arachosians. The
next, which confront Arachosia southward, toward part of the
Arachotæ, are the Gedrosi; and on the North side the Paro-
pamisadæ. The Town Cartana, named afterwards Tetra-
gonis, is at the foot of Caucasus. This Region lieth over
against the Bactriani: then its principal Town Alexandria,
named from its Founder: Syndraci, Dangulæ, Parapiani,
Cantaces, and Maci. At the Hill Caucasus standeth the
Town Cadrusi, built likewise by *Alexander.* Below all these
Regions lieth the Coast of the Indus. The Region of the
Arians, scorched with parching Heats, and environed with

Deserts : but many shadowy Places lie between.   Cultivators
are assembled especially about the two Rivers, Tonderos and
Arosapes.   The Town Artaccana.   The River Arius, which
runneth by Alexandria, built by *Alexander*.   The Town containeth in Compass 30 Stadia.   Artacabanè, as much more
ancient as it is more beautiful, which by *Antiochus* the King
was walled the second time, and enlarged to 50 Stadia.
The Nation of the Dorisci.   The Rivers Pharnacotis and
Ophradus.   Prophtasia, a Town of the Zarasparæ.   The
Drangæ, Argetæ, Zarangæ, and Gedrusi.   Towns Peucolais
and Lymphorta ; the Desert of the Methoricori ; the River
Manais, the Nation of the Augutturi.   The River Borru ;
the People Urbi ; the Navigable River Ponamus, in the
Borders of the Pandæ.   Also, the River Ceberon, in the
Country of the Soraræ ; with many Harbours in its Mouth.
The Town of Condigramma ; the River Cophes ; into which
run the Navigable Rivers, Sadarus, Parosphus, and Sodinus.
Some will have the Country Daritus to be a part of Ariana,
and they set down the Measure of them both to be in Length
1950 Miles, and in Breadth less by half than India.   Others
have said that the Country of the Gedrusi and Scyri containeth 183 Miles   Being past which, are the Ichthyophagi,
surnamed Oritæ, who speak not the proper Indian Tongue,
for 200 Miles.   And beyond it are situated the People of the
Arbians, for 200 Miles.   Those Ichthyophagi *Alexander* forbade to feed on Fish.[1]   Beyond them are the Deserts ; and
then comes Carmania, as well as Persis, and Arabia.   But
before we treat distinctly of these Countries, I think it meet
to set down what *Onesicritus* (who having the conduct of the

---

[1] Fish was a favourite diet among the people bordering on the
Mediterranean Sea, and therefore the objection of Alexander could not
be to this, simply as an article of food   It may be supposed that various
tribes living on the sea-coast were accustomed to feed on this diet alone,
on the principle of caste or sect, thereby rendering themselves exclusive
in their communications with others   To remove such barriers to civilis-
ation may be supposed to have been the prevailing motive with Alexander in this edict ; which regulated rather than forbade the use of a
wholesome article of food — *Wern   Club*

Fleet of *Alexander*, sailed out of India, about the Mediterranean parts of Persis) reporteth, according to the Information which came lately from *Juba* · in like manner this
Navigation in these years ascertained, is even at this day preserved.   The Reports made by *Onesicritus* and *Nearchus* of
their Navigation possess neither the Distance nor the Names
of the several Resting-places.   And to begin with Xylene-
polis, built by *Alexander*, from which they entered first on
their Voyage, it is not satisfactorily put down by them, either
in what Place it is situated, or near what River.   Yet these
Particulars are by them reported worthy the Remembrance .
as that in this Voyage *Nearchus* founded a Town · that
the River Nabrus is able to bear great Vessels : overagainst
which there is an Island, at the Distance of 70 Stadia ·
that *Leonatus* founded Alexandria in the Frontiers of
that Nation, by Commandment of *Alexander* ; Argenus is a
safe Harbour : that the River Tuberum is navigable, around
which are the Paritæ.   After them the Ichthyophagi, who
occupy so long a Tract, that they were 20 Days in Sailing
along by their Coasts   The Island of the Sun, named also
the Bed of the Nymphs, is red, and in which almost every
Creature is consumed for no certain cause.   The Origeus ·
Hytanis, a River in Carmania, with many Harbours, and
Plenty of Gold   And here first they observed that they had
a sight of the North-pole Star (Septentriones).   The Star
Arcturus they saw not every Night, nor at any Time all
Night long.   Furthermore, the Archæmenides reached thus
far : and they found Mines of Copper, Iron, Arsenic, and Ver-
milion . then is the Cape of Carmania . from which to the
Coast overagainst them of the Macæ, a Nation of Arabia, is
50 Miles.   Three Islands, of which Organa only is inhabited,
having Abundance of Fresh Water, and distant from the Continent 25 Miles · four Islands in the very Gulf before Persia.
About these Islands Sea Serpents, twenty Cubits long, as they
came swimming toward them, put the Fleet in great Terror.
The Island Acrotadus . likewise the Gauratæ, wherein the
Nation of the Chiani inhabit.   In the middle of the Persian
Gulf is the River Hiperis, able to bear Ships of Burden.   The

River Sitiogagus, upon which a Man may pass in seven Days to the Pasargadæ. A River that is Navigable called Phirstimus, and an Island without a Name. The River Granius, which runneth through Susianè, carrieth but small Vessels. Along the Right Bank of this River dwell the Deximontani, who prepare Bitumen. The River Oroatis, with a difficult Mouth, except to skilful Pilots: two little Islands. Past which, the Sea is very shallow, like a Marsh, but there are some Channels wherein they may sail. The Mouth of the Euphrates The Lake which the Eulæus and Tigris make, near to Characis. Then on the Tigris, Susa. There they found *Alexander* keeping Feast-days of Festivity in the seventh Month after he had parted from them at Patalæ, and the third Month of his Voyage. And thus much concerning the Voyage of *Alexander's* Fleet. Afterwards from Syagrus, a Promontory in Arabia, it was counted to Patalè 1332 Miles, and that the West Wind, which the people of that Country call Hypalus, was thought most proper to sail with to the same Place. The Age ensuing discovered a shorter and safer Course; namely, if from the said Promontory they set their Course directly to the River Zizerus, an Harbour in India. And in truth this Passage was sailed for a long time, until at length a Merchant found out a more compendious Course, and India was brought near for Gain for every Year they sailed thither, and because Pirates very much infest them, they embark in their Ships Companies of Archers. And because all these Seas are now first certainly discovered, it is not amiss to shew the whole Course from Egypt. It is worthy to be observed, that there is not a Year but it costs our State to furnish into India, 500,000 Sesterces, (fifty millions of Sesterces.) For which the Indians send back Merchandise, which at Rome is sold for a hundred times as much as it cost. From Alexandria it is two Miles to Juliopolis: from whence on the Nilus they sail 303 Miles to Coptus, which may be done in twelve Days, with the Etesian Winds blowing. From Coptus they travel upon Camels, and for the sake of Water there are Places appointed for Lodging. The first is called

Hydreuma, 32 Miles. The second, one Day's Journey, in a Mountain. The third, at another Hydreuma, 95 Miles from Coptus. The fourth, again, in a Mountain. Again, at the Hydreuma of *Apollo,* from Coptus, 184 Miles. Again, in a Hill. And then to Hydreuma the New, from Coptus, 234 Miles.[1] There is another called Hydreuma the Old, named also Troglodyticum, where, two Miles out of the direct way, is a Garrison, four Miles distant from New Hydreuma. From thence to the Town Berenicè, where is an Harbour of the Red Sea, 258 Miles from Coptus. But as the Journey is for the most part performed by Night, because of the excessive Heat, and Travellers rest all the Day, twelve Days are set down for the whole Journey between Coptus and Berenicè. They begin to sail at Midsummer, before or close upon the rising of the Dog-star; and in about 30 Days they arrive at Ocelis in Arabia, or else at Cana, within the Country of Incense. A third Port there is besides, called Muza, to which there is no Resort of the Merchants of India: neither by any but Merchants that traffic in Incense and Spices of Arabia. The Indus hath Towns.[2] Its Region is called Saphar. and another called Sabè. But for them that would make a Journey to the Indians, the most commodious place from whence to set forward is Ocelis: for from thence, and with the West Wind called Hypalus, they have a passage of forty Days' Sailing to the first Town of Merchandise in India, called Muziris. However, this Port is not to be ventured in, because of the neighbouring Pirates, which keep ordinarily about a place called Hydræ; and it is not richly stored with Merchandise. And moreover, the Station of the Ships is far from the Land, so that they must convey their Wares in little Boats which they use for the purpose. At the time when this Account was written, the King that reigned there was named *Celebothras.* There is another Harbour that is more commodious, belonging to the Nation

---

[1] So as it appeareth that every day's journey was about thirty-two miles

[2] This is an unfinished sentence, perhaps from the author's not being able to obtain the names of these towns — *Wern. Club*

Necanidon, which they call Bêcarè: the King's Name at
present is *Pandion ;* far off is another Town of Merchandise
within the Land, called Modusa. The Region from whence
they transport Pepper in small Lighters made of one piece
of Wood to Bêcarè, is named Cotona : of all which Nations,
Ports, and Towns, there is not a Name found in any of the
former Writers. By which it appeareth, that there hath
been great Change in these places. From India, our Merchants return in the Beginning of our Month December,
which the Ægyptians call Tybis : or at farthest before the
Sixth Day of the Ægyptian Month Machiris, which is before
our Ides of January : and by this reckoning they may pass
and return within the compass of One Year. When they
sail from India they have the (North-East) Wind, Vulturnus,
with them : and when they have entered into the Red Sea,
the South or South-west. Now will we return to our pro-
posed Discourse concerning Carmania : the Coast of which,
after the reckoning of *Nearchus,* may take in Circuit 12,050
Miles. From its Beginning to the River Sabis is 100 Miles,
from whence as far as to the River Andanim, are Vineyards
and Corn-fields, well cultivated. The Region is called Ar-
muzia. The Towns of Carmania are Zetis and Alexandria.
In this part the Sea breaketh into the Land in two Arms ;
which our Countrymen call the Red Sea,[1] and the Greeks
Erythræum, from a King named *Erythras ·* or (as some
think) because the Sea, by reason of the Reflexion of the Sun,
seemeth of a reddish colour. Others suppose that this Redness
is occasioned of the Sand and Ground, which is Red : and others
again, that the very Water is of its own nature so coloured.

CHAPTER XXIV.
The Persian and Arabian Gulfs

THIS Red Sea is divided into Two Gulfs. That from the
East is named the Persian Gulf, and is in Circuit 2500 Miles,

[1] Another reason for the name is to be found in Esau, the son of the
patriarch Isaac, and whose dominion was on its borders   Bruce and others
have advanced opinions with regard to the origin of the name of this celebrated sea ; but its most ancient name may be rendered the Weedy Sea
— *Wern Club*

by the computation of *Eratosthenes*. Overagainst this Gulf
is Arabia, which is in Length 1200 Miles   On the other
side there is another called the Arabian Gulf, which runneth
into the Ocean, called Azanius.   The Mouth of the Persian
Gulf is Five Miles wide, though some have made it but
Four.   From this to its deepest recess, by a straight Course,
is known to be 1125 Miles; and it is fashioned like a Man's
Head.   *Onesicritus* and *Nearchus* have written, that from
the River Indus to the Persian Gulf, and from thence to
Babylon by the Marshes of the Euphrates, is 2500 Miles.
In an angle of Carmania the Chelonophagi inhabit, who feed
on the Flesh of Tortoises, and cover their Cottages with their
Shells.   They inhabit from the River Arbis to the very Cape,
they are Hairy over all their Body except their Heads, and
wear no other Garment but Fish-skins

Chapter XXV.

The Island Cascandrus: and the Kingdoms of the Parthians

Beyond this Tract of the Chelonophagi, toward India,
there lieth, Fifty Miles within the Sea, the Island Cascan-
drus, by report all desert ; and near it, with an Arm of the
Sea between, another Island called Stois; having a lucrative
Trade in Pearls.   Beyond the Cape of Carmania, you enter
upon the Armozei.   Some say, that the Albii are between
both; and that their Coasts contain in the whole 402 Miles.
There are the Port of the Macedonians, and the Altars of
Alexander on the very Promontory itself   The Rivers Saga-
nos, and then Daras, and Salsos: beyond which is the Cape
Themistheas, and the Island Aphrodisias, which is inhabited
Then beginneth Persis, which extendeth to the River Oroatis,
that divideth it from Elymais   Overagainst Persis, these
Islands, Philos, Cassandra, and Aratia, with an exceeding
high Mountain in it   and this Island is consecrated to *Neptune*.   Persis itself, westward, hath the Coasts lying out in
Length 450 Miles.   The People are Rich, even to Luxury;
and long since they are become subject to the Parthians, and
have lost their own Name.   We will briefly now speak of

their Empire. The Parthians have in all Eighteen Realms
under them : for so they divide the Provinces about the
Two Seas, as we have said, the Red Sea lying southward,
and the Hircan Sea, toward the north. Of these Eleven,
which are called the Higher Provinces, take their beginning
from the Border of Armenia, and the Coasts of the Caspian ;
and they reach to the Scythians, with whom they have equal
Intercourse on the other side. The other Seven are called
the Lower Provinces. As for the Parthians, their Land
always lay at the Foot of those Mountains of which we have
so often spoken, which enclose all those Nations. It hath
on the East the Arii, and southward Carmania and the
Ariani ; on the west side the Pratitæ and Medi ; and on
the North the Hircani ; and is compassed about with Deserts.
The farthest Nations of the Parthians are called Nomades :
beyond the Deserts their Cities toward the West, are Issaris
and Calliopè, of which we have written before , but toward
the North-east, Europum ; and South-east, Mania In the
Midland the City Hecatompylos, and Arsacia The noble
Region of Nysæa in Parthyenes, where is Alexandropolis,
(so called) from its Founder.

Chapter XXVI

Media, Mesopotamia, Babylon, and Seleucia.

It is needful in this place to describe the Situation of the
Medi, and to discover the Face of those Countries, as far as
to the Persian Sea, in order that the Description of other
Regions may be the better understood. For Media on the
West runneth obliquely, confronteth the Parthiæ, and encloseth both these Realms. Therefore on the East side it
hath the Parthians and Caspians: on the South, Sittacenè,
Susianè, and Persis ; Westward, Adiabenè ; and Northward,
Armenia. The Persians always dwelt about the Red Sea, on
which account it was called the Persian Gulf. The Maritime Coast thereabout is called Cyropolis, and that part
which bordereth upon the Medes Elymais. There is a Place
called Megala, in the ascent of a steep Mountain, through a

narrow Passage by Steps to Persepolis, the Head of the Kingdom, and destroyed by *Alexander*   Moreover, in the Frontiers standeth Laodicea, built by King *Antiochus*. From thence towards the East the Magi hold the Castle of Passagardæ, wherein is the Tomb of *Cyrus*.   Also the Town Ecbatana belonging to the Magi, which *Darius* the King caused to be translated to the Mountains.[1]   Between the Parthians and the Ariani are extended the Paræraceni These Nations and the River Euphrates serve to limit the lower Realms.   Now are we to discourse of the Parts remaining of Mesopotamia ; setting aside one point thereof, and the People of Arabia, whereof we spoke in the former Book.   All Mesopotamia belonged to the Assyrians, dispersed in Villages, except Babylon and Ninus.   The Macedonians collected it into Cities on account of the goodness of their Soil.   Besides the above-named Towns, it hath Seleucia, Laodicea, and Artemita : likewise within the Nation of the Arabians named Aroei and Mardani, Antiochia : and that which, being founded by *Nicanor*, Governor of Mesopotamia, is called Arabis.   Upon these join the Arabians, but within the Country are the Eldamarii.   Above them is the Town Bura, situated upon the River Pelloconta ; beyond which are the Salmani and Masei, Arabians.   Then there join to the Gordiæi the Aloni, by whom the River Zerbis passeth, and so is discharged into the Tigris.   The Azones and Silices, Mountaineers, together with the Orentes ; on the side of whom the Town Gaugamela.   Also Suè among the Rocks ; above are the Sylici and Classitæ, through whom the Lycus runneth out of Armenia.   Toward the South-east, Absittis, and the Town Azochis.   Presently in the Plains the Towns Diospagè, Polytelia, Stratonicea, and Anthemus   Nicephorion, as we have already said, is seated near the River Euphrates, where *Alexander* caused it to be founded, for the convenient Situation of the Place.   Of the City Apamia we have before

---

[1] Pliny's statement as to the building of the palace, and indeed the whole city of Shushan, by Darius Hystaspes, is contradicted by all Greek and Oriental writers, who represent the city as extremely ancient—*vide* "Horne."—*Wern Club*

spoken in the Description of Zeugma : from which they that
go eastward meet with a strong fortified Town, formerly
in Compass 65 Stadia, and called the Royal Palace of their
Satraps, to which they brought Tributes; but now it is
formed into a Castle.   But there continue still as they
were, Hebata and Oruros, unto which, by the Conduct of
Pompey the Gieat, the Bounds of the Roman Empire were
extended; and it is from Zeugma 250 Miles   Some Writers
say that the Euphrates was divided by a Governor of Mesopotamia, and one Arm of it brought to Gobaris, which was
done lest the River should endanger the City of Babylon.
They affirm, moreover, that the Assyrians generally called it
Armalchar,[1] which signifieth a Royal River.   On the Place
where it is tuined there stood Agrani, one of the greatest
Towns of that Region, which the Persians utterly destroyed

Babylon,[2] the Capital of the Chaldean Nations, for a long
time possessed an illustrious Name through all the World: in
iegard of which the other Part of Mesopotamia and Assyria
was named Babylonia   and embracing 60 Miles.   The Walls
were 200 Feet in Height, and 50 broad : reckoning to every
Foot three Fingers' Breadth more than our ordinary Measure.   Through the midst passeth the River Euphrates · with
a wonderful Work, on both Sides.   To this Day the Temple

---

[1] Or rather, Nahal Nalca, *i. e* the King's River

[2] Herodotus, in the first book of his history, describes this most
splendid of cities; the walls of which were classed among the wonders of
the world.   But contrary to the report by which Pliny professes to be
guided, this ancient Greek author represents them to have been built in
the form of a square, and although the lapse of time may have caused a
variety of changes to take place in other particulars regarding this city,
we can scarcely suppose that these changes can have extended to the
dimensions or situation of its stupendous walls, by which alone its form
would be influenced.   It is surprising that among the authors which
Pliny had consulted in drawing up his account of these regions, he makes
no mention of this illustrious Greek writer, though he quotes him in
other places   Philostratus, Solinus, Diodorus, Quintus Curtius, and
more especially the Bible, may be consulted for a variety of curious particulars regarding this eminent and powerful city, whose walls and
splendour are now buried in a desert — *Wern Club*

of *Jupiter Belus* continueth there entire. He was the first
Discoverer of the Science of the Stars. Nevertheless it is
reduced to a Desert, having been exhausted by Seleucia,
which standeth near it : and which was for that very purpose
built by *Nicator* within the Fortieth Stone, at the Place of
meeting of the New Channel of Euphrates with the Tigris ·
nevertheless it is named Babylonia, a free State at this Day,
of independent Jurisdiction , but they live after the Manners of the Macedonians. And by report there are 600,000
common Citizens. The Position of the Walls, by report, is
in the form of an Eagle spreading out her Wings : and the
Soil is the most Fertile in all the East. The Parthians,
again, to exhaust this City, built Ctesiphon within the Third
Stone from it, in Chalonitis; which now is the Head
of the Kingdom. But when it advanced nothing, King
Vologesus founded another Town near it, called Vologeso
Certa. There are also in Mesopotamia the Cities Hyp-
parenum, a City likewise of the Chaldæans, and ennobled
for Learning, and, as well as Babylon, situated near the
River Narraga, which gave the Name to the City The
Persians destroyed the Walls of this Hypparenum. There are
also in this Tract the Orcheni, toward the south , and a Third
Sect of the Chaldæans. Beyond this Region are the Notitæ,
Orthophantæ, and Græciochantæ *Nearchus* and *Onesi-*
critus report, That from the Persian Sea to Babylon, by the
Voyage up the Euphrates, is 412 Miles. But later Writers
count from Seleucia 490 Miles *Juba* writeth, that from
Babylon to Charax is 175 Miles. Some affirm that beyond
Babylon the River Euphrates floweth in one Channel 87
Miles, before it is divided to water the Country : its entire
Course being 1200 Miles. This variety in Authors is the cause
of the Uncertainty of the Measure, considering that even the
very Persians agree not about the Dimensions of their
Schœni and Parasangæ, but have different Measures of them.
Where the River Euphrates ceaseth to defend by its own
Channel, at the portion approaching the Border of Charax,
there is great danger of the Robbers called Attalæ, a Nation
of the Arabians Beyond them are the Scenitæ The Arabian

Nomades occupy the circuit of the Euphrates, as far as to the Deserts of Syria: from which place we said that it turned into the South, abandoning the Deserts of Palmyra.[1] From the beginning of Mesopotamia to Seleucia, by sailing on the Euphrates, is 1125 Miles; and from the Red Sea, if you go by the Tigris, 320 Miles; from Zeugma 527 Miles; and to Zeugma from Seleucia in Syria, upon the Coast of our Sea, is 175 Miles   This is the Breadth there of the Land between the two Seas.   The Kingdoms of Parthia contain 944 Miles. Finally, there is a Town of Mesopotamia on the Bank of the Tigris, near where the Rivers meet, which they call Digba.

Chapter XXVII.

The River Tigris.

It is also convenient to say somewhat of the River Tigris itself.   It beginneth in the Region of Armenia the Greater, issuing out of a great Source in the Plain. The place beareth the Name of Elongosinè.   The River itself, so long as it runneth slowly, is named Diglito; but when it beginneth to be rapid, it is called Tigris, which in the Median language signifieth a Dart.   It runneth into the Lake Arethusa, which beareth up all that is cast into it; and the Vapours that arise out of it carry Clouds of Nitre.   In this Lake there is but one kind of Fish, and that entereth not into the Channel of the Tigris as it passeth through; as likewise the Fishes of the Tigris do not swim out into the Water of the Lake   In its Course and Colour it is unlike the other: and when it is past the Lake and meeteth the Mountain Taurus, it loseth itself in a Cave, and so runneth under, until on the other

---

[1] This is Tadmor in the wilderness, built by Solomon, king of Israel, and further illustrious from being the city where the critic Longinus was the prime minister of the Queen Zenobia   It is now truly in a wilderness, but is still celebrated for its remains of antiquity chiefly of Greek construction   There are many streams coming down from the adjacent mountains, and there can be no doubt that if a settled tribe fixed themselves there, the tract would become as fine an oasis as ever — *Wern. Club*

Side it breaketh forth again in a Place which is called Zoro-
anda. That it is the same River is evident by this, that it
carrieth through whatever was cast into it. After this second
Spring, it runneth through another Lake, named Thospites,
and again taketh its Way under the Earth through Gutters,
and 25 Miles beyond it is returned about Nymphæum
Claudius Cæsar reporteth, that in the Country Arrhenè, it
runneth so near to the River Arsanias, that when they both
swell they join, but without mingling their Water; for Arsanias, being the lighter, floateth over the other, for almost the
Space of four Miles; but soon after they part asunder, and it
turneth its Course toward the River Euphrates, into which
it entereth. But Tigris receiving the famous Rivers out of
Armenia: Parthenis, Agnicè, and Pharion, so dividing the
Arabians, Aroeans, and the Adiabeni, and by this means
making, as we have said, Mesopotamia to be an Island, after
it hath passed by and viewed the Mountains of the Gordiæi,
near Apamia, a Town of Mesenè on this side Seleucia, surnamed Babylonia, 125 Miles. Dividing itself into two Channels, with the one it runneth southward to Seleucia, watering
the Country of Mesenè; and with the other it windeth to
the north, on the back of the said Mesenè, and cutteth
through the Plains of the Cauchians. When these two
Branches are united again, it is called Pasitigris. After this
it receiveth out of Media the Coaspes; and so passing between Seleucia and Ctesiphon, as we have said, it poureth
itself into the Lakes of Chaldæa, which it replenisheth with
Water for the Compass of threescore and ten Miles: which
done, it issueth forth, gushing out with a very great Stream,
and on the right of the Town Charax is discharged into the
Persian Sea, by a Mouth ten Miles over. Between the
Mouths of these two Rivers were 25 Miles, or, as some say,
seven: and both of them were navigable. But the Orcheni
and other neighbouring Inhabitants long since turned the
Course of Euphrates aside to water their Fields, insomuch
that it is conveyed into the Sea, only through the Tigris.
The next Country bordering upon the Tigris is called Para-
potamia. in it is Mesenè, of which we have spoken. Its

Town is Dibitach. Chalonitis is joined with Ctesiphon, noble
not only with Date-trees, but also with Olive, Apple, and
Pear-trees, and generally with all sorts of Fruit. Unto this
Country extendeth the Mountain Zagrus, coming out of Armenia, between the Medes and Adiabeni, above Parætacenè
and Persis. Chalonitis is distant from Persis 480 Miles.
Some write, that by the nearest Way it is so much from the
Caspian Sea to Assyria. Between these Nations and Mesenè
lieth Sittacenè, the same that is called Arbelitis and Palæs-
tinè The Towns therein are Sittacè of the Græcians, toward
the east, and Sabata; but on the West, Antiochia, between
two Rivers, Tigris and Tornadotus. Also Apamia, which
Antiochus so called after his Mother's Name. This City
is environed with the River Tigris, and divided by the River
Archous. Somewhat lower is Susianè, wherein (is) Susa,
the ancient Region of the Persians, founded by *Darius*, the
Son of *Hystaspes*, and from Seleucia Babylonia, it is distant
450 Miles; and as much from Ecbatana of the Medes,
through the Mountain Charbanus. Upon that Channel of
the Tigris which taketh its Course northward, standeth the
Town Babytacè: and from Susa it is 135 Miles. The People
of this Country are the only Men in the World that hate
Gold: and they bury it, that it may serve for no use to any
one. To the Susiani eastward are joined the Cossæi Robbers, and forty Nations of the Mizæi, free and wild. Above
these lie the Parthusi, Mardi, Saitæ, and Hyi, who are
spread abroad above Elemais, which joineth to the maritime
Coasts of Persis, as is above said. Susa is from the Persian
Sea 250 Miles. On that Side where the Fleet of *Alexander*
came up the Pasitigris, there standeth a Village upon the
Lake Chaldais, named Aphlè: from which to Susa is 65½
Miles by Water. The next that border upon the Susiani
eastward are the Cossæi, and above the Cossæi northward
lieth Mesobatené, under the Mountain Cambiladus, which is
a Branch of the Caucasus: and from thence is the most easy
Passage to the Bactri. The River Eulæus maketh a Parti-
tion between Elimais and Susianè. This River riseth in the
Country of the Medi, and in the midst of its Course loseth

itself in the Ground; but rising again, and running through
Mesobatenè, it passeth round the Castle of the Susi and the
Temple of *Diana*, the most august Temple among those
Nations: and the very River itself is ceremoniously regarded: so that the Kings drink of no other, and therefore
they carry it to a great distance. It receiveth the River
Hedypnus, which cometh along by the Asylum of the Persians, and one from among the Susiani. A Town there is near
it, called Magoa, 15 Miles from Charax Some place this Town
in the utmost Borders of Susiana, close to the Deserts   Beneath Eulæus lieth Elymais, joining to Persis on the Sea-
coast; it is 240 Miles from the River Oroates to Charax. The
Towns in it are Seleucia and Sositarè, situated upon the
Mountain Casyrus.   The Coast which lieth before it is, as
we have said before, no less dangerous than the Lesser Syrtes,
because of the Mud and Slime which the Rivers Brixia and
Ortacea bring down; and Elimais itself is so moist that
there is no Way to Persis but by taking a Circuit about
it.   It is also much infested with Serpents, which those
Rivers bring down: but that part of it is the least passable
which they call Characenè, from the Town (Charax), which
limiteth the Kingdoms of Arabia: of which we will speak
by and by, after we have set down the Opinion of *M. Agrippa;*
for he hath written, that Media, Parthia, and Persis, are
bounded on the East by the Indus; on the West, by the
Tigris; on the North, by the Taurus and Caucasus; and on
the South, by the Red Sea: also, that they extend in Length
1320 Miles, and in Breadth 840.   Moreover, that Mesopotamia by itself is enclosed eastward by the Tigris, westward by
the Euphrates, on the North by the Taurus, and on the South
by the Persian Sea; being in Length 800 Miles, and in
Breadth 360.   Charax is the inmost Town of the Persian
Gulf, from which Arabia, called Eudæmon (happy) runneth
forth in Length; it is situated upon a Mount artificially
raised between the Confluence of Tigris on the right Hand,
and Eulæus on the left: with an Expansion of three Miles.
It was first founded by *Alexander* the Great; who, having
drawn Colonists out of the royal City Durinè (which then

was ruined), and leaving there behind him those Soldiers which were not fit for service, ordained that this Town should be called Alexandria; and the District about it, Pellæum, from his native Country : and he peopled it only with Macedonians. This Town was destroyed by the Rivers. Afterwards, *Antiochus*, the fifth of the Kings, rebuilt it, and named it from himself. But when it was injured again, *Spasines*, Son of *Sogdonacus*, King of the adjoining Arabians, and not (as *Juba* reporteth) a Lord (Satrap) under *Antiochus*, restored it by Moles opposite each other, and called it after his own Name. He thus fortified the Site of it three Miles in Length and little less in Breadth. At the beginning it stood upon the Sea-coast, being from the Water-side ten Stadia; and even from thence it hath false Galleries but by the Report of *Juba*, in his Time, 50 Miles. At this Day the Arabian Ambassadors, and also our Merchants that come from thence, affirm it is from the Sea-shore 125 Miles : so that it cannot be found in any Place that the Earth hath gained more, or in so short a Time by means of the Mud brought down by Rivers. And it is the more wonderful, that the Tide which riseth far beyond this Town doth not carry it away again. In this very Town I am not ignorant that *Dionysius*, the latest of our modern Geographers, was born : whom *Divus Augustus* sent before into the East to write a Description of whatever he found, for the Information of his elder Son, who was about to proceed into Armenia, in an Expedition against the Parthians and Arabians. It has not escaped me, nor is it forgotten, that in my first Entrance into this Work, I professed to follow those who had written of their own Countries, as being the most diligent in that behalf. Nevertheless, in this Place I choose rather to follow the Roman Officers that have warred there, and King *Juba*, in Books written to *C. Cæsar* (*Caligula*) concerning the same Arabian Expedition.

Chapter XXVIII.

Arabia, Nomades, Nabatæi, and Omani: the Islands Tylos and Ogyris.

ARABIA cometh behind none of the Nations for its great Length and Extent; for it beginneth at the Descent of the Mountain Amanus, overagainst Cilicia and Comagenè, as we have before said; where it is peopled with many Nations of them, brought by *Tigranes* the Great to inhabit that Quarter; and in old Time it descended naturally as far as to our Sea and the Egyptian Coast, as we have shewn: yea, and it extendeth into the midland Parts of Syria to the Mountain Libanus, where the Hills reach to the very Clouds: to which are joined the Ramasi; then the Taranei, and after them the Patami. The Peninsula itself of Arabia runneth out between two Seas, the Red and the Persian, by a certain Workmanship of Nature, resembling Italy in Form and Magnitude, with its Sea-coasts also in the manner of Italy. It also regardeth the same Quarter of the Heaven without any Difference. This Tract, for the rich Seat it hath, is named Felix (happy). The Nations therein dwelling, from our Sea to the Deserts of Palmyra, we have treated of already, therefore we pass them by. The Nomades, and those Robbers that trouble the Chaldæans, the People called Scenitæ, border on it as we have before said; they also are Wanderers, but are so called from their Tabernacles, which they make of Hair-cloths, and they encamp under them as they please. Being past them you find the Nabatæi, who inhabit a Town named Petra, in the Valley, little less than two Miles large; environed with very steep Mountains, and having a River running through the midst of it. It is distant from Gaza (a Town of our Coast) 600 Miles; and from the Persian Gulf, 122. And here meet both the Highways, that is, the one which Passengers travel to Palmyra in Syria, and the other wherein they come from Gaza. Beyond Petra the Omani inhabit as far as to Carax, in the celebrated Towns built by *Semiramis*, namely, Abesamis and Soractia. But now all is a Wilderness. Then come you to a Town named Forath, situated upon the Bank of the Pasitigris, and subject to the King of the Caraceni · to which they resort from Petra; and from thence to Charax they sail with a favourable Tide for the Space of twelve Miles. But they that come by Water out of the Parthian Kingdom, meet with a Village called Teredon, below the Place where Euphrates and Tigris meet. The Chaldæans inhabit the left Bank of the River, and the Nomades called Scenitæ, the right. Some affirm, that as you sail on the Tigris, you pass by two other Towns, distant from each other: the one called formerly Barbatia, and afterwards Thumata, which our Merchants report to be ten Days' Sail from Petra, and to be subject to the King of the Characeni: and the other named Apamia, situated in the Place where the Overflowing of Euphrates joineth with the Tigris; and therefore they prevent the Invasion of the Parthians, by breaking up the Banks and so procure an Inundation of the Waters. Now being past Charax, we will discourse of the Coast first explored by *Epiphanes*. The Place where the Mouth of the Euphrates was. A River of Salt Water, the Promontory Chaldone, where the Sea is more like a Whirlpool than a Sea, for 50 Miles The River Achana; Deserts for 100 Miles, until you come to the Island Ichara: the Bay Capeus, which the Gaulopes and Chateni inhabit: the Bay Gerraicus, and the Town Gerra, five Miles in extent; and fortified with Towers made of square Masses of Salt. Fifty Miles from the Sea-side is the Region Attenè: and overagainst it the Island Tylos, as many Miles from the Shore, with a Town bearing the Name of the Island, much celebrated for Abundance of Pearls and not far from it is another somewhat less, twelve Miles from the Cape of the aforesaid Tylos. Beyond these there are discovered by Report some great Islands; but they have not been visited by our Merchants. This last Island is 112 Miles and a half in Circuit, and is far from Persis; and Access to it is only by one narrow Channel The Island Asgilia; the Nations Nocheti, Zurachi, Borgodi, Cataræi, and Nomades: the River Cynos. Beyond that, *Juba* saith, there is no more Navigation discovered on that Side, by reason of the Rocks. He hath made no mention of the Town Batrasabè of the

Omani, nor of Omana, which former Geographers have
held to be a Harbour of great Importance in Carmania.
Also, Omnè and Athanæ, which our Merchants report to be
at this Day two very famous Towns, frequented from the
Persian Gulf. Beyond the River Canis, as King *Juba*
writeth, there is a Hill which seemeth all scorched. The
Nations of the Epimaranitæ: and soon after the Ichthyophagi . a desert Island ; the Nations Bathymi. The Mountains Eblitæi ; the Island Omœnus ; the Port Machorbæ, the
Islands Etaxalos, Onchobricè, the Nation Chadæi. Many
Islands without a Name : but of Importance, Isura, Rhinnea ;
and another very near, wherein are Pillars of Stone inscribed
with unknown Characters The Port of Gobœa; and the
desert Islands Bragæ. The Nation of the Thaludæi the
Region Dabanegoris the Mountain Orsa, with a Port:
the Bay Duatus, and many Islands. The Mountain Tricory-
phus : the Region Cardalena, the Islands Solanidæ, Capina.
Also the Islands of the Ichthyophagi· and after them the
Glari. The Shore called Hammæum, where are Gold Mines
The Region Canauna. The Nations Apitami and Gasani.
The Island Deuadœ; the Fountain Goralus; the Garpheti;
the Islands Aleu and Amnamethu. The Nation called
Darræ, the Islands Chelonitis, and many of the Ichthyophagi. The Isle Eodanda, which is Desert, and Basagè ;
many others of the Sabæi. The Rivers Thamar and Amnon ;
the Islands Dolicæ; the Fountains Daulotes and Dora ; the
Islands, Pteros, Labanis, Coboris, Sambracatè, with a Town
so named on the Continent. On the South side are many
Islands, but the greatest of them is Camari. The River
Mysecros; the Port Leupas, and the Sabæans, called Scenitæ. Many other Islands ; their Chief Town of Merchandise
is Acila, where the Merchants embark for their Voyage to
India. The Region Amithoscuta, and Damnia. The Mizi,
the Greater and Less . the Drimati and Macæ. The Promontory of these People is overagainst Carmania, and distant
from it 50 Miles. A wonderful thing is reported there : that
Numenius, Chief Commander under King *Antiochus*, over
Mesena, conquered the Navy of the Persians in a Sea-fight,

and on the same Day, with the return of the Tide, subdued their Horsemen: in memorial of which he erected in
the same Place two Trophies, one in honour of *Jupiter*,
and the other of *Neptune*. Far out at Sea there lieth an
Island called Ogyris, distant from the Continent 125 Miles,
and containing in Circuit 112; much renowned for the
Sepulchre of King *Erythra*, who was buried there. Another
there is no less famous, called Dioscoridu, in the Sea Azanium; and it is from Syagrum, the extremest Cape, 280
Miles. There remain yet not spoken of, the Autarides,
toward the South, in the Mountains, which continue for
seven Days' journey: the Nations Larendani, Catabani, and
Gebanitæ, who have many Towns, but the greatest are Nagia
and Tamna, with 65 Temples within it, which is a mark how
great it is. A Promontory, from which to the Continent of
the Trogloditæ is 50 Miles. The Toani, Acchitæ, Chatramotitæ, Tomabei, Antidalei, Lexianæ, Agrei, Cerbani; and
Sabæi, of all the Arabians most famous for their Frankin-
cense; their Nations reaching from Sea to Sea. Their Towns
on the Coast of the Red Sea are Maranè, Marma, Corolia,
and Sabatra; within-land are the Towns Nascus, Cardava,
Carnus, and Tomala, whence they convey their Commodities
of Aromatics. One part of them are the Atramitæ, whose
Capital City, Sobotalè, had within its Walls Sixty Temples.
But the Royal City of the whole is Nariaba, situated on a
Gulf that reacheth into the Land ninety-four Miles, full of
Islands, having Odoriferous Trees. Upon the Atramitæ,
within the Mainland, are joined the Minæi: but the Ela-
mitæ inhabit the Sea (Coast), where standeth a City also called
Elamitum. To them are joined the Cagulatæ; and their
Town is Siby, which the Greeks name Apatè. Then the
Arsicodani, and Vadei, with a great Town: and the Barasei:
Lichenia, and the Island Sygaros, which Dogs will not enter;
and if any be put there, they wander about the Shore until
they die. A Deep Bay, in which are the Leanitæ, who gave
name to it. Their Royal City is Agra: but Leana, or, as
others have it, Ælana, is in the Bay. And hence our
Writers have called that Bay Ælaniticum, which others

have termed Ælenaticum ; *Artemidorus*, Aleniticum ; and *Juba*, Læniticum. Arabia is reported to take in Circuit from Charax to Leana, 4870 Miles ; but *Juba* thinketh it somewhat less than 4000. It is widest in the North Parts, between the Towns Herous and Characè. Now it remaineth that we speak of other Parts within the Midland thereof. The Ancients joined the Nabatæi to the Thimanei ; but at this Day there are the Taveni, Suellem, and Sarraceni : the Town is Arra, wherein all Business is assembled. The Hemnatæ and Analitæ ; the Towns Domada and Eragè ; the Thamusians, with their Town Badanatha ; the Carrei, and their Town Chariati ; the Achoali, and their Town Phoda. Furthermore, the Minæi, descended, as some think, from *Minos*, King of Crete ; whose Town Charmæi is 14 Miles (in Compass) ; Mariaba, Baramalacum, a Town not to be despised ; likewise Carnon, and the Rhamei, who are thought to spring from *Rhadamanthus*, the Brother of *Minos*. The Homeritæ, with the Town Massala ; the Hamirci, Gedranitæ, Anapræ, Ilisanitæ, Bochilitæ, Sammei, and Amathei ; with the Towns, Nessa and Cennesseri. The Zamareni, with the Towns Saiacè, Scantatè, and Bacascani ; the Town Rhiphearma, which in the Arabian Tongue signifieth Barley : also the Autei, Raui, Gyrei, and Marhatæi ; the Helmodones, with the Town Ebodè ; the Agacturi in the Mountains, having a Town 20 Miles in Circuit, wherein is a Fountain called Emischabales, which signifies the Camel's Town ; Ampelonè, a Colony of the Milesii ; the Town Actrida ; the Calingii, whose Town is named Mariaba, which signifies Lords of all. Towns Pallon and Murannimal, near a River, by which they think that the Euphrates springeth forth. The Nations Agrei and Ammonii ; the Town Athenæ ; the Caurarani, which signifieth very rich in Cattle. The Caranitæ, Cæsani, and Choani. There were also Towns in Arabia, held by Greeks, as Arethusa, Larissa, and Chalcis, which were destroyed in various Wars. The only Roman until this day that carried our Arms into those Parts was *Ælius Gallus*, of the Knightly Order. For *Caius Cæsar*, the Son of *Augustus*, did but look only into Arabia ; but *Gallus* destroyed Towns, not named by Authors that wrote before : Egra, Annestum,

Esca, Magusum, Tammacum, Labecia, and the above-named Marieba, in Circuit Six Miles: likewise Caripeta, the furthest that he went to. The other matters he made report of were, that the Nomades live on Milk and Wild Animals; the rest express Wine, as the Indians do, out of Dates; and Oil of Sesama. That the Homerites are the most Populous; the Minæi have Fruitful Fields, full of Palm-trees and Vine-yards, but their Riches is in Cattle. The Cembani and Arii excel in Arms, but chiefly the Chatramotitæ. The Caræans have the largest Territories and most Fertile Fields. The Sabæi are Richest in the Fertility of their Woods, that bring forth Aromatic Gums: also in Mines of Gold; having Water to refresh their Lands, and plenty of Honey and Wax. Of the Spices that come from thence we will speak in a Book by itself. The Arabians wear Mitres,[1] or go with their Hair long; their Beards they shave, except on the upper Lip; and yet some there are that suffer their Beards to grow long. But one thing is surprising, that out of such a very great number of People, the one-half live by Robbery, and the other by Merchandise. On the whole they are exceedingly rich; for with them the Romans and Parthians leave very large Sums, for the Commodities out of their Woods and Seas which they sell them; and them-selves buy nothing of them in return. Now will we speak of the other Coast opposite to Arabia. *Timosthenes* hath set down, that the whole Gulf was from one End to the other Four Days' Sailing · and from Side to Side, Two Days'; the Breadth of the Straits being Seven Miles over. *Eratosthenes* saith, that taking the Measure at the very Mouth, it is every way 1300 Miles.

CHAPTER XXIX.

*The Gulf of the Red Sea: likewise of the Trogloditic and
Æthiopian Seas.*

ARTEMIDORUS saith, that the Red Sea toward the side of Arabia is 1450 Miles. but on the Coast of the Trogloditæ 1182,

---

[1] It is a question whether these are not rather turbans, as at present extensively worn through Asia.—*Wern. Club.*

until you come to Ptolemais but Agrippa 1322, without any distinction of the Sides. Most Geographers have set down the Breadth to be 462 Miles: and the Mouth of it against the Sun-rising in Winter, (*i. e.* South-west) some say, is 7 Miles Broad; and others 12. The Situation of it is this: Beyond the Bay called Ælaniticus there is another Bay which the Arabians call Æant, on which standeth the Town Heroon. There was also Cambisu, between the Neli and Marchandæ, into which the sick Soldiers were conveyed. The Nation of Tyra , the Port Daneon, from which *Sesostris,* King of Egypt, was the first that imagined to conduct a Navigable Channel into the Nile, in that part where it runneth to the Place called Delta, for the Space of 62 Miles; which is between the River and the Red Sea. This Enterprise was followed by *Darius,* King of the Persians : and afterwards by *Ptolomæus,* who also made a Channel 100 Feet in Breadth, and 30 Deep, for Thirty-Seven Miles and a Half in Length, even to the Bitter Fountains. But this Design went no farther, through fear of an Inundation : the Red Sea being found to lie Three Cubits above the Land of Egypt Some allege that this was not the true cause, but that if the Sea were let into the Nile the Water thereof (of which only they drink) would be corrupted. Nevertheless the Way is well frequented from the Egyptian Sea ; and there are Three ordinary Ways there · one from Pelusium over the Sands, where, unless Reeds be set up in the Ground for direction, no Path would be found, because the Wind bloweth the Sand over the Tracts of the Feet. A second beginneth Two Miles beyond the Mountain Casius, which after sixty Miles returneth into the Pelusiac Way. Here the Arabians called Autei inhabit. The Third beginneth at Gereum, which they call Adipson, and passeth through these same Arabians, being Sixty Miles nearer, but full of craggy Hills, and altogether destitute of Water. All these Ways lead to Arsinoe, which was built upon the Gulf Charandra by *Ptolemæus Philadelphus,* and bearing his Sister's Name · and he was the first that searched narrowly into the Region Trogloditicum ; and the River that passeth

by Arsinoë he called Ptolemæus. Within a little of this
Place there is a small Town named Aennum, for which
some write Philotera. Beyond them are the Azarei: wild
Arabians from Marriages of the Troglodítæ. The Islands
Sapyrenè and Scytala: and within a little, Deserts, unto
Myros-hormos, where is the Fountain called Tadnos; the
Mountain Eos; the Island Lambè, many Harbours; and
Berenicè, a Town bearing the Name of the Mother of *Phila-
delphus;* to which there is a Way lying from Coptos, as we
have said: the Arabians called Autei, and Gnebadei. Tro-
gloditicè, which the Ancients called Michoe, and others
Mìdoé: the Mountain Pentedactylos. Certain Islands called
Stenæ-deíræ; and others no fewer in number, named Halon-
nesi: Cardaminè, and Topazos, which gave the Name to the
precious Stone. A Bay full of Islands, of which that which
is called Mareu is well supplied with Water: another, called
Eratonos, is altogether Dry. There were Governors there
under the King. Within-land inhabit the Candei, whom
they call Ophiophagi, because they are accustomed to feed
on Serpents; and in truth there is no other Region that
breeds them more than this. *Juba,* who seemeth to have
very diligently searched into these things, hath omitted in
this Tract (unless there be some fault in his Original), to
speak of a second Berenicè, which is denominated Pan-
chrysos; as also of a third called Epidires, renowned for its
Situation; for it stands upon a Neck of Land running a long
way, where the Mouth of the Red Sea is not above Four
Miles and a Half from Arabia. There is the Island Cytis,
itself producing Topazes. Beyond this are Woods, where
Ptolemæus, surnamed *Philadelphus,* built a City for Hunting the Elephant, near the Lake Monoleus, and named it
Epitheras. This is the Region mentioned by me in the
Second Book; wherein for Forty-five Days before Mid-
Summer, and as many after, at the Sixth Hour of the Day,
no Shadows are to be seen: which being past, all the Day
after they fall into the South; and on other Days they fall
to the North; whereas, in Berenicè, which we mentioned
first, on the very Day of the Solstice, at the Sixth Hour, the

Shadows are wholly lost; and otherwise there is nothing
new to be observed for the space of 600 Miles about Ptolemais: a thing worthy of observation, and a place of great
Curiosity, that gave great Light to the World; for *Eratosthenes*, upon this undoubted argument of the Shadows, took
in hand to deduce the Measure of the Earth. Beyond this
is the Sea Azanium, and the Promontory which some have
written by the name of Hispalus; also the Lake Mandalum;
the Island Colocasitis, and in the deep Sea many, wherein
are numerous Tortoises. The Town Suchæ, the Island
Daphnis, and the Town Aduliton, built by Egyptian Slaves
who escaped from their Masters. This is the greatest Town
of Traffic of the Troglodıtæ, as well as of the Egyptians: and
it is (from Ptolemais) Five Days' Sailing. Thither are brought
very much Ivory and Horns of the Rhinoceros, Skins of the
Hippopotamus, Tortoise Shells, Monkeys, and Slaves. Above
are the Ethiopians, called Aroteres: also the Islands named
Alıæu: and Islands named Bacchias, Antibacchias, and
Strathonis; beyond them there is a Gulf in the Coast of
Ethiopia. as yet not known, a thing to be wondered at, considering that Merchants search into remoter Parts. Also a
Promontory, wherein is a Fountain named Cucios, much
desired by Sailors. Beyond it is the Port of Isis, distant
from the Town of the Adulıtæ ten Days rowing with Oars:
and thither is Myrrh collected by the Troglodıtæ. Before
this Harbour are two Islands, named Pseudopylæ; and as
many further within, called Pylæ; in one of them are some
Pıllars of Stone, engraved with unknown Characters. Beyond this is the Bay Abalites · the Island Dıodorı, and others
lying Desert. Also along the Contınent there ıs much Wilderness; the Town Gaza; the Promontory and Port Mossylites, unto which Cinnamon is brought. Thus far marched
Scsostrıs with his Army. Some Writers place one Town of
Ethiopia beyond this, on the Sea-side, called Baradaza.
Juba would have the Atlantic Sea to begin at the Promontory Mossylites: on which Sea a Man may Sail with a north-
west Wind, by the Coasts of his Kingdoms of Maurıtania to
Gades: and the whole of his Opinion cannot be contradicted

on this point. From a Promontory of the Indians called
Lepteacra, and by others Drepanum, to the Isle of Malchu,
he layeth it down that by a straight Course it is 1500
Miles, beside those Parts that are burnt up. From thence
to a place called Sceneos is 225 Miles: and from it to the
Island Sadanum, 150 Miles: and thus it is made to the open
Sea 1885 Miles. But all other Writers have been of opinion
that there could not be any Sailing on it, for the exceeding
Heat of the Sun. Moreover, the Arabians named Ascitæ do
much harm from the Islands to the Trade: for these Arabians join Bottles made of Ox Leather, two and two together, as if they were a Bridge, and exercise Piracy by
shooting their Poisoned Arrows. The same *Juba* writeth,
that there are Nations of the Troglodıtæ, named Thero-
thoes, from their huntings, of wonderful Swiftness: as
the Ichthyophagı from Swimming, as if they were Water
Creatures. He nameth also the Bargeni, Zageræ, Chalybæ,
Saxinæ, Syrecæ, Daremæ, and Domazanes. Also he affirmeth,
that the People inhabiting along the Sıdes of the Nile, from
Syenè to Meroë, are not Æthiopians, but Arabians, who for
the sake of Fresh Water approached the Nile, and there
dwelt: as also that the City of the Sun,[1] which we said before in the Description of Egypt, standeth not far from Memphis, was founded by the Arabians. There are some also
who assign the further side of the Nile to Africa and not to
Ethiopia. But leaving every Man to his own Pleasure, we
will set down the Towns on both sides in that order in which
they are declared. And to begin with that side toward
Arabia, after you are past Syenè, is the Nation of the Catadupi, and then the Syenitæ. The Towns Tacompson, which
some have called Thatice, Aranium, Sesanium, Sandura,
Nasaudum, Anadoma, Cumara, Beda and Bochıana, Leuphi-

---

[1] "City of the Sun," or Heliopolıs. This is the Egyptıan city, of
which the father of the patrıarch Joseph's wife was prıest. It may have
proceeded from the Arabian descent of the people of this place, that the
worshıp of the sun was more agreeable to the dısposition of the mınds of
the inhabitants, than that of any of the animal deıtıes, which obtained so
much favour in other cities of Egypt.—*Wern. Club.*

thorga, Tantarenè, Mæchindira, Noa, Gophoa, Gystatæ, Megeda, Lea, Rhemnia, Nupsia, Direa, Pataga, Bagada, Dumana, Rhadata, in which a Golden Cat is worshipped as a God. Boron in the Midland part, and Mallos, the next Town to Meroe. Thus hath *Bion* set them down. But King *Juba* hath arranged them otherwise. Megatichos, a Town on a Mountain between Egypt and Ethiopia, which the Arabians call Myrson; next to it Tacompson, Aranium, Sesanium, Pidè, Mamuda, and Corambis; near it a Fountain of Bitumen Hammodara, Prosda, Parenta, Mama, Thessara, Gallæ, Zoton, Graucomè, Emeum, Pidibotæ, Hebdomecontacomertæ, and the Nomades, who live in Tents. Cystè, Pemma, Gadagalè, Palois, Primmis, Nupsis, Daselis, Patis, Gambrenes, Magases, Segasmala, Cranda, Denna, Cadeuma, Thena, Batha, Alana, Macum, Scammos, and Gora within a Island. Beyond these Abala, Androcalis, Seres, Mallos, and Agocè. On the Side of Africa they are reckoned in this way: another Tacompsos, with the same Name or perhaps a part of the former: then, Magora, Sëa, Edosa, Pelenaria, Pyndis, Magusa, Bauma, Linitima, Spyntuma, Sydopta, Gensoa, Pindicitora, Eugoa, Orsima, Suasa, Mauma, Rhuma, Uibubuma, Mulona, which Town the Greeks call Hypaton; Pagoargas, Zamnes; and there begin the Elephants to come in, Mamblia, Berresa, Cetuma. There was formerly a Town named Epis, overagainst Meroe, but destroyed before *Bion* wrote. These were recorded until you come to Meroë; of which at this Day scarcely anything is to be found on either side. The remainder is a Wilderness, by report made to the Prince *Nero* by the Prætorian Soldiers sent thither from him under the Command of a Tribune, to make Discoveries. at the time when amongst his other Wars, he thought of an Expedition against the Ethiopians. But in the Days of *Divus Augustus*, the Roman Arms penetrated thither under the conduct of *Publius Petronius*, a Knight of Rome, and Prefect of Egypt. He conquered all those Towns in Ethiopia, which he found in this order following; Pseleis, Primis, Aboccis, Phthuris, Canbusis, Attena, Stadissis, where the River Nile casteth itself

down with such a Noise that the Inhabitants living close by
lose their Hearing. He won also Napata. He marched
forward a great way into the Country, even 870 Miles beyond Syenè; but this Roman Army laid not all Waste in
those parts. It was the Egyptian Wars that wasted Ethiopia;
sometimes by Ruling, and at others by Servitude; it was Illustrious and Powerful until the Reign of King *Memnon*, who
ruled in the Time of the Trojan War, so that Syria was subject to it; as also our own Coast in the Time of King *Cepheus*,
as appeareth by the Fables of *Andromeda*. In the same
manner they disagree about the Measure of Ethiopia. And
first, *Dalion* passing far beyond Meroe; after him, *Aristocreon*, *Bion*, and *Basilis*; also *Simonides* (the Lesser) who
dwelt in Meroe Five Years, when he wrote of Ethiopia.
Timosthenes, the Admiral of the Fleet of *Philadelphus*, hath
left in record, that from Syenè to Meroè is Sixty Days'
Journey, without particularizing the Measure. But *Eratosthenes* precisely noteth, that it is 625 Miles: *Artemidorus*,
600. *Sebostus* affirmeth, that from the Frontiers of Egypt it
is 1675 Miles; from whence the last rehearsed Writers count
1270. But all this difference is lately determined by the
Report of those Travellers whom *Nero* sent to Discover those
Countries, who have related that it is 862 Miles from Syenè
in this manner: from Syenè to Hiera-Sycaminon, Fifty-four
Miles; from thence to Tama, Seventy-five Miles; from Tama
to the Euonymites Country, the first of the Ethiopians, 120;
to Acina, Fifty-four; to Pitara, Twenty-five; to Tergedum,
106 Miles. That in the midst of this Tract lieth the Island
Gagandus, where they first saw the Birds called Parrots;
and beyond another Island called Attigula they saw Monkeys;
beyond Tergedum they met with the Creatures Cynocephali.
From thence to Napata Eighty Miles, which is the only
little Town among all the beforenamed; from which to the
Island Meroe is 360 Miles. They reported, moreover, that
about Meroë, and not before, the Herbs appeared greener;
and the Woods shewed somewhat in comparison of all the
way besides; and they espied the Tracts of Elephants and
Rhinoceroses. The Town itself of Meroë was from the

Entry of the Island Seventy Miles, and just by, there was
another Island called Tatu, which formed a Port for them
that approached by the Channel on the Right.   The Buildings
within the Town were few; the Isle was subject to a Queen
named *Candaocè,*[1] a name that for many years already hath
passed in succession from one Queen to another.   Within
this Town is the Shrine of *Hammon* for Devotion; and in all
that Tract many Chapels.   Finally, so long as the Ethiopians
were powerful this Island was very famous.   For by report,
they were accustomed to furnish of Armed Men 250,000, and
to maintain of Artisans 400,000.   Also it is at this day reported
that there have been Forty-five Kings of the Ethiopians.

<h2 style="text-align:center">Chapter XXX.</h2>

The Manifold and Wonderful Forms of Men.[2]

But the Nation in general was in old time called
Ætheria;[3] afterwards Atlantia; and finally from *Vulcan's*
Son *Æthiops,* it took the name of Ethiopia.   It is no wonder, that about the remote Borders of it there are produced
both Men and Beasts of monstrous Shapes, considering the
Agility of the Fiery Heat to frame Bodies and carve them
into strange Shapes.   It is reported by some, that far within
the Country eastward there are Nations without Noses, but
having their Visage all Plain and Flat: that others are
without any Upper Lip, and some without Tongues; also,
there is a kind of them that have the Mouth grown together, and are without Nostrils; so that at the same Orifice
only they take in Breath, receive Drink by drawing it in
through an Oaten Straw, and Feed themselves with the
Grains of Oats which grow of their own accord for their
Food.   Others there are, who instead of Speech make Signs
by nodding their Heads, and moving their Limbs.   There
are also some that before the Time of *Ptolemæus Lathyrus*

[1] See Acts of Apostles, viii. 27
[2] See further, Book vii. c. 2.
[3] As all Pliny's authors were Greek or Roman, he was ignorant that
a much more ancient name was Cush. — *Wern. Club.*

King of Egypt, knew no use of Fire. Some Writers have
reported, that in the Country near the Marshes from whence
the Nile hath its Source there inhabit a Nation of Pygmei.
But where we left off there is a continual range of Mountains, all Red, as if they were Burning. Beyond Meroë
there is a Country lying above the Troglodita and the Red
Sea; where Three Days' Journey from Napata toward the
Red Sea, in most places they save Rain Water for their ordinary Use; all the Country between is very abundant in
Gold. All beyond this Region is Inhabited by the Atabuli,
a People of Ethiopia. The Megabari, whom some have
named Adiabaræ, lie overagainst Meroë, and have a Town
bearing the Name of *Apollo*. Part of them are Nomades,
who live on Elephant's Flesh. Just against them in a part
of Africa are the Macrobii. Again, beyond the Megabari
are the Memnones and Daveli; and Twenty Days' Journey
from them the Critensi. Beyond them are the Dochi and
the Gymnites, who are always naked. Soon after you find the
Anderæ, Mathitæ, Mesagebes, Hipporeæ, of a Black Colour,
but who paint their Bodies with a kind of Red Chalk called
Rubrica. But upon a part of Africa are the Medimni; beyond them are Nomades, who feed on the Milk of Cynocephali: and the Olabi and Syrbotæ, who are reported to be
Eight Cubits high. *Aristocreon* saith, that on the side of
Libya, Five Days' Journey from Meroe, there is a Town
called Tolè; and Twelve Days' Journey from thence is Esar,
a Town of the Egyptians, who fled from *Psammeticus*. It is
reported, that they have lived in it for 300 Years; another
Town of theirs called Daronis, on the opposite side, on the
Coast of Arabia. But that which *Aristocreon* nameth Esar,
Bion calleth Sapa; and he saith, the very word signifieth
Strangers come from other parts. Their Capital City is
within the Island Sembobitis; and Sai in Arabia is the Third.
Between the Mountains and the Nile are the Symbari and
the Phalanges; but upon the Mountains themselves live
the Asachæ, with many Nations; and they are by report
Seven Days' Journey from the Sea. They live by Hunting
Elephants. The Island in the Nile, of the Semberritæ, is

subject to a Queen. Eight Days' Journey from thence lieth the Country of the Ethiopians, named Nubæi. Their Town Tenupsis is seated upon the Nile. The Sambri, where all the Four-footed Beasts, and even the very Elephants, are without Ears. Upon the Border of Africa inhabit the Ptœambati and Ptœmphanæ, who have a Dog for their King, and they judge of his imperial Commands by his Motion. Their City is Auruspi, far distant from the Nile. Beyond them are the Achisarmi, Phaliges, Marigeri, and Casamairi *Bion* says, that beyond Psembobitis, there are other Towns in the Islands toward Meroe, for Twenty Days' Journey. The Town of the next Island is Semberritarum, under a Queen; another called Asar; and there is a second Island having in it the Town Daron, they call the third Medoe, wherein standeth the Town Asel; and a fourth named Garodè, as the Town is also. Then along the Banks, the Towns, Navos, Modunda, Andatis, Setundum, Colligat, Secandè, Navectabè, Cumi, Agrospi, Ægipa, Candrogari, Araba, and Summara. The Region above Sirbitum, where the Mountains end, is reported by some to have upon the Sea-coast Ethiopians called Nisicastes and Nisitæ, which means Men with Three and Four Eyes; not because they are so furnished, but because they are excellent Archers *Bion* affirmeth, moreover, that from that part of the Nile which stretcheth above the Greater Syrtes, toward the Southern Ocean, they are called Dalion, who use Rain-water only; and the Cisori and Longopori. Beyond Oecalices for Five Days' Journey, the Usibalci, Isucles, Pharusi, Valii, and Cispii. The rest is desert. But then he telleth fabulous Tales. as that westward there are People called Nigrœ, whose King hath but one Eye, and that in the midst of his Forehead: also, there are the Agriophagi, who live chiefly on the Flesh of Panthers and Lions; the Pomphagi, who Eat all things, the Anthropophagi, that Feed on Man's Flesh; the Cynamolgi, who have Heads like Dogs; the Artabatitæ, who wander about like Four-footed Savage Beasts. Beyond whom are the Hesperi and Peroesi, who, as we said before, are planted in

the Confines of Mauritania   In certain parts of Ethiopia
the People live on Locusts only,[1] which they preserve with
Salt, and hang up in Smoke to harden, for their yearly Provision ; and these live not above Forty Years at the most.
Agrippa saith that all the Land of Ethiopia, with the Red
Sea, containeth in Length 2170 Miles: and in Breadth,
together with the higher Egypt, 1291.   Some have taken
the Breadth in this manner; from Meroe to Sirbitum,
Twelve Days' Navigation ; from thence to the Davelli, Twelve ;
and from them to the Ethiopian Ocean, a Journey of Six
Days   But on the whole all Writers in a manner agree
that between the Ocean and Meroë it is 725 Miles ; and
from thence to Syenè, as much as we have set down before.
The Situation of Ethiopia lieth South-east and South-west
In the exact South, Woods of Ebony chiefly flourish ; toward
the midst of this Region, there is a lofty Mountain looking
over the Sea, that burneth continually, which the Greeks
call Theon-ochema, from which it is counted Four Days' Sail
to the Promontory called Hesperion-Ceras,[2] on the border of
Africa, near to the Hesperian Ethiopians.   Some Writers
hold, that this Tract is beautified with little Hills, pleasantly
clad with shady Groves, wherein are the Ægipanes and
Satyri.

[1] That locusts should form a portion of the food of the people who
live where they abound, cannot be regarded as surprising.   John
the Baptist fed on them, Matt. iii. 4, and Mark, i. 6.   They are still
occasionally used for food in the East.   When Khosru Purwis (Chosroes),
the Sassanian king of Persia, was summoned by Mohammed to adopt his
doctrine, he contemptuously dismissed the messengers of a chief of "naked
locust-eaters."   The Arabs eat the different species of the migratory
locusts, and are very fond of them, especially of the red locust, which
when fat is called *Jeràd mikken*   They eat them either fried or broiled,
or dried in an oven, or boiled with a sprinkle of salt, the locusts taste
like dried sprats   The female locust when fat and full of eggs, is a great
dainty, and greatly esteemed by the male population on account of its
aphrodisiac qualities.   (Niebuhr, *Beschreibung von Arabien*, p. 170, &c)
— *Wern. Club*
[2] Cap de Bonne Esperance.

Chapter XXXI.

The Islands of the Ethiopian Sea.

EPHORUS, Eudoxus, and *Timosthenes* agree, that there are very many Islands in all that Sea. *Clitarchus* witnesseth, that report was made to *Alexander* the King, of one which was so rich, that for Horses the Inhabitants would give Talents of Gold; also of another, wherein was a sacred Mountain adorned with a shady Wood, where the Trees distilled Odours of wonderful Sweetness. Overagainst the Persian Gulf lieth the Island named Cernè, opposite to Ethiopia, but how large it is, or how far off from the Continent, is not certainly known: but this is reported, that the Ethiopians only inhabit it. *Euphorus* writeth, that they who would Sail thither from the Red Sea, are not able, from the extreme Heat, to pass beyond certain Columns; for so they call the little Islands there. But *Polybius* affirmeth, that this Island Cernè, where it lieth in the utmost Coast of Mauritania, overagainst the Mountain Atlas, is but Eight Stadia from the Land. On the other hand, *Nepos Cornelius* affirmeth, that it is not above a Mile from the Land, overagainst Carthage; and that it is not above Two Miles in Circuit. There is mention made also of another Island before the Mountain Atlas, and which is named Atlantis. And Five Days' Sailing from it are the Deserts of the Ethiopian Hesperians, and a Promontory, which we have named Hesperion-Ceras, where the Coasts of the Land begin first to turn about their front to the westward, and the Atlantic Sea. Overagainst this Promontory, as *Xenophon Lampsacenus* reporteth, lie the Islands called Gorgates, where formerly the Gorgani kept their Habitation, two Days' Sailing from the Continent. *Hanno,* Commander of the Carthaginians (Poeni), penetrated to them, and reported that the Women were all over their Bodies hairy; and that the Men were so Swift of Foot that they escaped from him; but he placed the Skins of two of these Gorgon Women in the Temple of Juno, for a Testimonial, and as a Wonder, and

they were seen there until Carthage was taken. Beyond
these Isles also there are said to be two Islands of Hesperides.
But so uncertain are all things concerning these parts, that
Statius Sebosus affirmeth, it is Forty Days' Sailing from the
Islands of the Gorgones along the Coast of Atlas, to the
Isles of the Hesperides, and from thence to Hesperion-
Ceras, one.   As little certainty there is concerning the
Islands of Mauritania.   In this only they all agree, that *Juba*
discovered some few of them over against the Autololes, in
which he purposed to dye Gætulian Purple.[1]

Chapter XXXII.

Of the Fortunate Islands.

SOME Authors think, that the Fortunate Islands, and
some others besides them, are beyond the Autololes; among
whom the same *Sebosus* spoke of their Distances: and particularly that the Island Junonia is from Gades 750 Miles;
and that from it westward the Isles Pluvialia and Capraria
are as much: also that in the Island Pluvialia there is no
Water but what they have by Showers.   From them to the
Fortunate Islands is 250 Miles; they lie eight Miles from the
Coast of Mauritania to the Left Hand, called the Coast of
the Sun, in a Valley, because it is like a Valley or Hollow;
and it is also called Planaria, as resembling an even Plain.
This Valley containeth in Circuit 300 Miles· wherein are
Trees so luxuriant that they grow to the Height of 144
Feet.   Concerning the Islands named Fortunate, *Juba*
learned by diligent inquiry, that they lie from the South
near to the West 625 Miles from the Islands Purpurariæ:
so that to Sail thither a Man must pass 250 Miles above the
West, and then for 75 Miles bend his course Eastward.   He
saith, moreover, that the first of these Islands is called Om-
brion, wherein are no Tokens of Houses.   Also that among
the Mountains it hath a Marsh; and Trees resembling the
Plant Ferula, out of which they press Water: that which

---

[1] On which account in the next chapter these islands are called
Purpureæ.—*Wern. Club.*

issueth out of the Black Trees being bitter, and that from the White sort sweet and potable.　He saith that a second Island is named Junonia, in which there is one little House, or Chapel, made of Stone: beyond it, but near by there is a third of the same Name, but less in size: and then you come to one called Capraria, full of great Lizards.　Within sight of these is the Island Nivaria, which took this Name from the Snow that lieth there continually, it is also full of Mists. The next to it is Canaria, so called from the great number of very large Dogs, of which *Juba* brought away two · and in this Island there are some marks remaining of Buildings. And as all these Islands abound plentifully with fruitful Trees and Birds of all sorts, so this is replenished with Palm-trees that bear Abundance of Dates, and likewise with Trees that yield Pine Nuts.　There is also great plenty of Honey: and the Rivers produce the Papyrus Reed, and are well stored with the Fish Silurus: and in conclusion he saith, that these Islands are much infested with great Animals, that are very often cast out in a Putrid Condition. Thus having at large gone through the Description of the Globe of the Earth, as well without as within, it remaineth now to collect into a small space the measure of the Seas.

Chapter XXXIII.

A Summary of the Earth, digested according to its Dimensions.

POLYBIUS layeth it down, that from the Straits of Gibraltar by a straight Course to the Mouth of Mœotis is 3437½ Miles.　From the same starting-place by a right Course eastward to Sicily, it is 1260½ Miles; to Crete, 375 Miles, to Rhodes, 146½ Miles; to the Chelidonian Islands as much: to Cyprus, 325 Miles; from whence to Seleucia Pieria in Syria, 115 Miles.　Which computation makes the sum of 2340 Miles.　*Agrippa* also counteth 3440 Miles for all this distance from the Straits of Gibraltar directly forward to the Gulf of Issa.　In which reckoning I scarcely know whether there be an error in the number, because the same Writer hath set down the passage from the Sicilian Strait to Alexandria at 1250 Miles. But the whole Circuit through the above-said Gulfs, from the point where we began to the Lake Mœotis, summed together, is 15,600 Miles. *Artemidorus* added thereto 756 Miles. And the same Geographer writeth, that with Mœotis it cometh to 17,390 Miles This is the measure of unarmed Men, and the peaceful boldness of such as have not feared to provoke Fortune. Now are we to compare the greatness of each part, in spite of the Difficulty produced by the Disagreement of Authors. But most easily will this appear if we join Longitude and Latitude together. According to this prescribed rule the Magnitude of Europe is 8148 Miles. Africa (taking the middle Computation between them all that have set it down) containeth in Length 3748 Miles. The Breadth of so much as is inhabited in no Place exceedeth 250 Miles. *Agrippa* would have it to contain 910 Miles in Breadth, beginning at the Bounds of Cyrenè, and comprehending in this Measure the Deserts thereof as far as to the Garamantæ, so far as they are known ; and then the whole Measure collected into one sum amounted to 4608 Miles. Asia[1] is allowed to be in Length 63,750 Miles ; and its Breadth is truly reckoned from the Ethiopian Sea to Alexandria, situated near the Nile, so that the Measurement runs through Meroë and Syrene, 1875 Miles ; whereby it appeareth that Europe is little wanting of being half as large again as Asia : and the same Europe is twice as much again as all Africa, and a sixth part over. Reduce now all these sums together, and it will be found clear that Europe is a third part of the whole Earth, and something more than an eighth Portion over ; Asia a fourth part, with a fourteenth ; and Africa a fifth, with an over-plus of a sixtieth portion. To this Calculation we will add one sentence of Greek invention, which sheweth

---

[1] Pliny's ignorance of the extent of Africa is pardonable, for he knew no more of it than the small portion which had come under the Roman dominion ; but in his account of Asia he contradicts what he has already assigned to India, which is only a part of it, but which he truly represented to be larger than Europe.— *Wern Club*

their exquisite subtilty, in order that we may omit nothing
in this view of the Situation of the Earth; that when the
Position of every Region is known, a Man may likewise come
to the knowledge of what Society there is between one and
the other, either of the agreement of the Length of Days and
Nights, by the Shadows at Noonday, or by the equal Con-
vexity of the World.   To bring this about effectually, I must
arrange the whole Earth into certain Portions of the Heaven;
for there are very many of those Divisions of the World which
our Astronomers call Circles, and the Greeks, Parallels.

Chapter XXXIV.

The Arrangement of the Earth into Parallels and equal Shadows.

The beginning is at that part of India which turns to the
South.   It extends as far as Arabia and the Inhabitants of
the Red Sea.   Under it are comprised the Gedrosi, Persæ,
Carmani, and Elimæi; Parthyenè, Aria, Susianè, Mesopotamia, Seleucia, surnamed Babylonia, Arabia, so far as
Petræ, Cœle-Syria, and Pelusium in Egypt, the Lower
Coasts, which are called of Alexandria, the Maritime Parts
of Africa; all the Towns of Cyrenaica, Thapsus, Adrumetum, Clupea, Carthago, Utica, both Hippoes, Numidia, both
Realms of Mauritania, the Atlantic Sea, and Hercules' Pillars.   In all the Circumference of this Heaven, at Noon-tide
of an Equinoctial Day, the Umbilicus, which they call Gnomon, seven Feet Long, casteth a Shadow not above the
Length of four Feet.   The Longest Night or Day is fourteen
Hours, and the shortest, ten.   The following Circle beginneth from India, tending westward, and passeth through
the midst of Parthia, Persepolis, the nearest parts of Persis,
the nearer Arabia, Judæa, and the Borders of the Mountain
Libanus.   It embraceth Babylon, Idumæa, Samaria, Hieru-
solyma, Ascalon, Joppè, Cæsarea, Phœnicè, Ptolemais,
Sydon, Tyrus, Berytrus, Botrys, Tripolis, Byblus, Antiochia,
Laodicea, Seleucia, the Sea-coasts of Cilicia, Cyprus, the
South Part of Creta, Lilybeum in Sinalia, the North Parts

of Africa and Numidia. The Gnomon upon the Equinoctial Day, thirty-five Feet in Length, maketh a Shadow
twenty-four Feet Long. The Longest Day or Night is fourteen Hours Equinoctial, and the fifth part of an Hour. The
third Circle beginneth at the Indians next to the Imaus, and
goeth by the Caspian Gates very near to Media, Cataonia,
Cappadocia, Taurus, Amanus, Issus, the Cilician Gates,
Soli, Tarsus, Cyprus, Pisidia, Sydè in Pamphilia, Lycaonia,
Patara in Lycia, Xanthus, Caunus, Rhodus, Cous, Halicarnassus, Gnidus, Doris, Chius, Delus, the Middle Cyclades,
Gytthium, Malea, Argos, Laconia, Elis, Olympia, Messenè,
Peloponnesus, Syracusa, Catina, the Midst of Sicily, the
South Part of Sardinia, Carteia, and Gades. The Gnomon
of one hundred Inches yieldeth a Shadow of seventy-seven
Inches. The Longest Day hath Equinoctial Hours fourteen
and a half, with the thirtieth part of an Hour. Under the
fourth Circle lie those who are on the other Side of Imaus,
the South Parts of Cappadocia, Galatia, Mysia, Sardis,
Smyrna, Sipylus, the Mountain Tmolus in Lydia, Caria,
Ionia, Trallis, Colophon, Ephesus, Miletus, Samos, Chios,
the Icarian Sea, the Northern Cyclades, Athens, Megara,
Corinthus, Sicyon, Achæa, Patræ, Isthmos, Epirus, the
North Parts of Sicily, Narbonensis Gallia toward the East,[1]
the Maritime Parts of Spain beyond New Carthage, and so
to the West. To a Gnomon of twenty-one feet the Shadows
answer of seventeen Feet. The Longest Day is fourteen
Equinoctial Hours, and two-third parts of an Hour. The
fifth Division containeth from the Entrance of the Caspian
Sea, Bactra, Iberia, Armenia, Mysia, Phrygia, Hellespontus,
Troas, Tenedus, Abydus, Scepsis, Ilium, the Mountain Ida,
Cyzicum, Lampsacum, Sinopè, Amisum, Heraclea in Pontus,
Paphlagonia, Lemnus, Imbrus, Thasus, Cassandria, Thes-
salia, Macedonia, Larissa, Amphipolis, Thessalonicè, Pella,
Edessa, Berœa, Pharsalia, Carystum, Eubœa, Bœotia,
Chalcis, Delphi, Acarnania, Ætolia, Apollonia, Brundisium,
Tarentum, Thurii, Locri, Rhegium, Lucani, Neapolis, Pu-

---

[1] Languedoc.

teoli, the Tuscan Sea, Corsica, the Baleares, the Middle of
Spain A Gnomon of seven Feet giveth six of Shadow.
The Longest Day is fifteen Equinoctial Hours The sixth
Parallel compriseth the City of Rome, and containeth the
Caspian Nations, Caucasus, the North Parts of Armenia,
Apollonia upon Rhindacus, Nicomedia, Nicæa, Chalcedon,
Byzantium, Lysimachia, Cherrhonesus, the Gulf Melanè,
Abdera, Samothracia, Maronea, Ænus, Bessica, the Mid-
land Parts of Thracia, Pœonia, the Illyrii, Dyrrhachium,
Canusium, the utmost Coasts of Apulia, Campania, Hetruria,
Pisæ, Luna, Luca, Genua, Liguria, Antipolis, Massilia, Nar-
bon, Tarracon, the Middle of Spain called Tarraconensis,
and thence through Lusitania To a Gnomon of nine Feet
the Shadow is eight Feet. The Longest Day hath fifteen
Equinoctial Hours and the ninth part of an Hour, or the
fifth, as *Nigidius* is of opinion. The seventh Division be-
ginneth at the other Coast of the Caspian Sea, and falleth
upon Callatis, Bosphorus, Borysthenes, Tomos, the Back
Parts of Thracia, the Tribali, the rest of Illyricum, the
Adriatic Sea, Aquileia, Altinum, Venetia, Vicetia, Patavium,
Verona, Cremona, Ravenna, Ancona, Picenum, Marsi,
Peligni, Sabini, Umbria, Ariminum, Bononia, Placentia,
Mediolanum, and all beyond Apenninum: also over the
Alps, Aquitaine in Gaul, Vienna, Pyrenæum, and Celtiberia.
The Gnomon of thirty-five Feet casteth a Shadow thirty-six
Feet in Length; yet so, that in some part of Venetia the
Shadow is equal to the Gnomon. The Longest Day is fif-
teen Equinoctial Hours, and three-fifth parts of an hour.
Hitherto we have reported the exact Labours of the Ancients.
But the most diligent Modern Writers have assigned the rest
of the Earth not as yet specified, to three Sections. (The
first) from Tanais through the Lake Mœotis and the Sarmatæ, all the way to Borysthenes, and so by the Daci and a
part of Germany, the Galliæ, and the Coasts of the surrounding Ocean, where the Day is sixteen Hours long. A
second, through the Hyperborei and Britannia, where the
Day is seventeen Hours long. Last of all, is the Scythian
Parallel, from the Rhiphean Hills unto Thulè: in which (as

we have said) it is Day and Night continually by turns. The same Writers have set down two Circles, before those Points where the others began, and which we set down. The first through the Island Meroë, and Ptolemais upon the Red Sea, built for the Hunting of Elephants; where the Longest Day is but twelve Hours and an half: the second passing through Syenè in Egypt, where the Day hath thirteen Hours. And the same Authors have put to every one of the other Circles, even to the very last, half an Hour more.

THUS MUCH OF THE EARTH.

IN THE SEVENTH BOOK

ARE CONTAINED

THE WONDERFUL SHAPES OF MEN IN VARIOUS COUNTRIES.

In sum, there are in this Book, of Histories and Observations, 747.

***

LATIN AUTHORS ABSTRACTED ·

Verrius Flaccus, Cn Gellius, Licinius Mutianus, Mutius, Massurius, Agrippina wife of Claudius, M Cicero, Asinius Pollio, Messala, Rufus, Cornelius Nepos, Virgil, Livy, Cordus, Melissus, Sebosus, Cornelius Celsus, Maximus Valerius, Trogus, Nigidius Figulus, Pomponius Atticus, Pedianus Asconius, Sabinus, Cato Censorius, Fabius Vestalis.

FOREIGN WRITERS.

Herodotus, Aristeas, Beto, Isigonus, Crates, Agatharcides, Calliphanes, Aristotle, Nymphodorus, Apollonides, Philarchus, Damon, Megasthenes, Ctesias, Tauron, Eudoxus, Onesicritus, Clitarchus, Duris, Artemidorus, Hippocrates the Physician, Asclepiander the Physician, Hesiodus, Anacreon, Theopompus, Hellanicus, Damasthes, Ephorus, Epigenes, Berosus, Pessiris, Necepsus, Alexander Polyhistor, Xenophon, Callimachus, Democritus, Duillius, Polyhistor the Historian, Strato who wrote against the Propositions and Theorems of Ephorus, Heraclides Ponticus, Asclepiades who wrote Tragodamena, Philostephanus, Hegesias, Archimachus, Thucydides, Mnesigiton, Xenagoras, Metrodorus Scepsius, Anticlides, and Critodemus

THE SEVENTH BOOK

OF THE

HISTORY OF NATURE,

WRITTEN BY

C. PLINIUS SECUNDUS.

THE PREFACE.

THUS we have in the former Books treated of the World, and of the Lands, Nations, Seas, Islands, and remarkable Cities therein contained. It remaineth now to discourse of the Nature of the Living Creatures comprised within the same: a point which would require as deep a Contemplation as any other Part whatsoever, if the Mind of Man were able to comprehend all the Things. By right the chief place is assigned to Man, for whose sake it appears that Nature produced all other Creatures; though this great favour of hers is severe as set against all her other Gifts: so that it is hard to judge whether she is a kinder Parent to Man, or a cruel Step-mother. For, in preference to all other Living Creatures, the one she hath clothed with the Riches of others: to the rest she hath assigned a variety of Coverings. as Shells, Barks, Hard Hides, Spines, Shag, Bristles, Hair, Feathers, Quills, Scales, and Fleeces. The Trunks and

Stems of Trees she hath defended with Bark, which is sometimes double, against the injuries both of Heat and Cold!
Man alone she hath cast all Naked upon the bare Earth,
even on his Birth-day, immediately to cry and lament: so
that among so many Living Creatures there is none subject
to shed Tears and Weep like him from the very onset of his
Existence. And verily, however forward and active we may
be, to no one is it given to laugh before he is Forty Days old.
From this glimmering of Light he is bound fast, and hath
no Member at liberty; a thing which is not practised upon
the Young of any Wild Beast among us. The Child thus
unhappily born, and who is to rule all other, lieth bound[1]
Hand and Foot, weeping and crying; and receiveth the
auspices of Life with Punishments, to make satisfaction for
this only Fault, that he is born Alive. What madness in
such as think this the proper Beginning of those who are
born to be proud! The first Hope of our Strength, the first
gift that Time affordeth us, maketh us no better than four-
footed Beasts. How long ere we can go alone! How long
before we can speak, feed ourselves! How long continueth
the Crown of our Heads to palpitate,—the mark of our exceeding great weakness above all other Creatures! Then
the Sicknesses, and so many Medicines devised against these
Maladies: besides the new Diseases that spring up to
overcome us. Other Living Creatures understand their
own Nature; some assume the use of their swift Feet,
others of their Wings; some are Strong; others able to
Swim; but Man knoweth nothing unless he be taught.
not even to speak, or go, or eat: and, in short, he is
naturally good at nothing but to weep. And hence some
have insisted on it, that it is best for a man never to have
been born, or else speedily to die. To one only, of living

[1] The artificial bandages inflicted on new-born children are the swad-
dling-clothes referred to in St. Luke's Gospel, c. ii. v 7; but they can
scarcely be numbered among the necessary evils of humanity, for they
have long since been abolished in England. In the seventh chapter of
this Book the Author dwells again on the littleness and misery of the
human race.— *Wern. Club.*

Creatures is it given to mourn, one only is guilty of excess, and that in a vast variety of ways, and through every Member that he has. Who but we are ambitious? Who but we are avaricious? None but we possess the extravagant desire of living, are superstitious, anxious for our burial, and what shall be our fate when we are gone. To none is Life more frail; yet to no Creature is there a greater craving after every thing; none suffereth under a more terrifying Fear; and none more furious in his Rage. To conclude, other Animals live orderly according to their kind · we see them flock together, and stand against others of a contrary kind, the Lions, though savage, fight not one with another, Serpents sting not Serpents: and even the very Beasts and Fishes of the Sea war not upon their own kind: but, by Hercules! the greatest part of the evils that happen to Men are from the hand of Man himself.

Chapter I.

The wonderful Forms of Nations.

In our reports of Nations we have spoken in general of the Human Race spread over the Face of the Earth. Neither is it our purpose at present to describe particularly all their numberless Customs and Manners of Life, which are as many as there are Assemblies of Men. However, I think it good not to omit all, but to make relation of some things concerning those People especially who live furthest from the Sea; among whom, I doubt not but I shall find such matter as to most Men will seem both prodigious and incredible. For whoever believed that there were Ethiopians before he saw them? what is it that seemeth not a Wonder at the First Sight? how many things are judged impossible before they are done? and the Power and Majesty of Nature in every particular action seemeth incredible, if we consider the same severally, and do not embrace the whole at once in the Mind. For, to say nothing of the Peacocks' Feathers, of the Spots of Tigers and Panthers, of the Colours that ornament so many Creatures besides: let us come to one only point, which to speak of seemeth small, but being deeply weighed, is a matter of exceeding great regard; and that is, the Speech of so many Nations; so many Tongues; so much Variety of Utterance, that a Foreigner seems to be something different from a Man. Then to view the variety that appeareth in our Face and Countenance; although there be not more than Ten Members or a few more, among so many thousand of these, not Two Persons are to be found who are not distinct in Likeness: a thing which no Art can perform, in a small number out of so many. And yet thus much must I advertise my Readers, that I will not pawn my credit for many things that I shall deliver; but I will rather direct them to the Authors, who will answer them in all doubtful points: only let them not think much to follow the Greeks, whose Diligence hath been greater, and their Attention of longer standing.

CHAPTER II.

Of the Scythians, and the Diversity of other Nations.[1]

THAT there are Scythians, and even many kinds of them, who feed ordinarily on Man's Flesh, we have shewn

---

[1] The belief of the ancients in the existence of many anomalous races of mankind, was a portion of the science of the age, and not to have given it credit, and a place in his work, would have subjected the author to as much reproach for scepticism, as the notice he has taken of them has done for his alledged credulity. And so far as Greek authority extended, the degree of credit which Pliny assigned to these strange races, appears to have been well founded, for except in one or two instances, the errors appear to have sprung from misinterpretation, rather than from a positive departure from truth. Aristotle is sufficient authority for the existence of a race of pigmies, who are also mentioned by Herodotus; and in more modern times that excellent naturalist Belon is satisfied concerning them. Nor can we, even now, refuse to admit the possibility of finding their representatives in the Bushmen still existing in Southern Africa. On the other hand, the existence of men of enormous stature, of which some stupendous instances are given by Pliny (b. vii c. xvi), is attested by profane as well as by sacred history. Thus Pau-

already, (Book iv 12; vi. 1.) The thing itself would be thought incredible, if we did not consider that in the very Middle of the World, even in Sicily and Italy, there have been Nations of such Monsters, as the Cyclopæ and Lystrigonæ: and also very

samas (in his "Atticks," quoted by Bishop Cumberland in his translation of Sanchoniatho) says, that he saw in the Upper Lydia bones whose figure would satisfy any man that they were men's bones, but their bigness was above the now known size of men He also mentions the bones of Asterius, in the neighbouring country of the Milesians; giving the dimensions of his body to be no less than ten cubits long, and that he was the son of Anax, a name singularly corresponding with a race mentioned by Moses, and the sight of whom terrified and humbled the Israelitish spies. It is not a little strange, as Bishop Cumberland remarks, quoting from Cicero "de Natura Deorum," that there is reason to believe, one of the very ancient and gigantic persons known under the name of Hercules had six fingers on each hand, as is also noticed of the last descendants of this mighty race, in the second book of Samuel, c. xxi. The tradition that such enormous people existed in the early ages of the world is often referred to by Homer, and other ancient writers, who drew from thence the erroneous conclusion, that the whole human race had, since their day, become gradually weaker and more diminutive; whereas, in the only authentic history of these remote ages it is clearly intimated, that this vast stature was limited to particular families or nations, who even at that time were thought remarkable by all besides; and who were finally exterminated by their neighbours, perhaps as the only resource against their violence. The Macrocephali, or long heads, (mentioned b vi c. 4) may be supposed to have owed their peculiarity to the habit of employing pressure to mould their heads in early infancy into the compressed and elevated form, as is now practised by some tribes on the continent of America; and such as are mentioned with exceedingly short necks may, perhaps, have been marked only with a personal deformity, but the people with intensely black skin, to all of whom, however otherwise different, the ancients seem to have assigned indiscriminately the name of Ethiopians, are judged by Pliny to display a more remarkable phenomenon than all the strange forms he has occasion to notice; as we also should probably do, if living instances had not rendered it common We may include in another section those singular examples of the human race, which the author supposes to be comprised in nations, but which are more probably reported as of rare or casual occurrence, or perhaps nothing beyond an accidental monstrosity. Such we know to be the case with the Albinoes, with white hair and tender eyes, and perhaps also the monoculous king, and the Arimaspians, who are mentioned also by Herodotus, together with the other Cyclopæan

lately, on the other side of the Alps,[1] there are those that kill Men for Sacrifice, after the manner of those (Scythian) people, which differs but little from eating their Flesh. Moreover, near to those Scythians that inhabit Northward, not far from the very rising of the North-east Wind, and

people, whose singularities may have referred to some manner in the habitual use of the organ, rather than to an actual deformity. A third section of these supposed anomalous people may obviously be referred to the quadrumanous tribes a class of creatures so nearly approaching to the external form of humanity, that we cannot feel surprised if ignorant travellers, who viewed only at a distance, and with minds prepared to welcome every wonder — the oran outang and pongo — were not able to discern a generic difference between them and the truly human race. Such were the hairy men and women mentioned in the 31st chapter of this book, the satyrs, Choromandæ, and people with no noses, or having tails, a figure of the latter being found on an *abraxis*, or amulet, engraved by Montfauçon; but through the whole of his narrative we observe that the author is careful to give his authorities, as being aware that what appeared so strange must be made to rest upon the credit of those who had originally reported it Some of these instances, indeed, admit of no interpretation that we are able to afford them; but in regard to one of the strangest of them, Purchas gives the authority of Fitch, an Englishman " I went from Bengala into the country of Couchè, not far from Cauchin China The people have ears which be marvellous great, of a span long, which they draw out in length by devices when they be young " In addition to the strange forms of men mentioned by Pliny, Diodorus Siculus mentions some in an island discovered by Jambulus, whose bones were as flexible as nerves (tendons) the holes of their ears far wider than ours; and with tongues deeply cloven, so that they imitate the song of birds, and can ordinarily speak to two men at once.— *Wern Club*

[1] The people here referred to are the Gauls. Cæsar (de Bell. Gall. lib vi.) says, " The whole nation of the Gauls is much addicted to religious observances, and on that account, those who are attacked by any of the more serious diseases, and those who are involved in the danger of warfare, either offer human sacrifices or make a vow that they will offer them, and they employ the Druids to officiate at their sacrifices, for they consider that the favour of the immortal gods cannot be conciliated, unless the life of one man be offered up for that of another they have also sacrifices of the same kind appointed on behalf of the state. Some have images of enormous size, the limbs of which they make of wicker-work, and fill with living men, and setting them on fire, the men are destroyed by the flames."— *Wern. Club*

about that Cave out of which that Wind is said to issue, which place they call Geschthron, the Arimaspi are reported to dwell, who, as we have said,[1] are distinguished by having One Eye in the midst of their Forehead, and who are in constant War about the Mines with the Griffins,[2] a flying kind of Wild Beasts, which used to fetch Gold out of the Veins of those Mines, which savage Beasts (as many Authors have recorded, and particularly *Herodotus* and *Aristeas* the Proconnesian, two Writers of greatest Name) strive as eagerly to keep the Gold as the Arimaspi to snatch it from them   Above those other Scythians called Anthropophagi, there is a Country named Abarimon, within a certain extensive Valley of the Mountain Imaus, in which are Wild Men, wandering about among brute Beasts, and having their Feet directed backward behind the Calves of their Legs, but able to run very swiftly.   This kind of Men cannot live in any other Climate than their own, which is the reason that they cannot be conveyed to the Kings that border upon them; nor could they be brought to *Alexander* the Great, as *Beton* hath reported, who was the Surveyor of the Journeys of that Prince.   The former Anthropophagi whom we have placed in the North, Ten Days' Journey above the River Borysthenes, are accustomed to drink out of the Skulls of Men, and to wear the Skins with the Hair for Mantles before their Breasts, according to *Isigonus* the Nicean   The same Writer affirmeth, that in Albania there are produced certain Individuals who have the Sight of their Eyes of a bluish-grey Colour, who from their Childhood are grey-headed, and can see better by Night than by Day. He reporteth also that Ten Days' Journey above the Borysthenes, there are the Sauromatæ, who never eat but once in Three Days. *Crates* of Pergamus saith, that in Hellespont about Parium there was a kind of Men, whom he nameth Ophiogenes, who, if one were stung by a Serpent, with touching only will ease it; and if they lay their Hand upon the Wound, are able to

---

[1] Lib. iv. 12, and lib. vi. 17
[2] The griffins are again mentioned, book x chap. 49.—*Wern. Club*

draw forth all the Poison from the Body *Varro* also testifieth, that even at this Day there are a few who cure the Stinging of Serpents with their Spittle. *Agatharcides* writeth, that in Africa the Psylli,[1] who are so called from king *Psyllus,* whose Sepulchre is in a part of the Greater

---

[1] The earliest existing reference that we have to the Psylli, or serpent-charmers, is found in the 58th Psalm, the 8th verse ; and the art is yet practised in the East. These men were, and still are, distinct tribes in their several countries, professing the power they claim to be an inherent and natural function Lucan, in the 5th book of his " Pharsalia," gives a complete exposition of the ancient belief concerning the charming of serpents He chiefly describes the measures which were taken to protect the Roman camp. When the encampment was marked out, the serpent-charmers marched around it chanting their charms, the mystic sounds of which chased the serpents far away But not trusting entirely to this, fires of different kinds of wood were kept up beyond the furthest tents, the smell of which prevented the serpents from approaching Thus the camp was protected during the night But if any soldier when abroad in the day time happened to be bitten, the Psylli exerted their power to effect a cure. First they rubbed the wounded part around with saliva, to prevent, as they said, the poison from spreading while they assayed their arts to extract it —

> " Then sudden he begins the magic song,
> And rolls the numbers hasty o'er his tongue ,
> Swift he runs on, nor pauses once for breath,
> To stop the progress of approaching death ;
> He fears the cure might suffer by delay,
> And life be lost but for a moment's stay
> Thus oft, though deep within the veins it lies,
> By magic numbers chased, the mischief flies
> But if it hear too slow, if still it stay,
> And scorn the potent charmer to obey ,
> With forceful lips he fastens on the wound,
> Drains out and spits the venom to the ground "—Rowe.

Lane (" Modern Egyptian") gives a particular account of the different methods made use of by the Psylli of the present day when exhibiting their supposed powers As to the pretensions of ancient as well as modern serpent-charmers, of being in their own persons insensible to the poison of the reptiles, there is no satisfactory proof of it indeed numerous instances to the contrary have occurred , and where they escape unharmed, it is to be attributed to the poison fangs having been previously extracted, or to their fearless handling of the deadly creatures —See the note on Ps. lviii 5, in the " Pictorial Bible," by Dr. Kitto — *Wern Club*

Syrtes, could do the like. These Men had naturally in
their Bodies a Poison fatal to Serpents, so that by the
Smell of it they were able to stupify them. And by
this means they used to try the Chastity of their Wives
For as soon as their Children were born, they exposed
them to the most furious Serpents; for these would not fly
from them if they were begotten in Adultery. This Nation,
in general, hath been almost entirely extirpated by the
Nasamones, who now inhabit those parts; but a kind of
these Men remaineth still, descended from those who fled,
or else who were not present when the Battle was fought, but
they exist in small Companies   In like manner, the Nation
of the Marsi continue in Italy, who preserve the Reputation of being descended from a Son of *Circè*, and therefore
possess the same natural faculty.   Yet so it is that all Men
possess within them that which is Poison to Serpents: for
it is reported they flee from Man's Spittle, as they do from
the touch of Scalding Water; but if it penetrate into their
Mouth, especially if it come from a Man that is fasting, it is
present Death.   Beyond the Nasamonæ, and their Neighbours the Machlyæ, there are Androgyni, of a double Nature,
inter se vicibus coeuntes, as *Calliphanes* reporteth.   *Aristotle*
adds, that their Right Breast is like that of a Man, and the
Left that of a Woman   In the same Africa *Isigonus* and *Nymphodorus* avouch that there are certain Families of Charmers:
who, if they praise, destroy the Sheep, cause the Trees to
wither, and Infants to pine away to death.   *Isigonus* addeth
further, that there are People of the same kind among the Triballi and Illyrii, who charm with their Eyesight, and kill those
whom they look upon for a long time, especially if their Eyes
look angry. which Evil of theirs is more quickly felt by those
who are above the age of Puberty.   It is worthy of remark,
that they have two Pupils in each Eye.   Of this kind *Apollonides* saith, there are also Women in Scythia named Bithyæ.
Philarchus witnesseth, that in Pontus also the Race of
the Thibii, and many others, have the same Quality: of
whom he giveth these marks, that in one of their Eyes they
have two Pupils, and in the other the Resemblance of a

Horse   He reporteth also, that they cannot sink in the
Water, not even if weighed down with Apparel. *Damon*
reports that there is a sort of People not unlike these in
Ethiopia, called Pharnaces, whose Sweat, if it chance to
touch a Man's Body, presently causeth him to waste away
And *Cicero*,[1] a Writer of our own, testifieth, that all Women
everywhere who have double Pupils in their Eyes inflict
Injury with their Sight.   In such manner Nature, having
generated in Man this custom of Wild Beasts, to feed upon
the Bowels of Men, hath taken Delight also to generate
Poisons in their whole Body, and even in the very Eyes of
some; that there should be no evil in the whole World, that
might not be likewise found in Man.   Not far from the City
of Rome, within the Territory of the Falisci, there are a few
Families called Hirpiæ, which at their Yearly Sacrifice celebrated to *Apollo* upon the Mount Soractè, walk upon the
pile of Wood as it is on Fire without being burnt.[2]   On
which account, by a perpetual Act of the Senate, they possess
an Immunity from War and all other Public Services.
Some men have certain Parts of their Bodies naturally
working surprising Effects   As for example, King *Pyrrhus*,[3]
whose Great Toe of his Right Foot was a Remedy by its

---

[1] This must have been in some of the lost works of Cicero, as no
such opinion is found in any of his extant writings — *Wern Club*

[2] The art of treading bare-foot on burning embers, red-hot iron, &c,
which has its professors in the present day, is from this passage shewn to
be of great antiquity; Virgil also alludes to the same when he speaks of
the annual festival of the Hirpi on Mount Soracte, in Etruria, where
Chlorcus, the priest of Cybele, thus addresses Apollo (Æn xi 785) —

"O patron of Soractè's high abodes !
  Phœbus, the ruling power among the gods !
  Whom first we serve   whole woods of unctuous pine
  Are fell'd for thee, and to thy glory shine,
  By thee protected, with our naked soles,
Through flames unsinged we march, and tread the kindled coals."

DRYDEN — *Wern Club*

[3] According to Plutarch, in his life of Pyrrhus, the person of this king
was very extraordinary —" Instead of teeth in his upper jaw, he had one
continued bone, marked with small lines resembling the divisions of a row

Touch for them that had Diseased Spleens. And they say, that when the rest of his Body was Burned that Great Toe could not be consumed · so that it was preserved in a little Case in the Temple. But principally India and the whole Tract of Ethiopia is full of these wonderful Things. The greatest Animals are bred in India, as will appear by their Dogs,[1] which are much greater than those of other Parts. And there are Trees growing in that Country to such a Height, that a Man cannot shoot an Arrow over them. The reason of this is the Goodness of the Soil, the Temperature of the Air, and the Abundance of Water: which is the cause also that under a single Fig-tree,[2] if it can be believed, Squadrons of Horsemen may stand. There are Reeds also of such Length[3] that between every Joint they will yield sufficient to make Boats able to receive three Men There are many Men there who are above five Cubits in Height: never do they Spit · they are not troubled with Pain in the Head, Toothache, or any Disease of the Eyes, and seldom of any other Parts of the Body; so hardy are they through the Moderate Heat of the Sun. There are certain Philosophers, whom they call Gymnosophistæ,[4] who from Sunrising to its setting persevere in standing and looking full against the Sun without once

of teeth. It was believed that he cured the swelling of the spleen, by sacrificing a white cock, and with his right foot gently pressing the part affected, the patients lying on their backs for that purpose There was no person, however poor or mean, to whom he refused this relief, if requested He received no reward, except the cock for sacrifice, and this present was very agreeable to him. It is also said that the great toe of that foot had a divine virtue in it, for, after his death, when the rest of his body was consumed, that toe was found entire and untouched by the flames "—LANGHORNE The reader will here be reminded of the royal touch for the cure of scrofulous diseases once exercised by our own kings —*Wern Club*

[1] Pliny (lib viii 40) tells us of one of these Indian dogs that conquered a lion —*Wern. Club.*

[2] The *Ficus Religiosa*, well known to modern travellers —*Wern. Club*

[3] Lib xvi. 36

[4] It is remarkable to observe how exactly the austerities of these ancient gymnosophists are still practised by the Fakirs of India —*Wern. Club.*

moving their Eyes: and from Morning to Night stand sometimes on one Leg, and sometimes on the other, on the Burning Sand. *Megasthenes* writeth, that on a Mountain named
Milo, there are Men whose Feet are turned backward, and
on each Foot they have eight Toes. And in many other
Mountains there is a kind of Men with Heads like Dogs, clad
all over with the Skins of Wild Beasts, and who instead of
Speech used to Bark: they are armed with Nails, and they live
on the Prey which they get by Hunting Beasts, and Fowling.
Ctesias writeth that there were known of them above
120,000 in number, and that in a certain Country of
India the Women bear but once in their Life, and their
Infants presently become Grey. Likewise, that there is a
kind of People named Monoscelli, which have but one Leg,
but they are exceedingly Swift, and proceed by Hopping.
These same Men are also called Sciopodæ, because in the
hottest Season they lie along on their Back on the Ground,
and defend themselves with the Shadow of their Feet: and
these People are not far from the Trogloditæ. Again, beyond these westward, some there are without a Neck, but
carrying their Eyes in their Shoulders. Among the Western
Mountains of India there are the Satyri (the Country where
they are is called the Region of the Cartaduli), the swiftest
of all Animals: which sometimes run on four Legs, at
others on two Feet like Men: but so light-footed are they,
that unless they are very Old or Sick they cannot be taken.
Tauron writeth, that the Choromandæ are a wild People,
without any Voice, but uttering a horrible Noise. their
Bodies Hairy, their Eyes bluish-grey, their Teeth like Dogs.
Eudoxus saith, that in the South Parts of India the Men
have Feet a Cubit long, but those of the Women[1] are
so small that they are called Struthopodes. *Megasthenes*
writeth, that among the Indian Nomadæ there is a Nation

---

[1] This character is so applicable to Chinese women, that it seems to
point out the great antiquity to which the strange custom of binding their
feet can be traced. The name of Struthopodes, or ostrich-footed, can only
have been applied to them by foreigners, but is not badly descriptive of
the figure of this artificial deformity.— *Wern Club.*

that instead of Noses have only two small Orifices, and after
the manner of Snakes have wiry Legs, and are named
Syrictæ.   In the utmost Borders of India, eastward, about
the Source of the Ganges, there is a Nation called the
Asthomes, having no Mouths hairy over the whole Body,
but clothed with the Down of the Branches of Trees: they
live only by the Vapour and Smell which they draw in at
their Nostrils no Meat or Drink do they take, but only
various pleasant Odours from Roots, Flowers, and Wild
Fruits; which they carry with them when they take a Long
Journey, because they would not miss their Smelling; but if
the Scent be a little too strong they are soon deprived of
Life. Higher in the Country, in the Edge of the Mountains,
the Pygmæi Spithamei are reported to be; which are three
Spans in Length, that is, not exceeding three times nine
Inches   The Climate is healthy, and ever like the Spring,
by reason that the Mountains are on the North side of them.
And these People *Homer*[1] also hath reported to be much
annoyed by Cranes. The report goeth, that in the Time of
Spring they set out all in a great Troop, mounted upon the
Backs of Rams and Goats, armed with Darts, to go down to
the Sea-side, and devour the Eggs and Young of their
Winged prey. For three Months this Expedition continueth,
for otherwise they would not be able to withstand their future
Flocks. Their Cottages are made of Clay, Feathers, and
Egg-shells. *Aristotle*[2] writeth, that the Pygmæi live in
Caves. For all the other matters he reported the same as
all the rest. *Isigonus* saith, that the kind of Indians named
Cyrni live a hundred and forty Years. The like he thinketh
of the Ethiopian Macrobii and the Seræ, and those who

---

[1] Iliad, lib. iii 6 —

> "So when inclement winters vex the plain
>   With piercing frosts, or thick descending rain,
>   To warmer seas the cranes embodied fly,
>   With noise, and order, through the mid-way sky
>   To pygmy nations wounds and death they bring,
>   And all the war descends upon the wing."—Pope

[2] Hist. Anim. lib. viii. 15.

dwell upon Mount Athos and of these last, because they
Feed on Vipers'[1] Flesh, and therefore it is that no offensive
Creatures are found on their Heads, nor on their Clothes.
Onesicritus affirmeth, that in those Parts of India there are
no Shadows, that the Men are five Cubits and two Palms in
Stature, that they live one hundred and thirty Years. and
never bear the Marks of Age, but die as if they were in the
middle of their age. *Crates* of Pergamus nameth those
Indians, who live above an hundred Years, Gymnetæ· but
not a few call them Macrobii. *Ctesias* saith there is a Race
of Indians, named Pandorè, inhabiting certain Valleys, who
live two hundred Years: in their youthful Time their Hair is
White, but as they grow old it becometh Black. On the
other hand, there are some who are Neighbours to the
Macrobii, who exceed not forty Years, and their Women
bear but once in their Lifetime. And this also is avouched
by *Agatharcides*, who addeth, that they feed on Locusts, and
are swift of Foot. *Clitarchus* and *Megasthenes* name them
Mandri, and number up three hundred Villages in their
Country: also, that the Women bear Children when they
are but seven Years old, and are aged at forty. *Artemidorus* affirmeth, that in the Island Taprobana the People
live exceeding long without any Bodily Infirmity. *Duris*
maketh report, that certain Indians have fellowship with
Beasts, of which acquaintance are bred a mixed and half
Savage Race; that among the Calingi, a Nation of India,
the Women conceive at five Years of Age, and live not above
eight. In another Tract of that Country, there are Men with
shaggy Tails and of great Swiftness. and some again that
with their Ears cover their whole Body. The Orites are
divided from the Indians by the River Arbis. They are
acquainted with no other Food but Fish, which they split
in Pieces with their Nails, and Roast against the Sun,
and then make Bread of it, as *Clitarchus* makes Report.
Crates of Pergamus saith, that the Troglodítæ above Ethiopia
are swifter than Horses, and that there are Ethiopians above

---

[1] Lib xxix. 6

eight Cubits High: that this Nation of Ethiopian Nomades is called Syrbotæ, and dwelleth along the River Astapus, toward the North. The Nation called Menismini dwell Twenty Days' Journey from the Ocean, and live on the Milk of certain Animals which we call Cynocephali,[1] of which they keep Flocks of the Females, but they kill the Males, except only enough to preserve the Race. In the Deserts of Africa you will meet oftentimes with Appearances in the shape of Men, but they vanish in an instant. Ingenious Nature disposes this and such-like things, as a Pastime to her, but which are Miracles to us. And indeed, who is able to recount every one of her Sports, which she accomplishes daily and even hourly? Let it suffice therefore, in order to declare her Power, that we have set down those prodigious Works of hers, as displayed in whole Nations. And now we proceed to a few Particulars that are well known in regard to Man.

Chapter III.

Of Prodigious Births.[2]

That Women may bring forth three at one Birth, appeareth evidently by the example of the *Horatii* and *Curiatii*. But to exceed that number is reputed to be among the Portents; except in Egypt, where Women are more fruitful by drinking the Water of the Nile. Of late Years, about the latter end of the Reign of *Divus Augustus*, a Woman at Ostia named *Fausta*, of ordinary Rank, was delivered of two Boys and as many Girls, but this was a Portent beyond

[1] The *cynocephalus anubis* of modern zoologists is without doubt here intended.—*Wern Club*

[2] "Prodigious births:" that is, not simply out of the common course of nature, but such as were believed to be prophetic of some remarkable events, and so reported by augurs to the proper authorities. What, at the end of this chapter, Pliny reports that he had himself seen, is of no uncommon occurrence, and would be regarded among us as nothing beyond a monstrous birth, an irregular formation of nature; but the incident he mentions last can only be regarded as a proof of the great agitation of the public mind, at a period when the danger was a sufficient motive to raise and propagate the strangest reports.—*Wern Club.*

doubt of the Famine that ensued   In Peloponnesus also there is found a Woman, who brought forth at four Births twenty Children, and the greater Part of them lived. *Trogus* is the authority, that in Egypt a Woman hath borne seven at a Birth.   It falleth out, moreover, that there come into the World Children of both Sexes in one, whom we call Hermaphrodites.   In old Time they were known by the Name of Androgyni, and reputed for Prodigies, but now Men take Pleasure in them.   *Pompey* the Great, in the Theatre which he adorned with remarkable Ornaments, as well for the subject as the most exquisite Hand of the great Artists, among other Images represented *Eutichè*, a Woman of Tralles, who after she had borne thirty Births, was carried by twenty of her Children to the Funeral Fire for to be burnt.   *Alcippè* was delivered of an Elephant, and that certainly was a monstrous Token.   Also in the beginning of the Marsian War a Bondwoman brought forth a Serpent.[1]

[1] We know how prone vulgar ignorance or superstition is to compare an ordinary monstrous birth to some fancied animal   Such is within the knowledge of living observers   But what shall we say to the following ? "Lemnius tells us of a monster, that a certain woman was delivered of, and to whom he himself was physician and present at the sight, which at the appearing of the day filled all the chamber with roaring and crying, running all about to find some hole to creep into ; but the women at the length stifled and smothered it with pillows "— *Wanley's Wonders of the Little World*   And from the same authority —" Johannes Naborowsky, a noble Polonian, and my great friend, (says Bartholini, " Hist Anat ") told me at Basil, that he had seen in his country two little fishes without scales, which were brought forth by a woman, and as soon as they came out of her womb did swim in the water as other fish "   The story given by Wormius, concerning the birth of an egg from a woman (and of which he gives a figure in his " Museum Wormianum,") is illustrated, and perhaps explained, as may all the others on the same principle, by another given in Wanley's book, of a woman " of good quality, who had made great preparations for her lying-in, but in the last month her distension subsided, and it is confessed that she plumped herself up with a stuffing of garments   However, the time must come at last, and she was delivered of a creature, very like unto a dormouse of the greater size, which to the amazement of the women who were present, with marvellous celerity sought out and found a hole in the chamber, into which it crept and was never seen after "   Instances somewhat similar have occurred in very

Many misshapen Creatures of various kinds are produced as
Monsters in the World *Claudius Cæsar* writeth, that in Thessaly an Hippocentaur was born, and that it died on the very
same Day. And when he was Sovereign we ourselves saw the
like sent to him out of Egypt, preserved in Honey. Among
the Instances there is one of a Child in Saguntum, in the Year
in which that Town was destroyed by *Annibal*, which, as soon
as it was born, presently returned again into the Womb

Chapter IV.

Of the Change of the Sex,[1] *and of Double Births.*

It is no fable, that Females may be turned to Males;
for we have found it recorded in the Annals, that in the Year
when *Pub Licinius Crassus* and *C Cassius Longinus* were
Consuls, there was at Cassinum a Maid who, under her
Parents, became a Boy · and by the order of the Aruspices
he was conveyed to a Desert Island. *Lucinius Mutianus* reporteth, that himself saw at Argos a Person named *Arescon,*
who had borne the Name of *Arescusa,* and even had been
Married but afterwards came to have a Beard, and the
general Properties of a Man, and thereupon married a Wife.
After the same sort he saw at Smyrna a Boy changed. I
myself was an Eye-witness, that in Africa *L. Cossicius,* a

recent times, to the great disappointment of expecting friends and the
laugh could only have been rendered the louder if, instead of a simple disappointment, an egg or dormouse, an elephant or serpent had been the
result   By law, "Ut monstrosos partus necare parentibus liceret,"— that
"it should be lawful to parents to put to death children that were born
monstrous;" but Dionysius Halicarnasseus adds, that it was necessary
they should call witnesses to prove that they were monstrous. although
the latter stipulation can scarcely be reconciled with another law, which
gave to parents the right of life and death over their children   According to the law of Tullus Hostilius, third king of Rome, when three children were born at one birth, they were to be brought up to the age of
maturity at the public charge —*Wern Club*

[1] Instances similar to these are scarcely uncommon, and the causes
are well known to anatomists   The remarks concerning the fate of twins
are so contrary to experience, that Pliny's error can scarcely be accounted
for —*Wern Club*

Citizen of Tisdrita, was turned from a Woman to a Man upon the very Marriage-day. If a Woman bring Twins, it is rare for them all to live, but either the Mother dieth, or one of the Babes, if not both But if the Twins be of both Sexes, it is rare for both of them to escape. Women grow old sooner than Men; and they grow to their Maturity more speedily than Men. It is certain that a Male Child stirreth oftener in the Womb, and lieth commonly more to the right Side; whereas Females incline to the left.[1]

Cap. V.

De Hominis Generando, et Pariendi Tempore per illustria Exempla a Mensibus septem ad undecim.[2]

Cæteris animantibus statum, et pariendi, et partus gerendi tempus est; homo toto anno, et incerto gignitur spatio. Alius septimo mense, alius octavo, et usque ad initia decimi undecimique. Ante septimum mensem haud unquam vitalis est. Septimo non nisi pridie posterove plenilunii die, aut interlunio concepti nascuntur Translatitium in Ægypto est et octavo gigni. Jam quidem et in Italia tales partus esse vitales, contra priscorum opiniones. Variant hæc pluribus modis Vestilia C. Herditii ac postea Pomponii atque Orfiti, clarissimorum civium, conjunx, ex his quatuor partus enixa, Sempronium septimo mensi genuit, Suillium Rufum undecimo, Corbulonem septimo, utrunque Consulem postea Cæsoniam Caii[3] principis conjugem, octavo. In quo mensium numero genitis, intra quadragesimum diem maximus

[1] No signs are known by which the sex of the child before birth is in the least indicated — *Wern Club*

[2] The term of pregnancy natural to the human female is 280 days; by the Prussian laws, 300 days, by the French, 301 days are considered to mark the extreme limit From physiological reasons it is extremely improbable if the usual term of nine calendar, or ten lunar months, is ever exceeded by more than one lunar month.—*Wern Club*

[3] The emperor so named is better known by the name of Caligula, which was imposed upon him on account of the military shoe which, when a child, he wore in the camp. The wife's father here spoken of was the Emperor Augustus — *Wern. Club.*

labor. Gravidis autem quarto et octavo mense, letalesque in iis abortus. Massurius auctor est, L Papyrium Prætorem, secundo hærede lege agente, bonorum possessionem contra eum dedisse, cum mater partum se 13 mensibus diceret tulisse, quoniam nullum certum tempus pariendi statutum videretur.[1]

Cap. VI.

De Conceptibus, et Signa Sexus in gravidis prævenientia Partum.

A conceptu decimo die, doloris capitis, oculorum vertiginis tenebræque, fastidium in cibis, redundatio stomachi, indices sunt hominis inchoati. Melior color marem ferenti, et facilior partus · motus in utero quadragesimo die. Contraria omnia in altero sexu : ingestabile onus, crurum et inguinum levis tumor. Primus autem nonagesimo die motus. Sed plurimum languoris in utroque sexu, capillum germinante partu, et in plenilunio ; quod tempus editos quoque infantes præcipue infestat. Adeoque incessus, atque omne, quicquid dici potest, in gravida refert · ut salsioribus cibis usæ, carentem unguiculis partum edant, et, si respiravere, difficilius enitantur. Oscitatio quidem in enixu letalis est sicut sternuisse a coitu abortivum.

Cap. VII.

De Conceptu Hominum et Generatione.

Miseret atque etiam pudet æstimantem quam sit frivola animalium superbissimi origo, cum plerunque abortus causa fiat odor a lucernarum extinctu. His principiis nascuntur tyranni, his carnifex animus. Tu qui corporis viribus fidis,

---

[1] According to the Roman law · " Sei qua molier post virei mortem in decem proximeis mensebos pariat, quei, quave ex ea nascatur, sonus, suave, in verei familia heres estod ."—" If a woman is delivered of a child ten months after the death of her husband, let the child born, either boy or girl, be heir to his father." Ulpian's opinion is, that a child born eleven months after the death of his father is not able to inherit. The Emperor Adrian allowed a legitimate birth in the eleventh month, but this is explained by saying, that the eleventh month may be begun, but not ended — *Wern. Club.*

tu qui fortunæ munera amplexaris, et te ne alumnum quidem ejus existimas, sed partum tu cujus semper in victoria est mens, tu qui te Deum credis, aliquo successu tumens, tanti perire potuisti : atque etiam hodie minoris potes, quantulo serpentis ictus dente : aut etiam, ut Anacreon Poeta, acino uvæ passæ : ut Fabius Senator Prætor, in lactis haustu uno pilo strangulatus. Is demum profecto vitam æqua lance pensitabat, qui semper fragilitatis humanæ memor fuerit.

Cap. VIII.

De Agrippis.

In pedes procedere nascentem contra naturam est ; quo argumento eos appellavere agrippas, ut ægre partos : qualiter M. Agrippam ferunt genitum unico prope felicitatis exemplo in omnibus ad hunc modum genitis. Quanquam is quoque adversa pedum valetudine, misera juventa, exercito ævo inter arma mortesque, ad noxia successu, infelici terris stirpi omni, sed per utrasque Agrippinas maxime, quæ Caium et Domitium Neronem Principes genuere, totidem faces generis humani · præterea brevitate ævi quinquagesimo uno raptus anno, in tormentis adulteriorum conjugis, socerique prægravi servitio, luisse augurium præposteri natalis existimatur. Neronem, quoque paulo ante Principem, et toto Principatu suo hostem generis humani, pedibus genitum parens ejus scribit Agrippina. Ritu naturæ capite hominem gigni mos est, pedibus efferri

Cap. IX.

Monstruosi Partus excisi Utero.

Auspicatius enecta parente gignuntur, sicut Scipio Africanus prior natus, primusque Cæsarum a cæso matris utero dictus : qua de causa et Cæsones appellati.[1] Simili modo natus et Manlius, qui Carthaginem cum exercitu intravit.

---

[1] The Cæsarian operation, as it is now called, has been an unsuccessful one in modern times ; but this arises from the fact that it is now performed on the living mother to preserve her life, perhaps at the risk of that of

Cap X

Qui sint Vopisci.

Vopiscos appellabant e geminis, qui retenti utero nasce-
rentur, altero interempto abortu.   Namque maxima et rara
circa hoc miracula existunt

Cap. XI.

Exempla Numerosæ Sobolis

Præter mulierem pauca animalia coitum novere gravida   Unum quidem omnino, aut alterum, superfœtat [1]
Extat in monumentis etiam medicorum, et quibus talia con-
sectari curæ fuit, uno abortu duodecim puerperia egesta.
Sed ubi paululum temporis inter duos conceptus intercessit,
uterque perfertur: ut in Hercule et Iphiclo fratre ejus apparuit,
et in ea quæ gemino partu, altero marito similem, alterum
adultero genuit; Item in Proconnesia ancilla, quæ ejusdem
diei coitu, alterum domino similem, alterum procuratori
ejus; et in alia, quæ unum justo partu quinque mensium
alterum edidit.   Rursus in alia, quæ septem mensium edito
puerperio, insecutis mensibus geminos enixa est.   Jam illa
vulgata, varie ex integris truncos gigni, ex truncis integros,
eademque parte truncos: signa quædam, nævosque et cica-
trices etiam regenerari. Quarto partus Dacorum originis Nota
in brachio redditur.

Chapter XII.

Examples of those who have closely resembled one another [2]

In the Race of the *Lepidi* it is said there were three, not
successively one after another, who had when they were

the child, whereas it appears that anciently it was had recourse to only
after the mother had expired, to save the child which still gave signs of
life Cornelius Gamma says, that he performed it six times on as many
women, and that the children were preserved, but he says nothing of the
fate of the mothers.—*Wern Club*

[1] Superfœtation is an exceedingly rare occurrence in women, but some
modern instances place the certainty of this fact on certain grounds —
Wern Club

[2] This chapter is borrowed from Aristotle's " History of Animals,"
b xvii. c 6 —*Wern. Club*

Born, a Membrane growing over the Eye. Some have resembled their Grandfathers: and of Twins, one hath been like the Father, the other the Mother but he that was Born a year after hath been so like his elder Brother as if he had been one of the Twins. Some Women bring all their Children like themselves; others again resembling their Husbands, and some like neither the one nor the other. Some Women bring all their Daughters like their Fathers, and their Sons like the Mothers. The Example is undoubted, of *Nicæus*, a famous Painter of Byzantium, who having to his Mother a Woman begotten in Adultery by an Ethiopian, and nothing different in Colour from other Women, was himself begotten an Ethiopian Indeed, the Consideration of the Likenesses is in the Mind, in which likewise many other Accidents are thought to be very strong, whether they come by Sight, Hearing, and Memory, or Imaginations drunk in in the very instant of Conception.[1] The thought of either Father or Mother flying to and fro transporting the Soul in a moment, is supposed to stamp this Likeness, or to mix it. On this account it is that Men are more unlike one another than other Creatures. for the Quickness of the Thoughts, the Agility of the Mind, the very great variety of our Dispositions, imprint the great Multiplicity of Marks, whereas the Minds of other Creatures is immovable, being alike in all, and in every one according to its own Kind. *Artenon*, a Man of the common Rank, was so like in all points to *Antiochus* King of Syria, that *Laodicè* the Queen, after *Antiochus* was killed, effected the Succession of the Kingdom through his acting the part of Recommendation. *Vibius*, a certain Commoner of Rome, and *Publicius*, one from a Bondslave made a Freeman, were both of them so like *Pompey* the Great, that the one could scarcely be discerned from the other: so closely did they represent that open Countenance, and the singular Majesty which appeared in his Forehead The like cause it was that gave his Father also the Surname of *Menogenes*, from his Cook, although he

---

[1] The reader will scarcely fail to remember Jacob's singular stratagem with Laban's flock—Genesis, xxx and xxxi —*Wern Club*

was already surnamed *Strabo*, because of his Squint Eyes imitating a defect that existed in his Servant. So was one of the *Scipios* surnamed *Serapio* upon such an occasion, after the name of one *Serapio*, who was a base Slave of his, and the dealer in buying and selling his Swine. Another *Scipio* after him, of the same House, was surnamed *Salutio*, because of a certain Jester of that Name After the same manner one *Spinter*, a Player of the second Place,[1] and *Pamphilus*, a Player of the third Part, resembled *Lentulus* and *Metellus*, who were Consuls together. And this fell out very untowardly, that such resemblances of the two Consuls should be seen together on the Stage On the other hand, *Rubrius* the Player was surnamed *Plancus*, because he was so like *Plancus* the Orator. Again, *Burbuleius* and *Menogenes*, both Players, gave name, the one to *Curio* the Father, as did the other to *Messala Censorius* There was in Sicily a Fisherman who resembled *Sura* the Proconsul, not in general likeness only, but also in the grin when he spoke, in drawing his Tongue short, and in his thick Speech. *Cassius Severus*, the famous Orator, was reproached for being like *Mirmillo*, a Keeper of Cattle. *Toranius* sold to *Marcus Antonius*, at that time Triumvir, two very beautiful Boys as Twins, so like they were one to the other: although one was born in Asia, and the other beyond the Alps. But when *Antony* afterwards came to the knowledge of the fraud, which was detected by the Language of the Boys, he threatened him in great Anger Among other things complaining of the high Price that he had made him pay, for they cost him two hundred Sesterces. But the cunning Merchant answered, That this was the very cause why he had sold them at so great a rate : for it would not have been so wonderful if two Brothers of the same Mother had resembled one another, but that there should be any found, who were born in different Countries, so like in all respects, was above every thing deserving of a high Price. This answer of his produced a well-timed admiration,

---

[1] That is, he who supported the second or the third rate of characters on the ancient stage.— *Wern. Club.*

so that the Proscriptor, whose mind was enraged and uttered reproaches, was not only appeased, but also induced to be well pleased with his good Fortune.

Cap XIII.

Quæ sit Generandı Ratio.

Est quædam privatım dissociatio corporum ; et inter se sterıles, ubi cum aliis junxere, gignunt . sicut Augustus et Livıa. Item alıı alıæque fœmınas tantum generant, aut mares ; plerunque et alternant . sicut Gıacchorum mater duodecies, et Agrippina Germanici novies   Aliis sterilis est juventa, alııs semel in vita datur gıgnere. Quædam non perferunt partus : quales, si quando medıcina et cura vicere, fœmınam fere gignunt   Dıvus Augustus in relıqua exemplorum rarıtate, neptıs suæ nepotem vıdıt genitum quo excessıt anno, M Syllanum ; qui cum Asiam obtineret post Consulatum, Neronis Prıncipis successione, veneno ejus interemptus est.   Q. Metellus Macedonicus, cum sex lıberos relınqueret, undecım nepotes relıquıt, nurus vero generosque et omnes qui se patris appellatione salutarent, vıginti septem   In Actis temporum Dıvi Augusti ınvenitur, XII. Consulatu ejus L. quæ Sylla Collega, ad III Idus Aprilis, C. Crispinum Hılarum ex ingenua plebe Fesulana, cum lıberıs novem (ın quo numero filıæ duæ fuerunt) nepotibus XXVII., pronepotıbus XXIX., neptibus IX., prælata pompa, cum omnıbus in Capıtolio immolasse.[1]

[1] These ınstances are more than equalled by some which are mentioned ın the preface to " Hearne's Edıtion of Leland," vol. vi. p. 4. Mary, wıfe of Rıchard Honıwood, of Charınge, ın Kent, dıed at the age of nınety-eıght, ın the year 1620, leavıng by one husband sıxteen chıldren, 114 grand-chıldren, 228 great-grand-children, and nıne ın the fourth degree ın all 367 persons   Thomas Urqhart, laırd and sherıff of Cromarty, had by one wıfe twenty-five sons and eleven daughters   all ol whom he lıved to see ol considerable emınence ın the world   "In Dunstable church," says Hakewell (Apol) "ıs an epıtaph on a woman, testıfyıng that she bore three chıldren at a birth three several tımes, and five at a bırth two other tımes."   In the year 1553 the wıfe of John Gıssger, an Italıan, had twıns, and before the year was out she produced five children, three sons and two daughters   Thomas Fazel wrıtes that " Jane Pancıca,

Cap XIV.

De eodem multiplicius.

Mulier post quinquagesimum annum non gignit, major-
que pars quadragesimo profluvium genitale sistit   Nam in
viris Massinissam Regem, post LXXXVI. annum generasse
filium, quem Methymnatum appellaverit, clarum est : Cato-
nem Censorium octogesimo exacto, a filia Salonii clientis sui
Qua de causa, aliorum ejus liberorum propago, Liciniani
sunt cognominati, hi Saloniani, ex quibus Uticensis fuit.
Nuper etiam L. Volusio Saturnino in urbis præfectura ex-
tincto, notum est Corneliæ Scipionum gentis Volusium Sa-
turninum, qui fuit Consul, genitum post LXII. annum.
Et usque ad LXXXV. apud ignobiles vulgaris reperitur
generatio.

Cap. XV.

De Menstruis Mulierum.

Solum autem animal menstruale mulier est : inde unius
utero, quas appellarunt molas.   Ea est caro informis,
inanima, ferri ictum et aciem respuens.   Movetur, sistitque
menses ; ut et partus, alias lethalis, alias una senescens,
aliquando alvo citatiore excidens.   Simile quiddam et viris
in ventre gignitur, quod vocant scirron · sic ut Oppio Capi-
toni prætorio viro.   Sed nihil facile reperiatur mulierum
profluvio magis monstrificum.   Acescunt superventu inusta,
sterilescunt tactæ fruges, moriuntur insita, exuruntur horto-
rum germina, et fructus arborum, quibus insidere, decidunt ;
speculorum fulgor aspectu ipso hebetatur, acies ferri præ-
stringitur, eborisque nitor ; alvei apum emoriuntur ; æs
etiam ac ferrum rubigo protinus corripit, odorque dirus
aera ; et in rabiem aguntur gustato eo canes, atque insanabili
veneno morsus inficitur.   Quin et bituminum sequax alio-

wife of Bernard, a Sicilian, in thirty births produced seventy-three
children." The latter instances are from Wanley's " Wonders of the
Little World," where his authorities are given.—*Wern. Club*

quin ac lenta Natura, in Lacu Judææ (qui vocatur Asphaltites), certo tempore anni supernatans, nequit sibi avelli, ad omnem contactum adhærens, præterquam filo quod tale virus infecerit. Etiam formicis animali minimo, inesse sensum ejus ferunt; abjicique gustatas fruges, nec postea repeti. Et hoc tale tantumque omnibus tricenis diebus malum in muliere exsistit, et trimestri spatio largius Quibusdam vero sæpius mense; sicut aliquibus nunquam, sed tales non gignunt, quando hæc est generando homini materia semine e maribus coaguli modo hoc in sese glomerante, quod deinde tempore ipso animatur, corporaturque. Ergo cum gravidis fluxit, invalidi aut non vitales partus eduntur, aut saniosi, ut autor est Negidius.[1]

Cap. XVI.

Item de Ratione Partuum.

Idem, lac fœminæ non corrumpi alenti partum si ex eodem viro rursus conceperit, arbitratur Incipiente autem hoc statu, aut desinente, conceptus facillimi traduntur Fæcunditatis in fœminis prærogativam accepimus, inunctis medicamine oculis, salivam infici. Cæterum editis primores septimo mense gigni dentes priusque in supera fere parte, haud dubium est Septimo eosdem decidere anno, aliosque suffici Quosdam et cum dentibus nasci,[2] sicut M. Curium, quod ob id Dentatus cognominatus est, et Cn Papyrium Carbonem, præclaros viros In Women the same thing was counted inauspicious in the times of the Kings, for when *Valeria* was born toothed in this manner, the Augurs (*Aruspices*) being consulted about it, answered by way of Prophecy, that she would be the ruin of that City to which she might be conveyed; whereupon she was conveyed to Suessa Pometia,

---

[1] Much that is here stated is erroneous, and mere fable, the recondite subject of generation abounding in the marvellous —*Wern Club*

[2] However this might have been regarded in ancient times, on a superstitious account, it is not an uncommon circumstance The editor is acquainted with the fact, that in an instance of three children being born at one birth, all of them were furnished with teeth —*Wern. Club.*

which at that time was very flourishing · and the ruin of the place certainly followed *Cornelia*, the Mother of the *Gracchi*, is sufficient proof that it is an adverse omen, when Women are born with the Genital Parts grown together Some Children are born with a continued edge of Bone instead of a row of distinct Teeth,[1] as a Son of *Prusius* King of the Bythinians, who had such a Bone in his Upper Jaw. But Teeth are the only parts that are not subdued by the Fires, so that they are not consumed with the rest of the Body; but the same parts that are not conquered by the Flames are hollowed out and wasted by a Waterish Rheum. They may be made White by some Medicines They are worn away by use; and sometimes they fall first out of the Head, they serve not only to grind our Meat for our Nourishment, but they are necessary for the framing of our Speech. The Fore-teeth hold the Government over our Voice and Words by a peculiar accord, answering to the Stroke of the Tongue, and the series of their Formation, with their Size, cutting up, softening, or restraining the Words; but when they are fallen out all explanation of Words is lost. Moreover, it may be believed, that some Augury can be gathered from the Teeth. Men are in possession of two-and-thirty in all, except the Nation of the Turduli; and those who have above this Number suppose that they may calculate on longer Life. Women have not so many · they that have on the right Side in the upper Jaw two Eye-teeth, named Canine, may promise themselves the Favours of Fortune, as was the case in *Agrippina*, the Mother of *Domitius Nero* · but it is the contrary in the Left Side. It is not the Custom in any Country to burn in a Funeral Fire the dead Body of an Infant before the Teeth are come up but of this we will write more, when our History will take in the individual Members *Zoroastres* was the only Man we have heard of, who laughed the same day he was born · his Brain did so evidently pulsate, that it would lift up the Hand that was laid on it. a Presage of his future Learning. It is certain

[1] This was also the case with King Pyrrhus See note, lib vii 2 — *Wern. Club.*

that a Man at three years of Age is come to one-half of the
Measure of his Height. This also is observed for a Truth, that
generally all Men fall short of the full Stature in Times past;
and seldom are they taller than their Fathers: the Exube-
rance of the Seeds being consumed by the burning, in the
Changes of which the World now vergeth toward the latter
End. In Crete, a Mountain being cloven asunder by an
Earthquake, a Body was found standing, forty-six Cubits
high; which some judged to be the Body of *Orion*, and
others, of *Otus* It is believed from Records that the Body
of *Orestes*, when taken up by direction of the Oracle, was
seven Cubits long.[1] And that great Poet, *Homer*, who lived
almost a thousand Years ago, did not cease to complain that
Men's Bodies were less of Stature even then, than in old
Time. The Annals do not deliver down the Bulk of *Nævius
Pollio;* but that he was of great size appeareth by this, that
it was taken for a Wonder, that in a great Crowd of People
running together he was almost killed. The tallest Man
that hath been seen in our Age was one named *Gabbara*,
who in the Days of Prince *Claudius* was brought out of
Arabia; he was nine Feet high, and as many Inches There
were in the Time of *Divus Augustus* two others, named
Pusio and *Secundilla*, higher than *Gabbara* by half a Foot,
whose Bodies were preserved for a Wonder in a Vault in the
Gardens of the Salustiani. While the same (*Augustus*) was
President, his Niece *Julia* had a very little Man, two Feet
and a Hand-breadth high, called *Canopas*, whom she made
much of; and also a Woman named *Andromeda*,[2] the Freed
Woman of *Julia Augusta*. *M. Varro* reporteth that *Manius
Maximus*, and *M Tullius*, Roman Knights, were but two
Cubits high: and we ourselves have seen their Bodies em-
balmed in Presses. It is well known that there are some

---

[1] Ten feet and an half.

[2] The instance of the American who exhibited himself through Europe is of recent occurrence John Duck, an Englishman, was carried
about for a show in 1610, being two feet and a half high at forty-five years
of age Cardan says he saw a man in Italy, of full age, not above a cubit
high He was carried about in a parrot-cage —*Wern Club.*

born a Foot and a half high ; others again somewhat longer :
filling up the Course of their Life in three Years. We find
in the Chronicles, that in Salamis the Son of *Euthimenes*[1] in
three Years grew to be three Cubits high , but he was in
his Pace slow and in his Understanding dull ; but having
attained the State of Puberty, and his Voice having become
strong, at Three Years' end he died suddenly of a Contraction
of all the Parts of his Body. Some while since I saw myself
the like in almost all respects, except the Puberty, in a Son
of *Cornelius Tacitus*, a Roman Knight, and a Procurator for
the State in Belgic Gaul. Such the Greeks call *Ectrapelos ;*
in Latin they have no Name.

CHAPTER XVII.

Observations of Bodies.

WE see that the Length of a Man from the Sole of the
Foot to the Crown of the Head is equal to the Extent of his
longest Fingers when his Arms and Hands are stretched out.
As also, that most People are stronger on the right Side ;
others are as strong on one Side as on the other · and there are
some that are altogether Left-handed ; but that is never seen
in Women. Men weigh heavier than Women : and in every
kind of Creature, the bodies, when dead, are more heavy than
when alive , and the same Parties sleeping weigh more than
when awake. The dead Bodies of Men float with the Face

[1] In the year 1747, Mr Dawkes, a surgeon at St. Ives, near Hun-
tingdon, published a small tract called " Prodigium Willinghamense," or
an account of a surprising boy, who was buried at Willingham, near
Cambridge, upon whom he wrote the following epitaph · — " Stop, tra-
veller, and wondering know, here buried lie the remains of Thomas, son
of Thomas and Margaret Hall, who, not one year old, had the signs of
manhood, not three, was almost four feet high , endued with uncommon
strength, a just proportion of parts, and a stupendous voice , before six he
died, as it were, of advanced age   He was born at this village, October 31,
1741, and the same departed this life, September 3, 1747 " (See also
"Philosophical Transactions," 1744-45) As Dr Elliotson has observed
(Blumenbach's " Physiology "), this perfectly authentic case removes all
doubts respecting the boy at Salamis mentioned by Pliny.—*Wern. Club.*

upward, and Women with the Face downward, as if Nature
had provided to save their Modesty even when dead

Chapter XVIII

Examples of a Variety of Forms.

We have heard that some Men's Bones are solid, and so
live without any Marrow. They are known by the Signs, that
they never feel Thirst, nor put forth any Sweat: and yet we
know that a Man may conquer his Thirst by his Will, and
Julius Viator, a Roman Knight, descended from the Race of
the Confederate Voconti, in his younger Years being ill with
an Effusion of Water beneath the Skin, and forbidden by
the Physicians to use Fluids in any way, obtained a Nature
by Custom, so that in his old Age he forbore to drink.
Others also have been able to command their Nature in
many Cases.

Chapter XIX.

Examples of Diversity of Habits.

It is said, that *Crassus*, Grandfather to that *Crassus* who
was slain in Parthia, never laughed, and on that account
was called *Agelastus* and also that many have been found
to have never wept   *Socrates*, who was illustrious for his
Wisdom, was seen always to carry the same Countenance,
never being more cheerful nor more disturbed at one Time
than another   But this tendency of the Mind turneth now
and then in the End into a certain Rigour and Sternness
of Nature, so hard and inflexible that it cannot be ruled;
and so despoileth Men of the humane Affections; and such
are called by the Greeks *Apathes*, who had the Experience
of many such ⋅ and, what is surprising, some of them were
very eminent for Wisdom, as *Diogenes* the Cynic, *Pyrrho*,
Heraclitus, and *Timo;* the latter being carried away so far
as to hate the whole Human Race.   But these were Examples of depraved Nature.   Various remarkable Things are
known; as in *Antonia*, the Wife of *Drusus*, who was never

seen to spit, and *Pomponius* the Poet, a Consular Man, who never belched   Such as naturally have their Bones solid, who are seldom met with, are called *Cornei* (hard as Horn).

Chapter XX

Of Strength and Swiftness.[1]

VARRO, in his Treatise of prodigious Strength, maketh Report of *Tritanus*, who was little in Person, but of incomparable Strength, much renowned in the Gladiatorial Play, with the Armature of the Samnites.   He maketh mention also of a Son of his, a Soldier under *Pompey* the Great; and that he had all over his Body, as well as through his Arms and Hands, Sinews running straight and across like Network. and when an Enemy challenged him to a Combat, he overcame him with his right Hand unarmed, and in the End caught hold of him, and brought him into the Camp with one Finger.   *Junius Valens*, a Centurion in the Prætorium of *Divus Augustus*, was accustomed to bear up Waggons laden with Sacks, until they were discharged: with one Hand he would hold back a Chariot, standing firm against all the Force of the Horses   He did also other wonderful Things, which are to be seen engraved on his Tomb: and therefore *Varro* saith that being called *Hercules Rusticellus*, he took up his Mule and carried him away   *Fusius Salvius* carried up over the Stairs two hundred Pounds' weight on his Feet, as many in his Hands, and twice as much upon his Shoulders   Myself have seen a Man named *Athanatus*, with a great deal of Ostentation walk upon the Stage clothed in a

---

[1] It is observable that in this, and chap xviii, Pliny's instances apply only to animal endurance   Martial took a more correct view of the mental property, when he said.—

> " Rebus in angustis facile est contemnere vitam
> Fortiter ille facit, qui miser esse potest "—B xi Ep 35

> When Fortune frowns, 'tis easy life to hate,
> But real courage is not crush'd by fate.

Wern Club

Cuirass of Lead weighing five hundred Pounds, and wearing high Shoes of the same Weight. When *Milo*, the great Wrestler of Crotonè, stood firm upon his Feet, no Man was able to make him stir in the least Degree · if he held an Apple, no Man was able to stretch out his Finger [1] It was a great matter, that *Philippides* ran 1140 Stadia, fiom Athens to Lacedæmon, in two Days; until *Anistis*, a Runner of Lacedæmon, and *Philonides*, belonging to *Alexander* the Great, ran from Sicyonè to Elis in one Day, 1200 Stadia. But now, indeed, we know some in the Circus able to endure the running of 160 Miles And lately when *Fonteius* and *Vipsanus* were Consuls, a young Boy, only nine Years old, between Noon and Evening ran 75 Miles. And a Man may wonder the more at this Matter, if he consider, that it was counted an exceeding great Journey that *Tiberius Nero* made in three Chariots in a Day and a Night, when he hasted to his Brother *Drusus*, then lying sick in Germany, which was but 200 Miles.[2]

[1] Two persons, successively porters to Kings James I and Charles, his son, were of great size and strength. The first, particularly, was able to take two of the tallest yeomen of the guard, one under each arm, and he ordered them as he pleased The Emperor Maximinus, who was eight feet and a half in height, was of enormous strength, even in proportion to his magnitude. — *Wern Club.*

[2] We have less examples of swiftness of foot, since more rapid conveyance is common Pliny's instances are the more surprising, as they imply continuance; but the English King Henry V. was so swift of foot, that with two of his lords, without any weapons, he would catch a wild buck in a large park. In Baker's "Chronicle" we are informed, that John Lepton, of Kepwick, in the county of York, one of the grooms of the Privy Chamber to James I., for a wager rode for six days successively between York and London which is 150 miles He accomplished the work of each day, beginning May 20, 1606, before it was dark; and having finished his wager at York on Saturday, on the following Monday he rode back to London, and on Tuesday to the court at Greenwich being as fresh and well as when he began In the year 1619, July 17, Bernard Calvert rode from St George's church, in Southwark, to Dover. thence by barge to Calais, and from thence back to St George's church, on the same day; beginning at three o'clock in the morning, and ending at eight in the evening, fresh and lusty, although roads were then less perfect than now. — *Wern. Club.*

Chapter XXI

Examples of good Eyesight.

We find in Histories almost incredible Examples of Sharpness of the Eyes. *Cicero* hath recorded, that the Poem of *Homer* called the Iliad, written on Parchment, was enclosed within a Nutshell. The same Writer maketh mention of one who could see to the Distance of 135 Miles. And *M. Varro* nameth the Man, saying that he was called *Strabo;* and that during the Carthaginian War he was accustomed to stand upon Lilybæum, a Promontory of Sicily, and discover the Fleet coming out of the Harbour of Carthage; he was also able to tell even the Number of the Ships. *Callicrates* made Emmets, and other equally small Creatures, out of Ivory, so that other Men could not discern the Parts of their Bodies. A certain *Myrmecides* was excellent in that kind of Workmanship; who of the same Material carved a Chariot with four Wheels, which a Fly might cover with her Wings. Also he made a Ship that a little Bee might hide with her Wings.[1]

Chapter XXII.

Of Hearing

Of Hearing there is one Example which is wonderful: that the Battle in which Sybaris was destroyed was heard at Olympia on the very same Day it was fought. For the Cim-

---

[1] Peculiarities of eyesight are also recorded in ancient authors. The Emperor Tiberius was able to see better than other men by night; and contrary to the usual habit, best when he first opened his eyes from sleep. Such was also the case with the philosopher Cardan. Fabricius ab Aquapendente knew a man who could see well by night, but not by day, and the Editor was acquainted with two brothers, whose vision was of this kind, and it may be accounted for by the fact, that they were destitute of eyebrows, and had very little eyelashes — *Wern. Club*

brian Victories and the Report of the Victory over the Persians made at Rome by the Castors, on the same Day that it was achieved, were Visions and the Presages of Divine Powers.

Chapter XXIII.

Examples of Patience.

MANY are the Calamities incident to Mankind, which have afforded innumerable Trials of Patience, in suffering Pains of the Body. The most illustrious among Women is the Example of *Leæna* the Courtesan, who, when she was tortured, did not betray *Harmodius* and *Aristogiton*, who slew the Tyrant Among Men is the Example of *Anaxarchus*, who, being tortured for a like Cause, bit off his Tongue with his Teeth, and spat his only Hope of Discovery into the Face of the Tyrant

Chapter XXIV.

Examples of Memory [1]

MEMORY is the greatest Gift of Nature, and most necessary of all others for Life, it is hard to say who deserved the

---

[1] The orator Hortensius was famous for an extensive and accurate memory, which Cicero speaks of with admiration It is said of him, that once sitting at a place where things were exposed to public sale for a whole day, he recited in order all the things that had been sold, their price, and the names of the buyers, and it was afterwards found that he was minutely correct Cicero, comparing him with Lucullus, says, that Hortensius's memory was greater for words, and that of Lucullus for things,—an important distinction, for it is commonly found that those who best remember the one, are deficient in the other Seneca had a remarkable memory for words, so that he was able to repeat two thousand names in the order they were pronounced The art of memory, to which some moderns have made great pretensions, is very ancient; and it was much in use in the middle ages. But it applies to words rather than things, and it requires to be studied as an individual object, and not as means to an end — *Wern Club.*

chief honour therein, considering how many have excelled in its Glory.   King *Cyrus* called every Soldier in his Army by his own Name   *L. Scipio* could do the like by all the Citizens of Rome.   *Cineas*, Ambassador of King *Pyrrhus*, the next Day after he came to Rome, saluted by Name the Senate and Equestrian Order.   *Mithridates*, the King of two-and-twenty Nations of different Languages, ministered Justice to them in that Number of Tongues: and when he made a Speech in the public Assembly respectively to every Nation, he performed it without an Interpreter.   A certain *Charmidas*,[1] a Grecian, rehearsed as if he was reading whatever any Man would call for out of any of the Volumes in the Libraries. At length the Practice of this was reduced into an Art of Memory, which was invented by *Simonides Melicus*, and afterwards brought to Perfection by *Metrodorus Scepsius*, by which a Man might learn to rehearse the same Words of any Discourse after once hearing.   And yet there is nothing in Man so frail, for it is injured by Diseases, Accidents, and by Fear, sometimes in part, and at other Times entirely.   One who was struck with a Stone forgot his Letters only.   Another, by a Fall from the Roof of a very high House, lost the Remembrance of his own Mother, his near Relations, and Neighbours.   Another when sick forgot his own Servants; and *Messala Corvinus*, the Orator, forgot even his own Name [2] So also it often endeavoureth to lose itself, even while the Body is otherwise quiet and in Health.   But let Sleep creep upon us, and it reckoneth, as an empty Mind inquireth, what place it is in.

---

[1] *Carneades*, according to Cicero and Quintilian

[2] A sudden loss of memory on a particular subject is common, though unaccountable   We are told that Curio, the orator, was much given to this ; so that, offering to divide a subject into three heads, he would forget one of them, or perhaps make four   He was to plead on behalf of Sextus Nævius, opposed to Cicero, who was on the side of Titania Corta , when he suddenly forgot the whole cause, and ascribed the fact to the witchcraft of Titania. — *Wern Club*

Julius Cæsar and Augustus.

Chapter XXV.

The Praise of C. Julius Cæsar.

For Vigour of Spirit I judge that *C. Cæsar*, the Dictator, was the most excellent. I speak not now of his Courage and Constancy, nor of his lofty Understanding of all Things under the Expanse of Heaven; but of that proper Strength and Quickness of his, as active as the very Fire. We have heard it reported of him, that he was accustomed to write and read at one Time, to dictate and hear. He would dictate Letters of the utmost Importance to four Secretaries at once: and when he was free from other Business, he would dictate seven Letters at one Time. The same Man fought fifty Battles with Banners displayed: in which Point he alone exceeded *M. Marcellus*, who fought thirty-nine Battles. For, besides his Victories in the Civil Wars, he slew in Battle 1,192,000 of his Enemies; but this, for my own Part, I hold no special Glory of his, considering the great Injury so inflicted on Mankind: and this, indeed, he hath himself confessed, by avoiding to set down the Slaughter that occurred during the Civil Wars. *Pompey* the Great deserveth honour more justly for taking from the Pirates 846 Sail of Ships. But what is proper and peculiar to *Cæsar*, besides what is said above, was his remarkable Clemency, in which he so far surpassed all others, that he himself regretted it. The Example of his Magnanimity was such, that nothing besides can be compared to it. For to reckon up the Spectacles exhibited, with the lavish Expense, with the Magnificence in this Portion of his Works, is to lend a countenance to Luxury. But herein appeared the true and incomparable Loftiness of his unconquered Mind, that when at the Battle of Pharsalia, the Writing-case containing the Letters of *Pompey* was taken, as also those of *Scipio* at Thapsus, he burnt them all with the utmost Fidelity, without having read them.

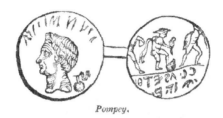

Pompey.

Chapter XXVI.

The Praise of Pompey the Great.

To relate all the Titles, Victories, and Triumphs of *Pompey* the Great, wherein he was equal in the splendour of his Exploits not only to *Alexander* the Great,[1] but even almost to *Hercules* and *Liber Pater*, would redound, not to the Honour only of that one Man, but also to the Grandeur of the Roman Empire. In the first place then, after he had recovered Sicily, from whence his first rising was as a follower of Sylla in the cause of the Republic, he appeared auspiciously

[1] It is clear from various ancient authorities, that it was the ambition of Pompey to imitate and be compared to Alexander; and it was with this view that the title of Great was highly acceptable to him. It was perhaps to humour this foible, and through it to secure him the more effectually to his party, that Sylla was accustomed to pay him extraordinary personal honours: returning his salutation of Imperator with the same title, rising from his seat to salute him when Pompey dismounted from his horse, and uncovering his head at the same time.—*Daleschampius.* In honour of Pompey's having restored the sovereignty of the sea, the reverse of a Roman denarius bears the figure of a Dolphin and Eagle, separated by a Sceptre, with the inscription, *Magn. Procos.*—*Wern. Club.*

fortunate. Having also wholly subdued Africa, and brought
it under obedience, he was brought back in a Triumphal
Chariot, with the name of Great, by reason of the Pillage
there captured, being then only a Roman Knight: a thing
that was never seen before. Immediately passing into the
West, and having brought under obedience 876 Towns,
between the Alps and the borders of Spain, he erected
Trophies on the Pyrenees, with the inscription of his Victory;
and with more nobleness of Mind, said nothing concerning
Sertorius. And after the Civil War was put an end to
(which drew after it all Foreign matters), this Roman Knight
triumphed the second time · being so many times a General
(Imperator), before he was a Soldier (Miles). Afterward
he was sent out on an Expedition to all the Seas, and then
into the East parts: From whence he returned with more
Titles to his Country, after the manner of those who win
Victories at the Sacred Games.[1] Neither, indeed, are those
Crowned, but they Crown their Native Countries; and
so *Pompey* gave as a Tribute to the City these honours
which he dedicated to *Minerva*,[2] out of (*manubiis*) his own
share of the Spoils, with an inscription in this manner
Cn. Pompeius *the Great, Imperator, having finished the
War of Thirty Years: having discomfited, put to flight, slain,
received to submission,* 2,183,000 *Men · sunk or taken* 846
*Ships. brought under his authority Towns and Castles to the
number of* 1538 : *subdued the Lands from the Lake Mæotis
to the Red Sea, hath dedicated of right this Vow to* Minerva.
This is the Summary of his Services in the East. But of the
Triumph which he led on the Third Day before the Calends
of October, when *M Messala* and *M Piso* were Consuls,
the Title ran thus: When he had freed the Sea-coast from
Pirates, had restored to the People of Rome the Sovereignty
of the Sea, he hath triumphed for Asia; Pontus, Armenia,
Paphlagonia, Cappadocia, Cilicia, Syria, the Scythians, Jews,
and the Albani; the Island Iberia, Crete, the Bastarni;
and above these, over the Kings *Mithridates* and *Tigranes.*
But the greatest Glory of all in him was this, (as himself

---

[1] Olympia, Nemæa, Pythia, Isthmia.   [2] Or Victory

said in an Assembly, when he discoursed of his own Exploits). that whereas Asia, when he received it, was the
remotest Province of his Country, he left it in the centre.
If a man would set *Cæsar* on the other side against him,
and review his actions, who of the two seemed greater,
he might indeed reckon up the whole World, which would
amount to an infinite matter.

Chapter XXVII.

The praise of the First Cato.

Many Men have differently excelled in various other
kinds of virtues. But *Cato*,[1] the First of the *Porcian* House,
was thought to have been the most excellent in three
things which are in the highest degree commendable in
Man	He was the best Orator; the best General; and the
best Senator. And yet, in my opinion, all these excellencies
shone out more brightly, although he was not first, in *Scipio
Æmilianus* To say nothing besides of the absence of the
Hatred of so many Men, which *Cato* laboured under. But
if you seek for one especial thing in *Cato*, this is. that he
was judicially called to his answer Forty-four times, and
never was there a Man accused oftener than he; yet he was
always acquitted.

Chapter XXVIII.

Of Valour.

It is a very extensive inquiry, to discover in whom the

---

[1] This Cato appears to have been more successful in obtaining the
esteem than the love of the people; and, indeed, from the evidence of his
"Treatise on Agriculture," appears to have been a niggardly and
shrewd master, whom no one could defraud, and who was ready to
secure every advantage in a bargain He recommends, with the same
indifference, the sale of an ox that was past labour, his rusty iron, and
sickly or worn-out slave

Narratur et prisci Catonis,
Sæpe mero caluisse Virtus — *Wern. Club.*

greatest degree of hardy Courage existed; and more especially if we admit the fabulous tales of Poets. *Q Ennius*
had in greatest admiration *T. Cæcilius Teucer,* and his
brother; and in regard of those Two he added to the others
the Sixth Book of his Annals. But *L. Siccius Dentatus,* a
Tribune of the Commons, not long after the Banishment of
the Kings, when *Sp. Tarpeius* and *A Æternius* were Consuls, by most Voices surpasseth in this kind, having Fought
120 Battles; having been Conqueror in Eight Combats with
a Challenge; being marked with 45 Scars on the front
of his Body, and none behind. Also he won the Spoils of
33 Enemies; he had been presented with 18 Spears, 25
trappings for Horses; 83 Chains; 160 Bracelets; 26
Crowns, of which 14 were Civic, eight of Gold: three
Mural, and one Obsidional, together with a Pension from
the Treasury; and ten Captives with twenty Oxen; and
thus he followed nine Imperators, who chiefly by his means
triumphed. Besides these things, he accused in open court
before the body of the People, which I suppose was the
worthiest act he ever did, *T. Romulus,* one of the lead-
ing Generals (who had been a Consul) and convicted him for
his ill management of his military command Scarcely
inferior to these were the exploits of *Manlius Capitolinus,* if
he had not forfeited them again with such an end of his life.[1]
Before he was seventeen years of age, he had gained two
spoils of his Enemies. He was the first Roman Knight that
received a Mural Crown, with six Civic Crowns, 37 Dona-
tions; and he carried the Scars in the forepart of his Body
of 33 Wounds. He rescued *P. Servilius,* Master of the
Horse, and (in the rescue) was himself wounded in the Arm

[1] Marcus Manlius was the means of preserving the Capitol when it was
nearly taken by the Gauls, from which exploit he obtained the surname
of Capitolinus. Becoming afterwards a warm supporter of the popular
party against the patrician order, he was accused of aiming at the kingly
power, and condemned to death According to Livy (lib vi) "the
tribunes cast him down from the Tarpeian rock; thus the same spot, in
the case of one man, became a monument of distinguished glory and of
the cruellest punishment."—*Wern. Club.*

and Thigh.   Above all other actions, he alone saved the
Capitol, and thereby the whole State, from the Gauls : if he
had not saved it for his own Kingdom !   In these examples
there is indeed much of courage, but yet Fortune hath had the
greater share, and in my judgment no one may justly prefer
any Man before *M. Sergius,* although *Catiline,* his Nephew's
Son, discredited his Name.   In the second Year of his Service
he lost his Right Hand, and in two Services he was wounded
three and twenty times by which means he had little use
of either his Hands or Feet.   But although thus disabled
as a Soldier, he went many a Time after to the Wars,
attended only by one Slave.   Twice he was taken Prisoner
by *Hannibal* (for he did not serve against ordinary Enemies),
and twice he escaped from his bonds, although for twenty
Months he was every Day kept Bound with Chains or
Shackles.   Four times he fought with his Left Hand only,
until two Horses were killed under him   He made himself
a Right Hand of Iron, and he fought with it fastened to his
Arm   He delivered Cremona from Siege, and saved Placentia.   In Gallia, he took twelve Camps of the Enemies:
All which Exploits appear from that Oration of his which he
made in his Prætorship, when his Colleagues repelled him
from the solemn Sacrifices because he was maimed.[1]   What
heaps of Crowns would he have built up if he had been
matched with any other Enemy !   For it is very important,
in our estimate of Courage, to consider in what Time the
Persons lived.   For what Civic Crowns yielded either Trebia
and Ticinus, or Thrasymenus ? what Crown could have been
gained at Cannæ, where the best service of Courage was to
have made an escape ? Others, truly, have vanquished Men ;
but *Sergius* conquered Fortune herself.

---

[1] The ancients were cautious not to admit a mutilated person to the
celebration of sacred rites, observing that such a defect was to be regarded
as a thing of ill-omen, and that, if the victim must be perfect, how much
more does it become the priest to be so ! How careful the Jews were
commanded to be in this respect, appears from the Law of Moses,
Levit. xx. xxi.—*Wern. Club.*

Chapter XXIX.

Of Ingenuities, or the Commendations of some Men for their Ingenuity.

Who is able to make a muster of them that have been
excellent in Ingenuity through so many kinds of Sciences,
and such a variety of Works and Things? Unless perhaps
we agree that *Homer*, the Greek Prophet, excelled all others,
considering either the subject matter or the happy fortune
of his Work   And therefore *Alexander* the Great (for in so
proud a decision I shall cite the Judgment of the highest,
and of those that are beyond Envy), having found among
the Spoils of *Darius*, king of the Persians, his Casket of
sweet Ointments, which was richly embellished with Gold,
Pearls, and precious Stones ; when his friends shewed him
many uses to which the Cabinet might be put, considering
that *Alexander*, as a Soldier engaged in War, and soiled with
its service, was disgusted with those Unguents By *Hercules*,
he said, let it be devoted to the care of *Homer's* Books, that
the most precious Work of the Human Mind should be preserved in the richest of all Caskets The same Prince, when
he took Thebes, commanded that the Dwelling-house and
Family of the Poet *Pindar*[1] should be spared He refounded
the native place (Patria) of *Aristotle* the Philosopher ; and
so mingled a kind Testimony for one who threw light on
all things in the World. *Apollo*, at Delphi, revealed the
murderers of *Archilochus* the Poet. When *Sophocles*, the
Prince of the Tragic Buskin, was dead, and the Walls of
the City were besieged by the Lacedæmonians, *Liber Pater*
commanded that he should be buried ; and he admonished
Lysander their King several times as he slept, to suffer his
delight to be interred   The King made diligent inquiry who

[1] "The Macedonian conqueror bade spare
The house of Pindarus, when temple and tower
Went to the ground "—Milton

lately had died in Athens and by relation of the Citizens
soon found out who the god had signified; and so gave them
peace for the burial.

CHAPTER XXX.

Of Plato, Ennius, Virgil, M. Varro, and M. Cicero.

DIONYSIUS the Tyrant, born otherwise to pride and
cruelty, sent out to meet Plato, the Chief of the Wise
Men, a Ship adorned with Ribbons; and himself went out
in a Chariot with four white Horses, to receive him on the
Shore. *Isocrates* sold one Oration for twenty talents of Gold.
Æschines, the famous Orator of Athens, having at Rhodes
rehearsed that accusation which he had made against
Demosthenes, read also his adversary's defence, by occasion
of which he had been driven into Banishment at Rhodes;
and when the Rhodians wondered at it he said, How much
more would you have wondered, if you had heard him de-
livering it himself! Yielding thus in his Calamity a noble
Testimony to his Adversary. The Athenians exiled *Thucydides* their General but after he had written his Chronicle
they called him home again, wondering at the Eloquence of
the Man whose Courage they had condemned. The Kings
of Egypt and Macedonia gave a strong Testimony how much
they honoured *Mænander* the Comic Poet, in that they
sent Ambassadors for him with a Fleet, but he won himself
greater fame by esteeming more his Studies, than the Favours
of Princes Also the Roman Nobles have afforded Testi-
monies even to Foreigners. Hence *Cn. Pompey*, when he had
ended the War against *Mithridates*, being about to enter the
House of *Posidonius*, the celebrated Professor of Wisdom,
forbad the Lictor to knock at the Door according to custom:
and he to whom both the East and the West parts of the
World had submitted, laid down the lictorial Fasces at the
Gate. *Cato*, surnamed *Censorius*, when there came to Rome
that noble embassage from Athens, consisting of three, the
wisest Men among them, having heard *Carneades* speak,

gave his opinion presently, that those Ambassadors were to be sent away with all speed, because, if that Man argued the case, it would be difficult to find out the Truth.[1] What a change is there now in Men's manners! His decision was, that by any means all Greeks should be expelled from Italy; but his nephew's Son, (*Pronepos*,) *Cato* of Utica, brought one of their Philosophers over with him from the Tribunes of the Soldiers, and another from the Cyprian Embassy. And it is worthy of notice to consider how the same Language was regarded by these two *Catoes*: for by the one it was rejected. But let us now discern the glory of our own Countrymen. *Scipio Africanus* the elder gave order that the Statue of *Q. Ennius*[2]

[1] The account of Cato's conduct with the Greek ambassadors, as given by Pliny, is very different from that by Plutarch, and, from Cato's acknowledged love of eloquence, we may judge more correct. It was not, therefore, the fear that eloquence would render the Romans effeminate, but because the peculiar eloquence of these men, with perhaps the general tendency of Greek studies, was calculated to foster habits of sophistry, and so confound the distinction between truth and falsehood.—*Wern Club.*

[2] He was emphatically the poet of the republic, and must have been a man of sterling worth to have been so highly esteemed by the family of Scipio, and by the censor Cato. "It was well known from a passage in Cicero, and another in Livy, that the sepulchre of the Scipios stood beyond the Porta Capena of Rome; and Livy describes it as being in his time surmounted by three statues· two of them of the Scipios, and the third, as was believed, of the poet Ennius. But it was not until the year A D 1780, that some labourers at work in a vineyard discovered a clue which led to further excavations; and thus the tombs, after having lain undisturbed for upwards of 2000 years, were most unexpectedly brought to light. The original inscriptions have been removed to the Vatican." The following is from "Roma Antica," but is also contained in Montfaucon's "Antiquities," and it must belong to that Scipio who is spoken of by Pliny in the thirty-fourth chapter of this book, though our author has erred in the application.—

> Honc oino ploirume consentiont . R .
> Duonoro optumo fuise . viro .
> Luciom Scipione . filios . Barbati .
> Consol . Censor . Aidilis Hic fuit . A . . .
> Hec cepit Corsica . Aleriaque . Urbe .
> Dedet . tempestatebus aide mereto .

the Poet should be set over his Tomb;[1] to the end that this illustrious name, or indeed the spoil that he had carried away from a third part of the World, should be read over his last ashes, with the title of the Poet   *Divus Augustus* forbad that the Poems of *Virgil* should be burned, contrary to the truth of his will, by which means there grew more credit to the Poet, than if himself had approved his own Verses. *Asinius Pollio* was the first that set up a public Library at Rome, raised from his portion of spoil, and in it he placed the image of *M. Varro*, even while he lived · a thing of as great honour, in my opinion (considering that among the multitude of learned Men he only received this Crown from a Citizen and an excellent Orator), as that other Naval Crown gained him, which *Pompey* the Great bestowed upon him

Thus interpreted :—

> Hunc unum plurimi consentiunt Romæ,
> Bonorum optimum fuisse virum,
> Lucium Scipionem, filius Barbati,
> Consol, Censor, Ædilis, Hic fuit; atque (or, apud vos,
>   or ad eos).
> Hic cepit Corsicam, Aleriamque urbem
> Dedit Tempestatibus ædem merito

"The Roman people agree in thinking this man, Lucius Scipio, the best of all good citizens He was the son of Barbatus, and consul, censor, and ædile among you   He took Corsica, and the city Aleria, and worthily dedicated a temple to the Seasons"

This inscription was dug up in 1616, but was rejected as spurious until the others were discovered   Africanus, the greatest of the Scipios, was not buried in the paternal tomb, but on the shore at Liternum; and the inscription on his tomb is supposed to have been, "Ingrata Patria, ne ossa quidem habes."   The place is supposed to be marked by a modern tower, which from the inscription still retains the name of "Patria."— *Wern. Club.*

[1] "Nor think the great from their high place descend,
    Who choose the Muses' favourite for a friend,
    When mighty Scipio, Rome well pleas'd could see,
    With Ennius join'd, in kindest amity"

Jephson's *Roman Portraits*

"L'intime liaison de Scipion avec le poete Ennius, avec qui il voulut avoir un tombeau commun, fait juger qu'il ne manquoit pas de goût pour les belles lettres"—*Hist Rom. par* Rollin, vol. vii

in the Pirates' War. There are innumerable Roman examples, if a Man would search them out · for this one Nation hath brought forth more excellent Men in every kind than all besides. But why should I be silent concerning the sacrifice of *M. Tullius?* or how shall I best declare his high excellency? how better his praises than from the most ample testimony of the whole body of the People in general, and the acts only of this Consulship, chosen out of the whole course of thy life? Thine Eloquence was the cause that the Tribes renounced the *Agrarian* Law . that is, their own Sustenance. Through thy Persuasion they pardoned *Roscius*, the Author of the Law of the Theatre;[1] they were content to be noted by the Difference of Seat. At thy Request the Children of the Proscribed felt ashamed to sue for honourable Dignities; *Catiline* fled from thy Ability; it was thou that proscribedst *M. Antonius.* Hail, thou who wast the first that wast saluted by the Name of Father of thy Country! the first in the long Robe that deserved a Triumph, and the Laurel for thy Language! the Father indeed of Eloquence and of the Latin Learning · and (as the Dictator *Cæsar*, who was at one Time thine Enemy, hath written of thee) hast obtained a Laurel above all other Triumphs, by how much more Praiseworthy it is to have enlarged the Bounds of Roman Learning than of Roman Dominion.

CHAPTER XXXI.

Of Majesty in Manners

THOSE who, among other Gifts of the Mind, have surpassed the rest of Mankind in Wisdom, were on that Account among the Romans surnamed *Cati*, and *Corculi*. Among the Greeks, *Socrates* was preferred to all beside by the Oracle of *Apollo Pythius*.

---

[1] The Roscian and Julian law, of which L. Roscius Otho, tribune of the people, was the author, which defined and regulated the order of sitting in the public theatre , where, before this, the people mixed indiscriminately with the knights The law seems to have been unpopular, and therefore to have required frequent renewal. Martial (b v ep. 8), has an amusing epigram on its enforcement by Domitian.— *Wern. Club*

Chapter XXXII.

Of Authority.

AGAIN, *Chilo* the Lacedæmonian was of such great Reputation among Men, that his Sayings were held for Oracles; and three Precepts of his were consecrated at Delphi, in these Words. *That each one should know himself. Set thy Mind too much on Nothing· Debt and Law are always accompanied with Misery.* Moreover, when he died for Joy, on receiving Tidings that his Son was Conqueror at Olympia, all Greece solemnised his Funeral

Chapter XXXIII.

Of a divine Spirit.

AMONG Women, in the *Sibyl*[1] there was a divine Spirit, and a certain very noble Companionship with celestial Beings. Of Men, among the Greeks, *Melampus,* and among the Romans, *Martius*

Chapter XXXIV.

Of Nasica

SCIPIO NASICA was judged once by the sworn Senate to be the best Man from the Beginning of Time: but the same Man is remarked to have twice suffered a Repulse by the People in his white Robe. And to conclude, it was not permitted him to die in his own Country; no more, by *Hercules,* than it was that *Socrates,* pronounced the wisest Man by *Apollo,* should die out of Bonds.

Chapter XXXV

Of Modesty.[2]

SULPITIA, Daughter of *Paterculus* and Wife to *Fulvius Flaccus,* by the Sentence in general of the Matrons was pro-

[1] The Sibyls will be referred to in the 34th book.— *Wern. Club.*

[2] It was an ancient law, "Ut Matronis de via decederetur, nihil obscœni presentibus iis vel diceretur vel fieret, neve quis nudum se ab iis conspici

nounced the most modest; and was elected out of a hundred principal Matrons to dedicate the Image of *Venus*, according to the Sybilline Books. *Claudia*, likewise was, by a religious Experiment (proved to be such), by bringing the Mother of the Gods to Rome.

Chapter XXXVI.

Of Piety [1]

TRULY, in all Parts of the World, there have been found infinite Examples of Piety; but one Example of this occurred at Rome, to which none beside can be compared. There was a young Woman of humble Condition among the common People, and therefore of no account, who lately had been in Childbed, and whose Mother was shut up in Prison for some great Offence; and when this Daughter obtained leave to have Access to her Mother, and constantly by the Jailer was narrowly searched, that she might not bring to her any Food, she was at last detected suckling her with the Milk of her Breasts On account of this astonishing circumstance the Life of the Mother was granted to the Piety of the Daughter, and both of them had continued Sustenance allowed them, and the Place where this happened was consecrated to this Deity (*Piety*). so that when *C. Quintius* and *M. Acilius* were Consuls, the Temple of Piety was built, in the very Place where this Prison stood, and where now standeth the Theatre of *Marcellus*. The Father of the *Gracchi*

pateretur, alioquin criminis capitalis reus haberetur" That they should give way to matrons, that no obscenity should either be spoken or done in their presence, and that no man should suffer himself to be within sight of them naked. if otherwise, he should be held guilty of a capital crime. —*Wern Club.*

[1] In the language of the ancients, piety is not to be understood as having a reference to God, but only as expressing the law of social kindness among the relations of blood or marriage. It proceeds only from revelation that the latter is made to be a duty flowing from the former, and hence, while among Heathens the most vicious of mankind in his general character might also be among the most pious, among Christians no such anomalies can exist.—*Wern Club*

having taken two Serpents within his House, received an Answer (from the Soothsayers), that if he would himself live the female Snake must be killed. Truly then, said he, rather kill the male, for *Cornelia* is young, and may have more Children This was in order to spare his Wife's Life, in consideration of the Good she might do to the Commonwealth. And so it fell out soon after. *M. Lepidus* so entirely loved his wife *Apuleia*, that he died when she was divorced from him. *P. Rutilius* was laid by from some slight Illness, but hearing of his Brother's Repulse in his Request for the Consulship, died immediately. *P. Catienus Philotimus* so loved his Master (*Patronus*), that though he was made his Heir to all that he had, yet he cast himself into his funeral Fire.

Chapter XXXVII.

Of the Excellency of many Arts, as Astrology, Grammar, and Geometry.

In the Knowledge of various Arts a great Number of Men have excelled, but we will only take the Flower of them, and touch them lightly. In Astrology, *Berosus* was eminent; to whom the Athenians, for his divine Predictions, caused a Statue with a golden Tongue to be erected in the public Gymnasium. In Grammar, *Apollodorus* was distinguished; and therefore he was highly honoured by the Amphitryons of Greece. In Medicine, *Hippocrates*[1] excelled; and having foretold a Pestilence that was approaching from Illyria, to cure it he sent his Disciples to the surrounding Cities. In Recompense of which good Desert, Greece decreed for him the like Honours as to *Hercules*. For the same Science, King *Ptolemy* gave to *Cleombrotus* of Cea, at the sacred Megalensian Rites, a hundred Talents, especially for curing King *Antiochus*. *Critobulus* likewise acquired great Fame for drawing an Arrow out of King *Philip's* Eye, and

[1] The remarkable observation at the end of the 50th chapter, which appears to be confirmed by the course of the most formidable epidemics of modern times, will account for this skill in this most eminent physician

so curing the Wound that the Sight remained, and only a
Blemish of the Mouth remained. But *Asclepiades* the Pru-
sian surpassed all others, having founded a new Sect; he
rejected the Ambassadors and large Promises offered by
King *Mithridates;* discovered a Method to make Wine medi-
cinable for the Sick; and recovered a Man to his former
state of Health, who was carried forth to be buried: and
chiefly he attained to the greatest Name for the Engagement
made against Fortune, that he would not be reputed a Physician if he ever were known to be in any way diseased. And
he was Conqueror; for when he was very aged he fell down
over the Stairs, and was killed. A high Testimony for Knowledge in Geometry and the making of Engines was given by
M. Marcellus to *Archimedes,* who in the storming of Syra-
cuse gave express Command concerning him alone, that no
Violence should be done to him; but military Imprudence
disappointed the Order. *Ctesiphon* of Gnosos is much praised
for having wonderfully erected the Temple of *Diana* at
Ephesus. *Philon,* likewise, was highly esteemed for making
the Arsenal at Athens, which was able to receive a thousand
Ships; and *Ctesibius* for a Method of forming Wind Instruments, and the Discovery of Engines to draw Water: *Dino-*

of antiquity, who had the benefit of access to the long series of records of
the family of the Asclepiadæ, and whose public spirit was equal to his
abilities and opportunities.— *Wern. Club.*

Medal of Hippocrates, from an engraving in Dr. Mead's Harveyan Oration, 1723.

crates, also, for devising the Model of Alexandria in Egypt, when *Alexander* founded it. To conclude, this great Commander (Imperator) forbade, by Edict, that any Man should paint him but *Apelles* · that any one should carve his Statue besides *Pyrgoteles* and that any one except *Lysippus* should cast his Image in Brass. In which Arts many have excelled.

Chapter XXXVIII.

Surprising Works of Artificers.[1]

King *Attalus* offered by Competition, for one Picture by *Aristides* the Theban Painter, a hundred Talents. *Cæsar* the Dictator bought for eight Talents two Pictures, the *Medea* and *Ajax* of *Timomachus*, which he meant to consecrate in the Temple of *Venus Genetrix* King *Candaulas* bought of *Butarchus* a Picture of the Destruction of the Magnetes, of no great Size, and weighed it in an equal Scale with Gold. King *Demetrius*, surnamed *Expugnator*, forbore to set Rhodes on Fire, because he would not burn a Picture by *Protogenes*, which was placed in that part of the Wall which he attacked. *Praxiteles* was ennobled on account of a marble Statue, the Gnidian *Venus*, remarkable particularly for the mad Love of a certain young Man; which Statue was so esteemed by King *Nicomedes*, that he endeavoured to obtain it in full Payment of a large Debt they owed him. The *Jupiter Olympius* still affordeth daily Testimony to *Phydias*. (*Jupiter*) *Capitolinus*, and *Diana* of Ephesus yield Testimony to *Mentor*: and the Instruments of this Art were consecrated by them in their Temples.

Chapter XXXIX.

Of Bondsmen.[2]

I have never obtained the Knowledge to this Day of a

---

[1] The subject of statues and paintings is more fully treated of in the 34th and 35th books — *Wern Club*

[2] The money which Marc Antony paid for a couple of boys is given in the 12th chapter of this book. — *Wern Club.*

Man born a Slave who was valued so high as *Daphnis*, the Grammarian, was : for *Cn. Pisaurensis* sold him for 300,700 Sesterces to *M Scaurus*, Prince of the City. In this our Age Stage-players have gone beyond this Price, and that not a little , but they had bought their Freedom. And no Wonder, for it is reported that the Actor *Roscius* in former Time had yearly earned 500,000 Sesterces. Unless any one may desire in this Place to hear of the Treasurer of the Armenian War, a little while before carried on on account of *Tyridates,* and who was made free by *Nero* for 120,000 Sesterces But, by *Hercules,* it was the War that cost so much, and not the Man. Like as *Sutorius Priscus* gave to *Sejanus* 3500 Sesterces for *Pæzon,* one of his Eunuchs : but this was more for Lust than for his Beauty But he executed this infamous Bargain at a Time when the City was in Sorrow, and no Man had any Leisure to utter a Word in reproach.

Chapter XL.

The Excellency of Nations.

It will be scarcely questioned, that of all Nations in the World, the Romans[1] are the most excellent for every Virtue ; but to determine who was the happiest Man is above the reach of human Understanding, considering that some fix

---

[1] The Romans were a haughty people; and they had much to be proud of for we have no records of a nation that ever understood the arts of government or war better than they. But of what is properly denominated science they knew little ; and the Chevalier Bunsen remarks, that they did not reverence or recognise human rights in any nation beside their own The love of knowledge and truth for their own sakes was altogether unknown among them, and they never conferred benefit except for their own advantage. Their calculating self-love made them, essentially, beneficial rulers , but they manifested no esteem for their subjects , and we may add, that the most probable motive which actuated Plutarch in writing his " Lives," and especially for arranging them in parallels, was to shew covertly that men, as great in all respects as any Romans, had lived in Greece. Germanicus is judged to have been an exception to this Roman constitution of mind ; and probably there were others of lower rank ; but they are to be regarded as simply the exceptions

their highest Advantage in one Thing, others in another,[1] and every one measureth it according to his several Disposition : but if we wish to form a correct Judgment, throwing aside all the Ambition of Fortune, it may be concluded, that there is not a Man in the World to be accounted happy. And, therefore, Fortune dealeth liberally and indulgently with any one, if he may justly be called not unhappy ; because if there be no other Things, yet surely a Man may be ever in Fear lest Fortune should grow tired of him but let him admit this Fear, and there can be no solid Happiness. What should I say, moreover, to this ? — that no Man is at all Times wise ? I wish that this were false, and not, in the Judgment of most Men, a Poet's Word only   But such is the Folly of mortal Men, that they are very ingenious in deceiving themselves so that they reckon after the Custom of the Thracians, who, by Stones marked with different Colours, which they cast into an Urn, institute the Trial of every Day, and at their last Day they separate these Stones one from another and count them : and thus give Judgment concerning

to the general rule   It is in the spirit of Pliny's remark that Martial begins his Epigram to Trajan, lib xii cp 8 —

> " Terrarum Dea, gentiumque Roma,
> Cui par est nihil, et nihil secundum "

> Goddess of lands and nations, Rome,
> Nothing to which can equal come,
> And nothing second   *Wern Club*

[1] The reader is referred to the fourth epistle of Pope's " Essay on Man," for a more extended and poetical developement of this sentiment

The sentiments in the latter part of this chapter are re-echoed in the Book of Ecclesiastes by Solomon, where he employs the advantages arising from his high situation and consummate wisdom in seeking to discover whether, on merely human principles, there was any such thing as human happiness in the world. The result was the same as is expressed by Pliny, but with the advantage on the side of the Hebrew sage, that he was able to find in his more elevated principles a security of which Pliny was altogether ignorant.   The value of the Life and Immortality which have been brought to light by the Gospel, can best be estimated when we see the gloom which occupied the mind of even such a man as Pliny without it   The highest happiness detailed in the next chapter (xli) is much below the aspiration of every Christian — *Wern Club*

each one. But what if the Day, flattered with a white Stone, have in it the Beginning of some Misfortune? How many a Man hath entered upon Empires, which have turned to their Affliction? How many have lost their Goods, and at last have been brought to utter Ruin? Certainly these are good Things if a Man could enjoy them fully for one Hour. But thus stands the Case, that one Day is the Judge of another, and the last Day judgeth all; and therefore there is no trust to be placed in them. To say nothing of this: that our good Fortunes are not equal to our bad even in Number; nor is any one Joy to be weighed against the least of our Sorrows. Alas for our empty and imprudent Diligence! We reckon our Days by Number, whereas we should estimate them by Weight.

Chapter XLI.

Of the highest Happiness.

LAMPIDO, a Lacedæmonian Lady, is the only Woman that ever was known to have been the Daughter of a King, a King's Wife, and the Mother of a King Also, *Pherenicè* alone was the Daughter, Sister, and Mother of them that won the Victory at the Olympian Games. In one Family of the *Curiones* there were three Orators, one after another, by descent from Father to Son. The Family of the *Fabii* alone afforded three Presidents of the Senate in succession, who were *M. Fabius Ambustus, Fabius Rullianus* the Son, and *Q. Fabius Gurges* the Nephew.

Chapter XLII.

Examples of Change of Fortune.

WE have innumerable other examples of the variety of Fortune: for what great Joys did she ever give, but such as sprung from some Evil? Or what great Calamities that have not followed upon the highest Joys?

Chapter XLIII

Of one twice Proscribed. of Q Metellus, and L. Sylla.

M. *Fidustius*, a Senator, having been Proscribed by *Sylla*, was preserved for six-and-thirty Years; but he was afterwards Proscribed the second time: for he outlived *Sylla* and continued to the time of *Antony;* and it so happened that by him he was Proscribed again, for no other reason but because he had been so before. Fortune was pleased that *P. Ventidius* alone should triumph over the Parthians: but she had led him, while a Boy, in the Asculan triumph of *Cn. Pompeius Strabo*, although *Massurius* testifieth, that he was so led in triumph twice. *Cicero* saith,[1] that he was at first but a Muleteer to serve the Camp with Meal. Many others affirm that in his Youth he was a poor Soldier, and served as a Footman in his Caliga (or Military Foot Clothing). *Balbus Cornelius* was also the Senior Consul but he had been judicially accused, delivered over to the Counsel of the Judges, so that the right of the Rods[2] was on him. But this Man was the first Roman Consul of Foreigners, and even of those born within the Ocean; having attained to that Dignity, which our Forefathers denied to Latium Among the distinguished is *L Fulvius,* who was Consul of the rebellious Tusculans; but when he had passed over to the Romans, he was presently by the whole People advanced to the same Honour among them · and he was the only Man who triumphed at

[1] Epist x 18

[2] This "right" was according to a law whose origin is disputed, but it seems to have been ancient According to Dalechampius' note on the passage, no Roman citizen could be sentenced by the magistrate to the rods, or be put to death, for any other crime than murder, and of the latter it was necessary that he should be regularly convicted But it would appear that he might be condemned to exile with little ceremony Before the passing of this law, a Roman citizen, as well as a foreigner, if sentenced to death, was scourged as a matter of course previous to the execution of the higher sentence The tendency of this law to confer protection is seen in the instance of St Paul, Acts of the Apostles, xvi 37, and xxii 25.—*Wern. Club*

Rome over them whose Consul he had been, even in the same Year in which he was himself an Enemy in the Field L. *Sylla* was the only Man, until our time, that challenged to himself the surname of *Felix*,[1] or the Fortunate, but the Title was adopted from shedding the Blood of Citizens, and by waging War against his Country. And by what arguments was grounded this good Fortune of his? That he was able to Proscribe, and put to Death, so many thousands of the Citizens! O mistaken interpretation, and unhappy even to future time! For were not they more blessed, who then lost their Lives, whose Death at this day we pity, than *Sylla*, whom no Man living at this day doth not abhor? Moreover, was not his end more cruel than the misery of all those who were Proscribed by him? for his own wretched Body consumed itself,[2] and bred its own torment. And although we may believe that he dissembled all this by his last Dream,[3] wherein he lay as if he were dead, upon which he gave out this Speech, that himself alone had overcome Envy by Glory; yet in this one thing he confessed, that his Felicity was defective, inasmuch as he had not Consecrated the Capitol. *Q. Metellus*, in that Funeral Oration which he made in commendation of *L. Metellus*, his Father, left it written of

[1] There was scarcely a title more coveted by the Romans than this of Fortunate, for they took it to be a decisive evidence of the ability which had led to success Appian says that there existed in front of the Rostra in Rome, a golden equestrian figure of Sylla, with the inscription, "Syllæ Imperat fortunato" But from Pliny we learn that his cruelty had caused his memory to be held in little estimation by posterity — *Wern Club*

[2] The cause of the death of Sylla is not quite certain Appian (De Bell Civ i 105) says he died of an attack of fever, while others inform us that the loathsome disease called *phthiriasis* was the cause of his death Of this latter opinion were Plutarch, Pliny, and Pausanias — *Wern Club*

[3] Plutarch says, "Sylla tells us," in his Commentaries, "that the Chaldæans had predicted, that after a life of glory he would depart in the height of his prosperity" He further acquaints us, that his son, who died a little before Metella, appeared to him in a dream, dressed in a mean garment, and desired him to bid adieu to his cares, and go along with him to his mother Metella, with whom he should live at ease, and enjoy the charms of tranquillity — *Wern Club*

him, that he had been Pontifex, twice Consul, Dictator, Master of the Horse, one of the Quindecimvirs deputed for Division of Lands, and that in the first Punic War he led many Elephants in triumph · moreover, that he had accomplished ten of the greatest and best Things, in seeking which the Wise spend their whole time. for his desire was to be among the foremost of Warriors, an excellent Orator, a very powerful Commander (Imperator); to have the conduct of the most important Affairs, to be in the highest place of Honour, to be eminent for Wisdom, to be accounted a principal Senator, to attain to great Wealth by good Means, to leave many Children behind him, and to be the noblest personage in the City. That these perfections fell to him, and to none but him since the Foundation of Rome, it were long and useless now to confute: but it is abundantly answered by one instance, for this same *Metellus* became Blind in his old Age; having lost his Eyes in a Fire, when he would have saved the Palladium[1] out of the Temple of *Vesta:* an act worthy of being remembered; but the event was unhappy In regard of which it is not proper to term him Unfortunate (Infelix); and yet he cannot be called Fortunate (Felix). The People of Rome granted to him a Privilege, which no Man before him in the World was known to have: that he should be conveyed in a Chariot to the Senate-house as often as he went to sit at the Council. a great and elevated Prerogative, but it was allowed him as a Compensation for his Eyes.

Chapter XLIV.

Of another Metellus

A Son likewise of this *Q Metellus*, who gave out those Commendations concerning his Father, is reckoned among

---

[1] It was one of the figments of Roman divinity, that this image of the tutelary Pallas had existed in ancient Troy, from whence, with Æneas, it had transferred the empire to the imperial city of Rome. A similar image existed at Ephesus (Acts of the Apostles, xxix 35), and it has been supposed that the fall from the sky, of at least the materials of the image, may not have been imaginary. The descent of an aerolite was, probably as common in ancient times as in modern — *Wern Club*

the most rare examples of human Felicity; for besides the most honourable Dignities, and the Surname of *Macedonicus*, he was borne to the Funeral Pile by four Sons, one being the Prætor, and the other three having been Consuls: of which two had triumphed, and one had been Censor: which remarkable things had happened to few. And yet in the very flower of these Honours, as he was returning from the Field, about Noon-day, he was seized by *Catinius Labeo*, surnamed *Macerio*, a Tribune of the Commons, whom he by virtue of his Censorship had expelled out of the Senate; and the Forum of the Capitol being empty, he took him away by force to the Tarpeian Rock, with an intention to cast him down headlong. A number came running about him of that company which called him Father; but, as was unavoidable in so sudden a case, slowly, and as if attending a Funeral; with the absence also of a right to make Resistance, and repel the inviolable Authority · so that he was likely to have Perished even for his Virtue and faithful Execution of his Censorship, if there had not been one Tribune found, with much difficulty, to step between and oppose himself, by which means he was rescued, even from the utmost point of Death. He lived afterwards by the liberality of other Men: for all his Goods from that day forward were devoted, from his Condemnation · as if he had not suffered Punishment enough to have his Neck so writhed, as that the Blood was squeezed out at his Ears. And truly I would reckon it among his Calamities, that he was an Enemy to the later *Africanus*, even by the Testimony of *Macedonicus* himself. These were his words to his Children: Go, my Sons, and do honour to his Obsequies; for the Funeral of a greater Citizen ye will never see. And this he said to them, when they had conquered Crete and the Balearic Islands, and had worn the Diadem in triumph · being himself already entitled *Macedonicus*. But if we consider that only injury offered to him, who can justly deem him happy, being exposed to the pleasure of his Enemy, far inferior to *Africanus*, and so to come to confusion? What were all his Victories to this one Disgrace? What Honours and Chariots did not Fortune

cast down by her violence, when a Censor was dragged through the middle of the City (the only way indeed to bring him to his Death); dragged to the Capitol itself, to which he had ascended triumphant · but he never so dragged along those Captives, for whose Spoils he triumphed. And this Outrage was the greater in regard of the Felicity which ensued ; considering that this *Macedonicus* was in danger to have lost so great an Honour as this solemn and stately Sepulture, in which he was carried forth to his Funeral Fire by his triumphant Children, as if he had triumphed again at his very burial. Truly that can be no sound Felicity, which is interrupted by any Indignity of Life, much less by so great a one as this. To conclude, I know not whether there be more cause to glory for the modest carriage of Men, or to grieve at the Indignity, that among so many *Metelli* so audacious a Villany as this of *Catinius* was never revenged.

Chapter XLV.

Of Divus Augustus.[1]

Also, in *Divus Augustus*, whom all the World declareth to be in this rank of fortunate Men, if we diligently consider all things, we perceive great Changes of the Human lot Driven by his Uncle from the Generalship of the Horse, and, notwithstanding his Petition, seeing *Lepidus* preferred to that place, he laboured under the reproach of the Proscription ; and for being one of the Triumvirate, united with the most wicked Citizens, and this with a less than equal share (of the Roman Empire), for *Antony* obtained the greatest Portion. He was Sick at the Battle of Philippi ; his flight, and while still Sick, for three Days his lying hidden in a Marsh ; so that (as *Agrippa* and *Mecænas* confess), he grew into a kind of Dropsy, and his Sides were distended with Water under the Skin, his Shipwreck in

---

[1] It is a proof of the imperfect manner in which history has been generally treated, that Suetonius has written the life of Augustus Cæsar without the mention of a great part of these particulars, and of none of them in the point of view here given.—*Wern Club*

Sicily, and there likewise he was glad to remain concealed in a Cave; then he was put to flight at Sea, and when the whole power of his Enemies was hard on him, he besought *Proculeius* to put him to Death; how he was perplexed by the Contentions at Perusium, the anxiety he was in at the Battle of Actium, and for the issue of the Pannonian War; for the fall of a Bridge, so many Mutinies among his Soldiers, so many dangerous Diseases of his Body, the suspected Allegiance of *Marcellus;* the shame of Banishing *Agrippa;* his Life so many times attempted by secret Plots, the suspected Deaths of his Children, the sad Afflictions thereby; and not altogether for his Childless condition; the Adultery of his Daughter, and her Contrivances for taking his Life away made known to the World; the reproachful Retreat of *Nero,* his Wife's Son, another Adultery committed by one of his Nieces: above all this, so many united Evils, as the want of Pay for his Soldiers, the Rebellion of Illyricum, the Mustering of Slaves; the Scarcity of Young Men; a Pestilence in the City; Famine and Drought through Italy, a deliberate Resolution of Dying, having to that end Fasted four Days and Nights, and in that time received into his Body the greater part of his own Death. Besides these things, the Slaughter of *Varius's* Forces, and the foul stain of his Honour; the putting away of *Posthumus Agrippa* after his Adoption, and the desire that he had for him after his Banishment, then the Suspicion that he conceived of *Fabius,* and the disclosing of his Secrets; and again his Opinions concerning his Wife and *Tiberius,* which surpassed all his other Cares. To conclude, that God, of whom I do not know whether he rather obtained Heaven than deserved it, left behind him for his Heir the Son of his Enemy.

Chapter XLVI.

Whom the Gods Judge the most Happy.

I cannot pass over in this Discourse the Oracles of Delphos, delivered from the God to chastise the Folly of Men. Two of them are these: That *Phedius,* who but a while before Died for his Country, was the most Happy. Again, being consulted by *Gyges*, the most sumptuous King in all the Earth, the answer was, that *Aglaus Psophidius* was the more Happy. This *Aglaus* was a Man somewhat advanced in Years, dwelling in a very narrow corner of Arcadia, where he had a little Estate, which himself cultivated; and it was sufficient with its yearly Produce to Support him plentifully, out of it he never went so that (as appeared by his course of Life,) as he coveted very little, so he experienced as little Trouble while he Lived.

Chapter XLVII.

Whom, while Living, they ordered to be Worshipped as a God [1]

By the appointment of the same Oracle, and by the approbation of *Jupiter*, the Sovereign of the Gods, *Euthymus* the Wrestler, who always was Conqueror at Olympia, except once, was Consecrated a God while he lived, and knew of it, he was born at Locri, in Italy, where one Statue of his, as also another at Olympia, were both on one Day struck with Lightning which I see *Callimachus* wondered at, as if nothing else were worthy of Admiration; and gave order that he should be Sacrificed to, as to a God. which was performed accordingly, both while he Lived and after he was Dead. A thing that I wonder at more than at any thing else that the Gods should have been pleased with such a thing.

[1] It was scarcely more reasonable to worship a man after he was dead than during his life, and yet Pliny must have joined in the worship of Augustus and Julius Cæsar, and have been conscious, as appears from several places of his writings, that the greatest gods of his country had formerly been living men. The egregious vanity of desiring to be supposed a god was felt by Alexander the Great, to whose application for recognition in this character the Lacedæmonians replied by an edict, that "If Alexander wished to be a god, he might be a god." Pliny lived to see the brother of his patron Titus, Domitian, exemplify the absurdity of which he complains, for it appears that the latter emperor was more than ordinarily fond of this assumption of divinity. — *Wern. Club*

Chapter XLVIII.

Of the longest Extent of Life.

The extent and duration of Man's Life are rendered uncertain, not only by the Situation of Places, but also from Examples, and the peculiar lot of his Nativity. *Hesiod*, the fiist Writer who has treated on this Subject, in his Fabulous Discourse (as I regard it), embracing many things about the Age of Man, saith that a Crow lives nine times as long as we; the Stags four times as long as the Crow; and the Ravens thrice as long as they. And his other remarks about the Nymphs and the Phœnix are still more Fabulous. *Anacreon* the Poet, assigneth to *Arganthonius*, King of the Tartessi, 150 Years: and to *Cyniras*, King of the Cypri, ten Years longer: to *Ægimius*, 200 *Theopompus* affirmeth that *Epimenides*, the Gnossian, died when he was 157 Years old. *Hellanicus* hath Written, that among the Epii, in Ætolia, there are some who continue full 200 Years. and with him agreeth *Damastes;* adding also, that there was one *Pictoreus* among them, a Man of exceeding Stature, and very Strong, who lived even to 300 Years. *Ephorus* saith, that the Kings of Arcadia usually lived to 300 Years *Alexander Cornelius* writeth of one *Dando* in Illyrica, who lived 500 Years. *Xenophon* in his " Periplus," maketh mention of a King of a People upon the Sea-coasts, who lived 600 Years. and as if he had not lied enough already, he saith, that his Son came to 800. All these strange reports proceed from ignorance of the times past, for some reckoned the Summer for one Year, and the Winter for another. Others reckoned every Quarter for a Year, as the Arcadians, whose Year was but three Months. Some, as the Egyptians, count every change of the Moon for a Year; and therefore some of them are reported to have lived 1000 Years. But to pass to things acknowledged as true, it is almost certain, that *Arganthonius*, King of Calais, reigned 80 Years; and it is supposed that he was 40 Years old when he began to Reign It is undoubted, that *Masanissa* reigned 60 Years; and also that

Gorgias the Sicilian lived 108 Years   *Q. Fabius Maximus* continued Augur for 63 Years.   *M. Perpenna*, and of late, *L Volusius Saturninus*, out-lived all those Senators who had sat in Council with them when they were Consuls. *Perpenna* left but seven of those Senators alive whom he had chosen in his Censorship: and he lived himself 98 Years   Where, by the way, one thing cometh to my Mind worth the noting. that there was one Space of five Years, and never but one, in which not one Senator died; and that was from the time that *Flaccus* and *Albinus* the Censors finished their Lustrum, to the coming in of the next Censors; which was from the Year after the Foundation of the City, 579   *M. Valerius Corvinus* lived 100 Years complete; and between his first Consulate and his sixth, were 46 Years. He took his Seat on the Curule Chair 21 Times, and no Man ever besides him so often.   *Metellus* the Pontifex lived full as long as he

To come now to Women. *Livia* the Wife of *Rutilius* lived more than 97 Years.   *Statilia*, a noble Lady, in the Time of *Claudius* the Prince, was 99 Years of Age: *Cicero's* Wife, *Terentia*, was 103 Years old.   *Clodia*, Wife to *Osilius*, saw 115 Years; and she had 15 Children   *Luceia*, a Comic Actress, appeared on the Stage for 100 Years.   *Galeria Copiola*, a Mimic Actress, was brought again upon the Stage when *Cn. Pompeius* and *Q. Sulpitius* were Consuls, at the solemn Plays vowed for the Health of *Divus Augustus*, when she was in the 104th Year of her Age: the first Time that she entered on the Stage was 91 Years before, when she was brought thither by *M Pomponius*, Ædile of the Commons, in the Year that *C. Marius* and *Cn. Carbo* were Consuls; and once again *Pompey* the Great, at the dedication of his great Theatre, returned the old Woman to the Stage for the wonder of the thing.   Also *Asconius Pædianus* writeth, that *Samula* lived 110 Years; and therefore I wonder the less that *Stephanio* (who was the first of the Long Robe who appointed Dancing) danced in both the Secular Games, as well those that were set out by *Divus Augustus*, as those which *Claudius Cæsar* exhibited in his fourth Consulship; considering that between the one and the other there were but 63 Years, and yet *Stephanio* lived for a considerable Time after *Mutianus* witnesseth, that in Tempsis, which is the Crest of the Mountain Tmolus, People lived 150 Years At that Age, *T. Fullonius*, of Bononia, entered his Name in the Census at the Time that *Claudius Cæsar* held the Registry, and that he was so old indeed, appeared by comparing together several Registries that he had before made, as also by circumstances that had occurred in his Lifetime; for the Emperor took care in that way to find out the Truth.[1]

Chapter XLIX

Of Differences in the Nativities.

This Point would require the Advice of the Science of the Stars; for *Epigenes* saith, that it is not possible for a Man to live a hundred and twenty-two Years; and *Berosus* is of opinion, that one cannot pass an hundred and seventeen. That Calculation holdeth good which *Petosiris* and *Necepsos* have delivered, and which they call *Tetartemorion*, from a portion of three Signs, according to which account it

[1] The length of life detailed in the Mosaic records was unknown to the Greeks, who had only retained an obscure traditionary remembrance of it, and of the great stature and strength with which it was supposed to be accompanied But that Pliny's mode of interpreting it, by a peculiar method of explaining the length of the year, will not apply to the narrative in the Book of Genesis, appears from the fact that the same history records the reduction of the length of human life, by sudden transitions, to at last threescore and ten years, which we are compelled to measure by the same scale as the former

As a general summary of the duration of life in historical times, the "History of Life and Death," by Lord Bacon, may be consulted Fuller mentions James Sands, of Horborne in Staffordshire, who lived 140 years, and his wife 120 The Countess of Desmond, known to Sir W Rawleigh, lived to about 140 years, and had new teeth three several times Thomas Parr was born in 1483, married at the age of eighty, and in the space of thirty-two years had only two children. At the age of 120 he had another child, and died aged 150 years.— *Wern Club*

is evident, that in the Tract of Italy, Men may reach to a
hundred and twenty-six Years. They denied that a Man
could possibly pass the ascendant Space of 90 Degrees
(which they call Anaphoras), and that even these are cut
short, either by the encounter of malevolent Planets, or by
the radiations of them or the Sun. Again, the Sect of *Ascle-*
piades[1] affirm, that the appointed Length of Life proceedeth
from the Stars, but concerning the utmost term, it is uncertain But they say, that the longer Ages are Rare, because
the greatest Number by far have their Nativity at the
marked Moments of the Hours of the Moon, or of Days
according to the Number of Seven or Nine (which are
Daily and Nightly observed): by the gradual declining Law
of the Years, called Climacteric,[2] and such as are so Born
scarcely exceed the fifty-fourth Year But here, first, the
Uncertainty of the Art itself declareth how doubtful this
matter is To this are added the Observations and Instances
of the very recent Census, which within the Space of four
Years, the Imperators, Cæsars, Vespasians, Father and
Son, Censors, have accomplished. And here we need not
search every Cupboard, we will only set down the examples
of the middle part, between the Apennine and the Po At
Parma, three Men were found of the Age of a hundred and

---

[1] In book xxvi c 3, Pliny gives a more precise, and not very com-
plimentary, account of this physician.— *Wern Club*

[2] A large portion of the physiological learning of ancient physicians
consisted in the arithmetical calculation of types and periods of vital and
diseased actions, in connexion with which they also arranged the motions
of the celestial bodies and their influences. It thus became necessary,
that he who was a physician in the modern meaning of the word should
also be able to interpret the stars, and to apply mathematical reasoning
to the laws of health and disease The calculation of climacterical
years, and the ultimate duration of human life, were thus decided by a
combination of intricate mathematical probabilities These climacteric
years were formed on the multiplication of the number seven by the
unit numbers, and at them the most important of the periodic changes
of the body were accomplished The highest number thus multiplied
formed the grand climacteric, after which the changes produced a retro-
gression towards feebleness and decay, the danger of which was ever
greatest at the climacterics See book ii c 52 — *Wern Club*

twenty Years: at Brixelus, one that was a hundred and twenty-five Years, at Parma, two of a hundred and thirty Years; at Placentia, one of a hundred and thirty-one; at Faventia, there was one Woman a hundred and thirty-two Years old, at Bonona, *L. Terentius*, the Son of *Marcus*, and at Ariminum *M. Aponius*, were a hundred and fifty. *Tertulla* was a hundred and thirty-seven. About Placentia there is a Town on the Hills, named Velleiacium, in which six Men brought a Certificate that they had lived a hundred and ten Years; four likewise brought one of about a hundred Years; one of a hundred and forty,[1] namely *M Mutius*, son of *Marcus* surnamed *Galerius Felix*. But because we will not dwell long in a matter so commonly allowed, in the eighth Region of Italy there were found in the Roll fifty-four Persons of one hundred Years of Age; fifty-seven of a hundred and ten; two, of a hundred and twenty-five; four, of a hundred and thirty, as many that were a hundred and thirty-five, or a hundred and thirty-seven Years, and three Men of a hundred and forty. Another inconstant variety in mortal Men: *Homer* reporteth, that *Hector* and *Polydamas* were born in one Night, though Men of such a different Fortune. While *C. Marius* was Consul, and *Cn. Carbo* with him, who had been twice before Consul, the fifth Day before the Calends of June, *M. Cæcilius Ruffus* and *C. Licinius Calvus* were born on the same Day, and both of them indeed were Orators· but their fate was very different And this is seen daily to happen throughout the World, that among those born in one Hour some are Kings, and others Beggars, some Lords and others Slaves.

CHAPTER L

Various Examples of Diseases

PUB. CORNELIUS RUFUS, who was Consul with *M. Curius*, dreamed that he had Lost his Sight, and so it proved when he awoke On the other Hand, *Phalereus* being given

---

[1] Dr Holland seems to have read "one hundred and fourteen"—
Wern Club

over by the Physicians for the Disease of Vomica, being
stabbed in his Breast, found a Remedy in his Enemy.   *Q.
Fabius Maximus,* Consul, engaging in a Battle with the Nations
of the Allobroges and Averni, near the River Isara, on the
sixth Day before the Ides of August; in which double
action he Slew of his Enemies 13,000; he was in the Contest
delivered from his Fever   This gift of Nature, truly, whatever is bestowed on us, is frail and uncertain   and in those
in whom it exists in the largest Measure, it is but short and
evil if we consider the whole Course of it from Beginning to
End   Because if we count our repose by Night, a Man
may be truly said to live but one half of his Life, for that
Half of it which is spent in Sleep may be compared to Death,
and if he cannot Sleep, it is a Punishment.   Nor are the
Years of our Infancy to be reckoned, for this Age is void of
Sense; nor those of old Age, which is the punishment of a
disposition to live   What shall I speak of so many kinds of
Dangers, so many Diseases, so many Fears, so many Cares,
so many Prayers for Death, that we Pray for nothing more
frequently? and therefore Nature knoweth not what better
thing to give a Man, than short Life.   The Senses[1] become
dull, the Members grow benumbed, the Eye-sight decayeth
betimes, the Hearing followeth, then the Supporters, the
Teeth also, and the very Instruments that serve for our
Food; and yet all this Time is counted a Part of our Life.
And therefore it is taken for a wonderful example, and that
to which we cannot find a fellow, that *Xenophilus* the Musician lived 105 Years, without any inconveniency in all his
Body. But all other Men, by *Hercules!* are vexed at certain
Hours, as no other Creatures are besides, with pestiferous
Heat and Cold in every part of their Members; which go

---

[1] How remarkably does this enumeration of the signs and evils of
age correspond with the more poetical representation of the same condition by Solomon, in the last chapter of the Book of Ecclesiastes!
Cicero, in his "Cato," laments the ills of age as more weighty than Ætna,
and others of the wisest heathens join in the lamentation, which ceases
to surprise us when we reflect that they were destitute of a hope in the
future — *Wern Club*

and come, not for certain Hours only, but by Day and by Night : one while every Third, and at others every Fourth Day and Night, even through the whole Year And it is some sort of Disease to die through wisdom, for Nature hath set down certain Laws, even to Diseases, as that the circle of a Quartan Fever never beginneth in the shortest Days of the Year, neither in the Months of Winter : that some Diseases are not incident to those that are above Sixty Years of Age; that others again pass away when young People come to the Age of Puberty, and especially this is observed in young Women   Old People are the least liable to take the Plague   Also there are Sicknesses that follow particular Regions, affecting the Inhabitants generally therein.   There are some again that take hold of Servants only ; others touch the highest Persons alone   and so from degree to degree. But in this Place it is to be observed, that a Pestilence beginneth in the South parts, and always goeth toward the West; and it scarcely ever doeth otherwise, except in Winter, and then it doth not exceed three Months.[1]

Chapter LI

Of the Signs of Death.[2]

Now let us take a View of the fatal Signs in Sickness In the Disease of Fury (Madness), to Laugh is such a Sign In the Sickness of Wisdom (Frenzy), to have a care of the Fringes of their Garments and Bedclothes, to smoothe them down ; the neglect of such things as would prevent their Sleep, the apologising letting go of their Water   It

[1] This remark has been already referred to c 37, p 221, and it is the more worthy of notice, since there is reason to believe that all the epidemics which have traversed Europe since the time when Pliny wrote have conformed to the same rule — *Wern Club*

[2] Celsus considers this subject, book ii c 6, and the medical nature and treatment of insanity, book iii c 18   By *furor is morbus* (madness or mania), and *sapientiæ ægritudine* (frenzy), he seems to mean, the former, insanity of the passions, and the latter, insanity of the understanding — *Wern Club*

may also be certainly seen in the aspect of the Eyes and Nose, as also in the manner of lying always upon the Back supine also by the unequal stroke of the Veins, as if an Ant crept under it, with other Signs which *Hippocrates*, the prince of Medicine, hath observed And whilst there are innumerable Signs that presage Death, there is not one that can assure a Man certainly of Life and Health For *Cato*[1] the Censor, writing to his Son concerning robust Health, hath delivered from some Oracle, that Youth resembling Age is a Sign of untimely Death. Diseases are so innumerable, that *Pherecydes*, of the Island of Syros, died of a great quantity of Creepers[2] bursting out of his Body Some are never free of a Fever, as *C. Mecænas*. The same Man, for three whole Years before he died, never was asleep for a single Minute *Antipater Sidonius* the Poet, once a year during his Life was seized with an Ague-fit upon his Birthday only, and at last he died in such a Fit in a good old Age.

Chapter LII.

Of such as were carried forth to their Funeral and revived again.

A VIOLA, who had been Consul, came to himself when he was on the Funeral Pile; but because the Flame was so Strong that he could not be got away, he was burnt alive

---

[1] Cato's knowledge of medical subjects may be judged of from the specimens of miserable quackery contained in his " Treatise on Agriculture " Much of it consisted of charms, in unintelligible jargon — *Wern Club.*

[2] Pliny sometimes employs unusual words to express plain and common things; or he may have adopted the term to avoid what among polite people would have excited loathing For the same reason another author speaks of the same creatures under the name of *animalia tetra*, or foul creatures It was the disease which afflicted Herod, Acts of the Apostles, xii 23, and in modern times Dr Heberden records a case, " Commentaries," c. lxxi · but it is not certain that they are of the same species as that which commonly attacks the human body. The fate of Sylla, from the same cause, is referred to in the 43d chapter of this Book. — *Wern Club*

The like accident is reported to have befallen *Lu. Lamia*, of Prætorian rank. That *C Ælius Tubero*, who had been Prætor, was brought Alive again from the Funeral Fire, *Messala Rufus* and many others assert Such is the condition of Mortal Men ; and to this kind of Fortune, and such as this, are we born so that in the case of Man there is no assurance, no, not even in his Death. We read in Chronicles, that the Soul of *Hermotimus Clazomenius* was accustomed to leave his Body, and wandering to a great distance, brought him backs News of such things as could not possibly have been known unless it had been present there , and all the while his Body lay half Dead. This manner he continued, until the Cantharidæ, who were his Enemies, took his Body and burnt it to Ashes ; and by that means disappointed his Soul when it came back again to its Sheath. Also it is said, that the Spirit of *Aristæas* in Proconnesus was seen to fly out of his Mouth in the form of a Raven , and many an empty Tale followeth thereon : for surely I take it to be no better than a Fable, which is in like manner reported of *Epimenides* the Gnossian, that when he was a Boy, and wearied with Heat and Travel, he laid himself down in a Cave, and there slept for 57 Years [1] At length he awoke, as if on the very next Morning, and wondered at the changed face of every thing he saw. Hence in an equal number of Days after, he grew Old, that at last he lived to the Age of 175 Years. Women, by reason of their Sex, are most subject to this danger,[2] by the turning of the Womb ; which, if it be corrected, they soon recover. To this belongs that noble Volume among the Greeks written by *Heraclides*, where he writeth of a Woman that for seven Days lay as Dead, but who in the end was restored to Life. Also *Varro* reporteth, that when the twenty Men were dividing Lands

---

[1] Gibbon refers to a similar story, which was widely believed, in the fifth century of Christianity (" Decline and Fall," c xxxiii), but he seems not to have been aware of this more ancient, and perhaps original, narrative of a similar event.— *Wern Club*

[2] That is, of the suspension of animation, one of the symptoms of Hysteria — *Wern Club*

at Capua. there was one carried forth on his Bier who came home again upon his Feet   Also, that the like happened at Aquinum   Likewise, that in Rome one *Confidius*, who had married his own Aunt by the Mother's side, after his Funeral had been set in order, revived again; and the Orderer of his Funeral was by him carried out to the same.   *Varro* also addeth some surprising things, which are worth the rehearsal at large   There were two Brethren of the Equestrian order, of whom the elder, named *Corfidius*, happened in all appearance to die, and when his last Will was opened, the younger Brother, who was appointed his Heir, gave orders for his Funeral. In the meanwhile the Man that seemed Dead, by clapping one Hand against the other,[1] raised the Servants in the House; and he recounted to them that he was come from his younger Brother, who had recommended his Daughter to him; and, moreover, that he had shewed to him in what place he had buried his Gold, without the knowledge of any Man · requesting him also to employ that Provision which he had prepared for him about his own Funeral   As he was relating this matter, his Brother's domestic Servants came in great haste to the House, and brought word that their Master was dead, and the Gold was found in the place he had pointed out.   And truly life is full of these Divinations, but they are not to be compared with these, as for the most part they are mere lies, as we will prove by one notable example: in the Sicilian War, *Gabienus,* one of the bravest Officers of *Cæsar's* Fleet, was taken prisoner by *Sex Pompey,* and by commandment from him his Head was almost stricken off, so that it scarcely hung to the Neck by the Skin, and in this condition he lay all day on the Shore   When it grew toward the Evening, and a Company were flocked about him, with a groan and prayers he requested that *Pompey* would come to him, or at least send some one of those who

---

[1] Clapping the hands together appears to have been an ordinary method of summoning the attendants before bells came into use for that purpose — *Wern Club*

were dear to him, because he was sent back from the Lower
Regions, and had a Message to deliver to him. Then *Pompey*
sent several of his friends, to whom *Gabienus* related that
the Infernal Gods were well pleased with the Cause and
pious Dispositions of *Pompey*, and therefore he should have
as good an issue of it as he could wish. Thus much, he said,
he was commanded to deliver; and as a proof of the truth,
so soon as he had done his errand he would immediately
expire: and so it came to pass　Histories also make mention of them who have appeared after they were committed
to Earth. But our purpose is to write of Nature's works,
and not to prosecute such Prodigious Matters.

Chapter LIII.

Of Sudden Deaths.

But among the principal things is sudden Death, which
is the greatest Felicity of Life; many examples of which we
have, that always seem strange, although they are common,
and as we shall shew, natural. *Verrius* hath set forth many,
but we will make choice among them all. Besides *Chilon*,
of whom we have spoken before, there died suddenly for Joy
Sophocles the Poet, and *Dionysius* the Tyrant of Sicily.
both of them, on Tidings brought to them that they had won
the best Prize among the Tragic Poets. Presently after the
famous battle of Cannæ, a Mother died immediately on the
sight of her Son unhurt, whom by a false Message she had
heard to have been Slain　*Diodorus*, a Professor of Dialectic
Learning, for shame that he could not readily resolve a frivolous Question at the demand of *Stilbo*, sunk away without
recovery. Without any apparent cause some have died,
particularly two of the *Cæsars*, the one a Prætor: the other
who had borne that Dignity, the Father of *Cæsar* the Dictator. both of them in the Morning when they were putting
on their Shoes, the one at Pisa, the former at Rome
Q. Fabius Maximus in his very Consulship, upon the last
Day of December, in whose place *Rebilus* made suit to be

Consul for a very few Hours.[1]   Also, *C. Vulcatius Gurges*, a
Senator: all of them in such sound and perfect Health, that
they expected to live Long. *Q. Æmilius Lepidus*, even as he
was going out of his Bed-chamber, hit his great Toe against
the Door-post and died from it   *C. Aufidius* was going
out of his House, on his way to the Senate, and stumbled
with his Foot in the Comitium.   The Ambassador of the
Rhodians also, who had to the great admiration of all that
were present pleaded their cause before the Senate, in the
very entry of the Counsel-house, as he was going out, fell
down Dead   *Cn. Bœbius Pamphilus*, who had been Prætor,
died suddenly as he was asking a Boy what it was o'clock.
A Pompeius, so soon as he had worshipped the Gods in the
Capitol; *M. Juventius Talia*, the Consul, as he was sacrificing ; *Caius Servilius Pansa*, as he stood at a Shop in the
Forum, at the second Hour of the Day, leaning on his
Brother, *P. Pansa , Bœbius*, the Judge, as he was adjourning
an Appearance in the Court , *M. Terentius Corax*, while he
was writing Letters in the Forum , no longer since than last
Year a Knight of Rome, as he was talking in the Ear of one
who had been Consul, before the Ivory Statue of *Apollo*,
which is in the Forum of *Augustus* · but above all others,
C Julius, a Physician, as he was dressing an Eye with
Ointment, and drawing the Surgical Instrument along the
Eye; also *L Manlius Torquatus*, a Consular Man, when at
Supper he reached for a Cake , *L. Durius Valla*, a Phy-
sician, while he was drinking a Draught of honeyed Drink ,
Appius Saufeius, being come out of the Bath, as he was
drinking honeyed Drink, and supping an Egg; *P. Quin-
tius Scapula*, as he was at Supper with *Aquillius Gallus* ,
Decimus Saufeius, a Scribe, as he sat at Dinner in his own
House, *Cornelius Gallus*, who had been Prætor, and *T.
Ætherius* a Roman Knight, died in the very act of *Venus*
The like befell in our Days to two of the Equestrian order,
with the same pantomimic Jester *Mithycus*, who was in
those days of surpassing Beauty   But *M Ofilius Hilarus*,

[1] Until the year was accomplished an honour which otherwise he
was not likely ever to attain — *Wern Club*

an Actor in Comedies, as is reported by ancient Writers, died with the most laboured security of Death, for after he had afforded much Pleasure to the People on his Birth-day he held a Feast, and when the Supper was set forth, he called for some hot Drink in a Basin: and casting his Eye on the Mask that he had worn that day, he took off the Chaplet from his Head, and set it on it, in this habit he became cold before any Man perceived it, until he that reclined next to him put him in mind that his Drink was growing cold These are examples of happy Deaths. But, on the other hand, there is a very great number of those that are miserable *L. Domitius*, descended from a noble Family, being vanquished by *Cæsar* near Massilia, and taken prisoner at Corsinium by the same *Cæsar*, for very irksomeness of Life poisoned himself; but after he had drunk the Poison he did all he could to save his life. We find in the Public Acts, that when *Felix*, one of the Red-coloured Chariot-drivers, was carried out to be burnt, one of those who favoured him threw himself into his Funeral Fire A frivolous matter it is to speak of, but they of the other side, that this act should not be ascribed to the honour of the Artist abovenamed, gave it out, that this Friend of his did it only because his Head was intoxicated with the strong smell of the Odours Not long before this *M. Lepidus*,[1] descended from a most noble Family, who (as is above said) died through Grief, was by the violence of the Flame cast off from the Funeral Pile, and as, because of the extreme Heat, no one could come near to lay him again on the place, he was burnt naked on a pile of dry Vine Cuttings, near the former.

Chapter LIV

Of Burial.

To burn the Bodies[2] of the Dead was not an ancient Custom among the Romans; but they Buried them in the

---

[1] The cause of his death is mentioned in the 36th chapter of this book — *Wern Club*

[2] The practice of burning the dead is of high antiquity, and as such is

Earth. But after they understood that the Bodies of the Men slain in the distant Wars were taken up out of the Earth again, it was appointed to Burn them   And yet many Families kept still to the old Customs · as in the House of the *Cornelii* no one is reported to have been burnt before *L Sylla*, the Dictator   And he willed it through dread that he should be so served as he had done by *C. Marius*, whose Corpse he had caused to be digged up   (In Latin) he is said to be *Sepultus*, who is bestowed in any way ; but *Humatus* signifieth that he is covered with the Earth.

Chapter LV

Of the Soul, or the Manes.[1]

After Sepulture there is very great Obscurity regarding the Manes ; but this is generally held, that in whatever Con-

familiarly spoken of by Homer   That it was more ancient among the Romans than is represented by Pliny appears from Ovid, who ("Fasti," c 4) speaks of its having been practised on the body of Remus, the brother of Romulus   The same is also negatively proved by Numa, who ordered that his body should not be burned, and by the laws of the Twelve Tables, regulations were instituted concerning it   chiefly to prevent extravagant expense in the ceremony.   The general fashion of burning, in preference to interment, succeeded to the example set by Sylla, after whose day it was practised even by people of inferior orders but neither burning nor burial were allowed by law within the bounds of the city   An ordinance of Numa forbade that a woman who died in childbirth should be buried, until the child was taken from her, and the usual ceremonies were to be omitted when the person had been killed by lightning —*Wern Club*

[1] "Manes" was a general term expressive of the souls of men after they were separated from the body   They were supposed to be arranged in classes, according to their moral condition   for which see a note, vol 1 p 24   But however situated, a kind of deityship was supposed to attach itself to them   and hence they were addressed as *Dii Manes* Such was the popular opinion, as referred to by Virgil, Ovid, and other writers who reflected the public mind, but it was scarcely an article of faith among philosophers and the higher classes, whose opinions fluctuated according to circumstances.   As a motive to moral obligation and responsibility it was exceedingly feeble.

Pliny's observation, " that in whatever condition they were before

dition they were before they were born, in the same they
remain when they are dead   For neither Body nor Soul
hath any more Sense after Death than they had before the
Day of Birth   But the Vanity of Men extendeth itself even
into the future, and in the very Time of Death flattereth
itself with a Life after this   For some attribute Immortality
to the Soul; others devise a Transfiguration, some again

they were born, in the same they remain after they are dead," may be
understood as referring to the Pythagorean doctrine of Transmigration,
which was the most plausible account of the disposition of the intelligent
principle that the Heathens could reach to, before Light and Immortality were revealed in the Gospel, but by the almost contemptuous
silence with which he passes it over in his argument, it appears that he
did not feel disposed to credit it   With regard to the station of the
manes, Plato supposes that impure spirits wander about among sepulchres
and monuments.   Homer represents Elpenor as prevented from rest
until the funeral rites were paid, and a commonly received doctrine was,
that there were days sacred to Dis and Proserpine, on which the whole of
the secret and deep places of the world were thrown open, and the disem-
bodied spirits were permitted to revisit the light   Varro supposes that
this occurs three times in the year. on the feast of Vulcanalia, tenth of
the Calends of September, or 23d of August; on the 3d of the Nones of
October, the Fontinalia, October 13, and the 6th of the Ides of November,
or 8th of that month

According to the doctrine of the Jewish Rabbis, derived, no doubt,
from ancient Oriental sources, "during the first twelve months after
death the souls of righteous men descend and ascend again" (Talmud, tr.
Sabbath) which Rabbi Joseph Albo, in the "Book of Principles," c xxxi,
explains by saying, that the soul does not directly and at once become
divested of those corporeal attachments to which it is accustomed, but
lingers about them until by habit it becomes weaned from them, and
assimilated to the new condition on which it has entered.

The gloomy views which even the more virtuous of the ancient Heathens took of an invisible world is shewn by Homer's representations in
the "Odyssey," b xi, and by so much of Etrurian learning as, from
their paintings and other representations, have descended to us   With so
much distaste of a wearisome life on the one hand (in which even Homer
joins, b xvii), and on the other the dim prospect of the dreary regions
below, we can scarcely wonder if even the virtuous Pliny should choose
rather to lie down in ashes without the prospect of living again   The
greater portion of his argument, however, is founded on his ignorance
his questions then so doubtful, are such as now even a child may answer
— *Wern Club*

bestow Sense on those who are in the Lower Regions; and they do Honour to the Manes, making a God of him who hath ceased to be a Man · as if the Manner of Man's Breathing differed from that of other living Creatures; or as if there were not to be found many other Things in the World, that live much longer than Men, and yet no Man foretells the like Immortality to them. But what is the Body that followeth the Material of the Soul? where lieth her Thought? how is her Seeing, how is her Hearing performed? what toucheth she? nay, what doth she at all? How is she employed? or what Good can there be without these? I would know where she hath her abiding Place? and what Multitudes of Souls, like Shadows, would there be in so many Ages? Surely these are but fantastical and childish Toys, devised by Men that would fain live always. The like Foolery there is in preserving the Bodies of Men. And the Vanity of *Democritus* is no less, who promised a Restoration to Life, and yet himself hath not come to Life again. And what an Instance of Madness to think (an Evil in itself) that Death should be the Way to a life! What Repose should ever Men have that are born, if the Sense of their Souls should remain on high, while their Shadows are among those below? Certainly, this sweet Inducement, and Credulity, destroyeth the Benefit of the best Gift of Nature, which is Death, and it doubleth the Pain of a Man who is to die, if he happen to consider what shall befall him in the Time to come. For if it be sweet to live, what Pleasure can one have, that hath already lived? But how much more easy and certain is it for each Man to trust to himself, and to gather Reasons from the Experience that he had before he was born?

Chapter LVI.

The first Inventors of Things in Life

Before we depart from this Discourse of Men's Nature, it seemeth convenient to point out their Inventions, and what each Man hath discovered. In the first Place, *Liber*

Pater appointed buying and selling; he also devised the Diadem, the Ornament of Kings, and the Triumph. *Ceres* shewed the use of Corn, whereas before Men lived on Mast. She taught also how to grind Corn, to knead Dough, and make Bread of it, in Attica, Italy, and Sicily, for which she was reputed a Goddess. She it was that began to make Laws; but others have thought that *Rhadamanthus* was the first Lawgiver. I am of opinion, that Letters ever were in Assyria; but some think, as particularly *Gellius*, that they were invented by *Mercury* in Egypt, and others will have it that they came first from Syria. True it is, that *Cadmus* brought into Greece from Phœnicè to the Number of sixteen; to which *Palamedes*, in the Time of the Trojan War, added four, in these characters, Θ, Ξ, Φ, Χ. And after him *Simonides Melicus*[1] produced the same Numbers, Ζ, Η, Ψ, Ω: the Force of all which Letters we acknowledge among ourselves. *Aristotle* is rather of opinion, that there were eighteen ancient Letters· Α, Β, Γ, Δ, Ε, Ζ, Ι, Κ, Λ, Μ, Ν, Ο, Π, Ρ, Σ, Τ, Υ, Φ, and that the other two, Θ and Χ, were added by *Epicharmus*, and not by *Palamedes*. *Anticlides* writeth, that one in Egypt named *Menon* was the Inventor of Letters, fifteen Years before the Time of *Phoroneus*, the most ancient King of Greece· and he endeavoureth to prove the same by Monuments. On the other Hand, *Epigenes*, an Author as renowned as any, sheweth, that among the Babylonians there were found Observations of the Stars for 720 Years, written on Bricks; and they who speak of the least, as *Berosus* and *Critodemus*, report the like for 480 Years Whereby it appeareth that the use of Letters was eternal. The Pelasgi brought their use into Latium. *Euryalus* and *Hyperbius*, two Brothers at Athens, invented the first Manufacture of Bricks and the Formation of Houses; for before their Time Caves were used for Houses. *Gellius* is of opinion that *Doxius*, the Son of *Cœlus*, devised the first Houses that were made of Clay; taking his Pattern from the Nests of Swallows Cecrops called a Town after his own Name, Cecropia; which at this

---

[1] Some copies read Medicus, "a physician"—*Wern Club*

Day is the Castle in Athens.   Some will have it that Argos
was built before it by King *Phoroneus*, and others again,
that Sycionè was before them.   The Egyptians affirm, that
long before that, their City Diospolis was founded   *Cinyra*,
the Son of *Agriopa*, invented the Slating of Houses, and
Mines of Brass: both within the Isle of Cyprus   He also
invented Pincers, the little Hammer, the Lever, and the
Anvil. *Danaus*, who was brought from Egypt to Greece,
which was then called Argos Dipsion, first sunk Wells.
Cadmus at Thebes, or, as *Theophrastus* saith, in Phœnicè,
found out Stone Quarries   *Thrason* was the first Builder
of Walls of Towers, the Cyclops, as *Aristotle* thinketh;
but the Tyrinthii, according to *Theophrastus*   Weaving
was the Invention of the Egyptians, and Dyeing Wool,
of the Lydians in Sardis. *Closter*, the Son of *Arachnè*,
taught the first making of the Spindle for Woollen Yarn:
and *Arachnè* herself, the Flax and Nets   *Nicias* the Megaren-
sian invented the Fuller's Art: *Boethius*, the Art of Sewing.
The Egyptians will have Medicine to have been discovered
among them; but others, that *Arabus*, the Son of *Babylo*
and *Apollo*, was its Author. The first Herbarist and Apothe-
cary was *Chiron*, Son of *Saturn* and *Phyllira*. *Aristotle*
thinketh that *Lydus* the Scythian displayed the melting and
tempering of Brass; *Theophrastus*, that it was *Delas* the
Phrygian. Some think the Chalybæ devised the working
into Vessels of Brass, and others attribute it to the Cyclopæ.
The Discovery of Iron was the Invention of those in
Crete, who were called Dactyli Idæi, according to *Hesiod*.
Erichthonius the Athenian discovered Silver, or, as others
say, *Æacus*. The Gold Mines, together with the melting of
the Metal, *Cadmus* the Phœnician first found out at the
Mountain Pangæus; but others say, *Thoas* and *Eaclis* in
Panchaia, or else *Sol* the Son of *Oceanus*, to whom *Gellius*
attributeth the Discovery of Medicine, and of Honey.
Midacritus was the first that brought Lead out of the Island
Cassiteris.[1]   And the Cyclops invented the working Iron to

---

[1] The Islands of Scilly —*Wern Club*

use; *Corœbus* the Athenian, the Potter's Art, and therein *Anacharsis* the Scythian, or according to some, *Hyperbios* the Corinthian, invented the forming into a Globe The Carpenter's Art was the Invention of *Dædalus*, as well as the Tools: the Saw, the Hatchet, the Perpendicular, the Auger, Glue, Fish-glue. The Square, the Level, the Lathe, and the Key, were invented by *Theodorus Samius* *Phidon* the Argive, or *Palamedes*, as *Gellius* rather thinketh, found out Measures and Weights *Pyrodes*, the Son of *Cilix*, first obtained Fire from the Flint; and *Prometheus*, the Means to preserve it in *Ferula* (or Fennel). The Phrygians invented the Waggon with four Wheels: the Pœni (Carthaginians), Merchandise. *Eumolpus* the Athenian discovered the cultivation of Vines and Trees. *Staphylus*, the Son of *Silenus*, taught how to mix Wine with Water. *Aristæus* the Athenian invented the making of Oil, and also the Press belonging to it. The same Man taught to draw Honey from the Combs. *Buzyges* the Athenian, or as others have it, *Triptolemus*, employed Oxen for the Plough The Egyptians were the first that had a royal City, and the Athenians a popular City After *Theseus*, the first Tyrant was *Phalaris* of Agrigentum. The Lacedæmonians first invented the Condition of Slavery. The first Judgment for Death was in the Court of Areopagus. The first Battle was fought between the Africans and Egyptians; and the same was done with Clubs, which they call Phalangæ. Shields were contrived by *Prœtus* and *Acrisius*, when they warred against each other; or by *Calchus*, the Son of *Athamas* *Midias* of Messenè invented the Cuirass, and the Lacedæmonians the Helmet, Sword, and Spear The Carians contrived Greaves, and Crests (upon Helmets): *Scythes*, the Son of *Jupiter*, the Bow and Arrows; although some say that *Perses*, the Son of *Perseus*, invented Arrows The Ætolians invented the Lance. the Dart with a Loop was by *Ætolus*, the Son of *Mars*. the light Javelins and the Pilum by *Tyrrhenus*; and *Penthesilea* the Amazon, the Battle-axe *Piseus* found out the Boar-spear and Chasing-staff. Among Engines to throw with, the Cretes invented the Scorpion. the Syrians, the

Catapult: the Phœnicians, the Balista and the Sling. *Piseus* the Tyrrhenian first used the brazen Trumpet; and *Arthemon* the Clazomenian, Tortoises The Engine to batter Walls (called sometimes the Horse, and now the Ram) was the Device of *Epeus* at Troy. *Bellerophon* shewed first how to ride on Horseback: *Pelethronius* invented the Saddle and Bridle for the Horse. The Thessalians, called Centaurs, inhabiting near the Mountain Pelius, were the first that fought on Horseback. The Nation of the Phrygians first joined two Horses to a Chariot; and *Erichthonius* four *Palamedes*, during the Trojan War, invented the manner of setting an Army in array: also the giving of a Signal, the Watch-word, and the Outposts (Vigiliæ) In the same War, *Sinon* devised Watch-towers *Lycanor* was the first Maker of a Truce: *Theseus*, of Alliances: *Car*, from whom Caria took its Name, observed first the Flight of Birds (Augury); to which *Orpheus* added the Signs from other Animals. *Delphus* invented Divination from the Entrails (Aruspices)· *Amphiaraüs*, that of the Inspection of Fire (Ignispex): *Tyresias*, the Theban, that of the Auspices of Birds. *Amphictyon* gave the Interpretation of portentous Sights, and of Dreams. *Atlas*, the Son of *Libya* (or, as some say, the Egyptians, and as others the Assyrians), invented Astrology, and in that Science, *Anaximander* the Milesian devised the Sphere The Explanation of the Winds was given by *Æolus*, the Son of *Helen*. *Amphion* invented Music The Flute and the single Pipe[1] were the Invention of *Pan*, the Son of *Mercury* The oblique Cornet was by *Midas* in Phrygia; and in the same Country *Marsyas* invented the Double Flute; *Amphion* taught the Lydian Measures; *Thamyras* the Thracian, the Dorian; and *Marsyas* of Phrygia, the Phrygian. *Amphion*, likewise (or, as some say, *Orpheus*, and according to others, *Linus*), played first on the Lute.[2] *Terpander* added seven Strings to it; *Simonides* added the eighth, and *Timotheus* the ninth. *Thamyras* was the first that played on the Lute without Song,

---

[1] Fistula and Monaulus. — *Wern. Club*   [2] Cithara — *Wern Club*

and *Amphion* sung with it, or, according to some, *Linus.*
Terpander adapted Songs to the Lute　*Dardanus,* the Trœ-
zenian, began first vocal Music to the Flute.[1]　The Curetes
taught to dance in Armour, and *Pyrrhus* the Pyrrhic Dance;
and both these were first practised in Crete.　The Heroic
Verse we owe to the Oracle of *Pythius* (*Apollo*)　About the
Original of Poems there is a great Question　They are
proved to have existed before the Trojan War.　*Pherecydes*
of Syros, in the Days of King *Cyrus,* invented the Writing
in Prose.　*Cadmus* the Milesian founded History.　*Lycaon*
appointed the first public Games of Strength in Arcadia;
Acastus in Iolcum, the first solemn Games at Funerals, and
after him *Theseus,* in the Isthmus　*Hercules* instituted the
Athletic Exercises at Olympia: and *Pythus* those of Play at
Ball.　*Gyges* the Lydian first practised Painting in Egypt;
but in Greece, *Euchir,* a Relative of *Dædalus,* as *Aristotle*
supposeth; and according to *Theophrastus,* it was *Polygnotus*
the Athenian.　*Danaus* was the first that sailed with a Ship,
and so he passed the Sea from Egypt to Greece, for before
that time they used Rafts, which were invented by King
Erythra, to cross from one Island to another in the Red Sea
But we meet with some Writers who suppose that the Tro-
jans and Mysians were the first that devised Navigation before them in the Hellespont, when they passed over-against
the Thracians.　And even at this Day in the British Ocean,
there are made Wicker Boats covered with Leather, and
stitched round about, in the Nile, of Papyrus, Cane-reed,
and Rushes.　*Philostephanus* witnesseth, that *Jason* first used
in Navigation the long Ship; but *Egesias* saith, that it was
Paralus.　*Ctesias* attributeth it to *Samyras, Saphanus,* to
Semiramis; and *Archimachus,* to *Ægeon.*　*Damastes* testifieth, that the Erythræans first made the Bireme (or Galley
with two Ranks of Oars)·*Thucydides,* that *Aminocles* the
Corinthian built the first Trireme (with three Rows of Oars):
Aristotle saith, that the Carthaginians were the first that set
to Sea the Quadrireme (with four Ranks of Oars): and

---

[1] Tibia —*Wern Club*

Nesichthon the Salaminian, set afloat the first Quinquireme (with five Ranks of Oars). *Zenagoras* of Syracusa brought up those of six Rows; and from it to those of ten, *Mnesigeton* was the Inventor It is said that *Alexander* the Great built Galleys with twelve Banks; and *Philostephanus* reporteth, that *Ptolemy Soter* rose to fifteen: *Demetrius,* the Son of *Antigonus,* to thirty: *Ptolemy Philadelphus,* to forty, and *Ptolemy Philopater,* surnamed *Tryphon,* to fifty *Hippus* the Tyrian invented Ships of Burden.[1] The Cyrenians first built the Pinnace, the Phœnicians, the Ferry-boat; the Rhodians, the Wherry, and last, the Cyprians, the Hulk. The Phœnicians were the first that in sailing observed the Course of the Stars. The Copeans devised the Oar, and the Plateans its broad End: *Icarus,* the Sails *Dædalus,* the Mast and the Yard. Vessels for transporting Horses were the Invention of the Samians, or else of *Pericles* the Athenian. The Thasii formed the long-covered Ships · for before their Time they fought only from the Stern and the Bow. *Piseus* added the Rostra; the Tyrrhenians, the Anchor; to which *Eupalamus* added the two Claws, and *Anacharsis* the Grappling-hooks The Stock was by *Pericles* the Athenian; and finally, the Steering-tackle by *Typhis.* The Chief that first fought in a Fleet was *Minos.* The first that killed a Beast was *Hyperbius,* the Son of *Mars;* and *Prometheus* first killed an Ox.[2]

[1] The names of these ships in the original are, Oneraria, Cymba, Celox, Cercuros — *Wern Club*

[2] It has been already remarked, that the Greeks regarded as the inventor of any art him who had communicated it to them; and Pliny seeks no further than to their writings for authority in these particulars, In the Book of Genesis (chap iv &c) we have more authentic particulars of the invention of musical instruments, of tents to dwell in, and of working in metal the latter by one whose name seems to have been the origin of that of Vulcan; and the following catalogue of discoveries in the most ancient times is derived from Sanchoniatho, the Phœnician —

"From Genus, the son of Protogonus and Œon, other mortal issue were begotten, whose names were Light, Fire, and Flame These found out the way of generating fire by the rubbing of pieces of wood against each other, and taught men the use thereof These begat sons of vast bulk and height, whose names were given to mountains on which they

Chapter LVII

Wherein first appeared the general Agreement of Nations

The first silent Consent of all Countries hath agreed in this, That they should use the Ionian Letters.

first seized   so from them were named Mounts Cassius and Libanus, Antilibanus and Brathys   Perhaps it is to these that allusion is made, Genesis, vi. 4   The Protogonus and Œon here spoken of, being the first generation of mortals, were the discoverers of the way of taking food from trees; and their children, Genus and Genea, in a time of scarcity in Phœnicia, first worshipped the sun, as Beelsamin, or only Lord of Heaven

" Hypsuranius, a Tyrian, first made huts of reeds and rushes, and the paper-reeds   His brother Usous first invented covering for his body, out of the skins of wild beasts which he could catch ; which may be reconciled with the narrative in Genesis, iii. 21   He consecrated two rude stone pillars to the fire and wind, and worshipped them with the sprinkling of the blood of wild beasts taken in hunting   He first ventured on the sea in a kind of raft , and on his death were first instituted anniversary feasts   Many years after him, Agreus and Halieus were the inventors of the arts, and it would appear, the fathers of tribes who pursued hunting and fish-ing.   The two brothers who invented the working of iron were their sons   One of these, named Chrysor, the same as Vulcan, employed charms and divinations, he invented the hook, bait, and fishing-line, and boats slightly made   perhaps those covered with leather, mentioned by Pliny as used in his day in Britain, and originally derived from this Eastern source   This Coracle, employed so late as the fourth or fifth century of Christianity in crossing the British Channel, is still used in Welsh rivers, and is figured, in its modern structure, by Mr Yarrell (" History of British Fishes," vol ii p 62, 2d edit)   a copy from an ancient relievo in Montfaucon is at the end of this volume   It was a subsequent race, the Cabiri, that formed the first complete ship   From the last generation, or Chrysor and his brother, sprang two brothers   one called Technites, or the artist, and the other, Geïnus Autochthon, the home-born man of the earth   These first mingled stubble with the brick earth, and dried the tiling in the sun   This accommodation was further improved by the for-mation of courts, fences, and cellars about houses   They were husband-men, and worshipped a statue carried about in a movable temple, drawn by oxen   This practice is alluded to by the prophet Amos, v 26, and perhaps 2 Samuel, vi 3 and 7   These were the first that employed dogs in the hunting of wild animals   Amynus and Magus, their sons, first

Chapter LVIII.

Of the ancient Letters [1]

THAT the old Greek Letters were almost the same as the present Latin appeareth by an antique Table of Brass, which came from the Temple at Delphos, and which at this Day is in the Library of the Palatium, dedicated to *Minerva* by the Emperors, with an Inscription like this on it: Ναυσικράτης Τισαμένου Ἀθηναῖος, κόρα καὶ Ἀθῆνα ἀνέθηκεν· *i. e. Nausicrates* (the Son) of *Tisamenus* an Athenian, caused this Table to be made and set up to *Minerva.*

formed villages and flocks, and their sons, Misor and Sydyc (Wellfreed and Just), discovered the use of salt

" Cronus first made a scimitar and spear· Dagon invented the use of bread and the plough. Inachus, whom Archbishop Usher makes contemporary with the Scriptural Nahor, was the inventor of honorary gold and silver chains The purple dye from shell-fish was discovered by the Phœnician Hercules, the great navigator Melcartus, who first passed through the Straits of Gibraltar, and visited Cornwall It is true, there seems some doubt whether there be not two individuals referred to under this name, one of whom lived in the days of Canaan, but if so, at least they were natives of the same country, and were both honoured by their countrymen as inventors of the arts by which the nation acquired riches and eminency Cronus first taught the use of the bow as a weapon: which took place in Crete, an island afterwards famous for this kind of skill ' Eupolemus says of Enoch, that he was the true Atlas, the inventor of astronomy ' Finally, the infamy of having first practised persecution for religion is ascribed to Cronus, who is supposed to be Ham, the son of Noah, with the concurrence of the Egyptian Thoth; but the Jews are inclined to derive its origin from the city of Ur, in Chaldæa, where Terah was put to death in the fire (Ur). but in either case the act was devised in support of false religion, or idolatry."—*Wern Club*

[1] In the beginning of the 56th chapter, Pliny has expressed his belief that the Assyrian letters are the most ancient in the world but whether these were the same as in recent times have been discovered among the antique monuments of Nineveh and Babylon the Chaldæan characters afterwards introduced among the Jews by Ezra, or the ancient Phœnician, now termed the Samaritan; in either case it is only by passing through great mutations that they can be traced to the Greek and Latin forms of the days of Pliny Sanchoniatho says that Taautus, called by

CHAPTER LIX.

When Barbers were first at Rome.

THE next Consent of all People was to entertain Barbers; but they were later among the Romans. The first that entered Italy came from Sicily, in the 454th Year after the Foundation of Rome. They were brought in by *P. Ticinius Mena*, as *Varro* reporteth: for before this they were unshorn. The first that took up the practice to Shave every day was *Scipio Africanus:* and after him cometh *Divus Augustus*, who always used the Rasor.[1]

CHAPTER LX.

When was the first Dial.[2]

THE third Consent of all Nations was in the observation of the Hours; and this was grounded upon Reason · but at what Time, and by whom this was Invented in Greece, we have declared in the Second Book , and it was late before this came up at Rome. In the Twelve Tables the East and West alone are mentioned ; after some Years the Noon was added, and the Consul's Officer proclaimed Noon when, standing at the Hall of the Council, he beheld the Sun in

the Greeks Hermes, found out the first letters, but these appear, from his subsequent remarks, to have been what we now term hieroglyphics. It may be the phonetic characters, of which Pliny ascribes the invention to Meno the Egyptian, but it is probable that they are all much more ancient. — *Wern Club*

[1] Slaves and servants were not permitted to be shaved. The Egyptians were the only people who universally used the rasor — *Wern. Club.*

[2] Lumisden has some observations on the Roman method of measuring time. "I do not conceive," he says, "how a sun-dial or any other instrument could point out the various hours, as time was computed by the ancient Romans. The time the earth takes to revolve once round its axis, or the space between the rising of the sun till its next rising, which makes a day and a night, divided into twenty-four equal parts, we call hours Now, the Romans divided the day and the night into twenty-four hours. Twelve of these, from the rising of the sun to its setting, con-

that Quarter between the Rostra and the Grecostasis　But when the Sun inclined downward from the Column named Mœnia, to the Prison, he proclaimed the last Quarter (of the Day). But this observation would serve only on clear Days, and yet it was so until the first Punic War. *Fabius Vestalis* writeth, that *L. Papyrius Cursor*, the Prince, twelve Years before the War with *Pyrrhus*, to do the Romans a pleasure set up a Sun-dial on the Temple of *Quirinus*, when it was dedicated, his Father having vowed it before him. But this Author sheweth not either the method of that Dial, or the Workman; nor yet from whence it was brought, nor in what Writer he found it so written. *M. Varro* reporteth, that the first Dial was set up in the common Market-place, upon a Column near the Rostra, in the first Punic War, by *M. Valerius Messala*, the Consul, presently after the taking of Catana, in Sicily; from whence it was brought, thirty Years after the report of the aforesaid Dial of *Papyrius*, in the Year of the City 477. And although the Lines of this Dial did not agree with the Hours, yet were the People governed by it for an hundred Years save one, until *Q. Martius Philippus*, who was Censor, with *L. Paulus*, set another by it, made more carefully. And this gift, among other things done by the Censor, was highly acceptable to the People. But notwithstanding this, if it were a cloudy Day the Hours were uncertain, and thus it

stituted their day, and the other twelve, from the setting of the sun to its rising, constituted their night　Thus, as the seasons changed, the length of their hours must have varied. In winter the twelve hours of the day were short, and those of the night long　in summer they were the reverse. How then could these hours, of an unequal length, and which daily varied, be measured by an instrument? I have not been able to discover any method by which this could be done. However, they had two fixed points, namely, mid-day and midnight, which they called the sixth hour　So that a meridian line would always point out the sixth hour, or mid-day "

That the dial was a very ancient instrument for measuring time appears from the 2d Book of Kings, xx 11, and Isaiah, xxxviii 8, where is the first mention of it on record　It probably was invented in Babylonia.— *Wern. Club*

continued five Years more. Then *Scipio Nasica*, the Colleague of *Lænas*, first divided the Hours, both of Day and Night equally, by Water. And this Horologe he dedicated under a Roof, in the Year of the City 595 from the Building of Rome. So long it was, that the People of Rome did not measure out the Light.

Now let us return to the other Living Creatures: and first, of Animals of the Land.

Coracle referred to in note at p. 256.—*Montfaucon, tom.* iv. *pl.* 49.

END OF VOL. II.

London:—George Barclay, Castle Street, Leicester Square.

The Wernerian Club.

1848–9

Those marked † are Honorary

Patrons.

The Right Honourable the EARL OF ELLESMERE, F.R S &c Belgrave Square
The Most Noble the MARQUIS OF NORTHAMPTON, Pres R S &c The Terrace, Piccadilly

President.

C J. B ALDIS, EsQ M. D and M A	*Physiology*	1 Chester Terrace, Chester Square

Treasurer and Director

CHARLES MOXON, EsQ	*Mineralogy, Geology*	Emmanuel College, Cambridge

Committee (in addition to the Officers)

W T CLARK, EsQ. FRS	*Mechanics*	Hammersmith
W G V. BARNEWALL, EsQ M A	*Classics*	.. Cavendish Hotel, Jermyn Street
F COLLIER, EsQ . .	*Mechanics* .. .	Hoe Street, Walthamstow
G ALEXANDER, EsQ F S A	*Architecture*	30 Bedford Square

Secretary

B W CROKER, EsQ C E	*Mineralogy, Mecha- nics*	Hammersmith

Secretary for Publications

HENRY WATKINS, EsQ.	*Agricultural Engi- neering* ..	19 Dorset Street, Baker Street

~~~~~~~~~~

G B. Greenough, Esq F R S.	*Geology*	Outer Circle, Regent's Park.
W Fairbairn, Esq. C E	*Mechanics* ..	Canal Street, Manchester.
T Taylor, Esq M.R C S . .	*Anatomy*	Bethnal Green Road
John Moxon, Esq .	*Literature* .	8 Hanover Terrace, Regent's Park
Edward Prior, Esq. F.R.B.S	*Literature*	48 York Terrace, Regent's Park
†John Nickols, Esq.	*Literature*	33 Seething Lane, Tower Street
Arthur Dean, Esq. C E	*Geology* . .	2 Broad Sanctuary, Westminster
Henry Twining, Esq.	*Literature* .	Wandsworth, Surrey
F. Brook, Esq. M.A.	*Classics*	Ufford Hall, Woodbridge, Suffolk
†Sir J F. W Herschel, Bart F.R.S	*Astronomy*	Collingwood, Hawkhurst, Kent.
G J Lyon, Esq F.B S E.	*Botany*	West Campbell Street, Glasgow
R. J. N. Streeten, Esq M D F.L.S. .	*Botany* . .	Worcester.
T. Shapter, Esq. M D.	*Botany, Geology*	Exeter.
Rev G. B Moxon, B A.	*Botany* ..	Sandringham, Lynn, Norfolk
R C. Pitts, Esq . . .	*Geology*	Norwich
W. J. West, Esq. F G S.	*Geology, Botany*	Tunbridge, Kent
T. Bodenham, Esq F B S.E	*British Ornithology*	Shrewsbury.
†Rev. T. Fulcher, B A	*Classics* .	Old Buckenham, Norfolk.
P N. Brockedon, Esq C.E.	*Geology*	29 Devonshire Street, Queen Square.
J W Slater, Esq.	*Entomology*	Fairfield, Manchester
Beverley R. Morris, Esq. M.D	*Natural History*	York
W Sherwood, Esq	*Entomology*	Rysome Garth, Patrington, Hull
O A. Moore, Esq. . .	*Botany* ..	York.
C. Parsons, Esq F.L S.	*Ornithology, Natural History*	North Shoebury Hall, near Rochford, Essex

Name	Subject	Address
Rev. G. Munford	Botany	East Winch, near Lynn, Norfolk
J. D. Salmon, Esq.	Ornith. and Oology	Godalming, Surrey.
James Bladon, Esq	Natural History	Pontypool, Monmouthshire
Henry Bull, Esq	British Botany	Portsmouth
†James E. Moxon, Esq	Botany	Algoa Bay, South Africa
William R Scott, Esq Phil D.	Ornithology	St Leonard's, Exeter
P L. Sclater, Esq.	Ornithology	Hoddington House, Odiham, Hants
Robert Embleton, Esq.	Zoology, Botany	Embleton, Northumberland
J W Barlow, Esq	Natural History	Park Place, Greenheys, Manchester
Mark Booth, Esq	British Ornithology	Killerby, near Catterick, Yorkshire
Rev. W Strong Hore, M.A	Botany	33 Trafalgar Place, Stoke, Devonport
Cornelius Nicholson, Esq.	Geology	Stand Lodge, Manchester.
Jonathan Couch, Esq F L S.	Zoology	Polperro, Cornwall
†Theod F Moss, Esq	Mineralogy	United States (Philadelphia)
John Sharp, Esq	Botany (Freshwater Algæ).	Tonbridge Wells.
David Moore, Esq.	Botany	Glasnevin, Dublin
J G. Harrison, Esq. M D	Physiology	4 Piccadilly, Manchester
Robert Cook, Esq	Entomology (Lepidoptera)	30 Colliergate, York
W. Rayner, Esq. M D	Anatomy, &c.	Stockport.
Octavius A. Ferris, Esq.	Geology	Victoria Park, Manchester.
E. J. Chapman, Esq.	Mineralogy	Addison Terrace, Kensington
W H Hatcher, Esq C E	Mineralogy	345 Strand
F W L Ross, Esq	Natural History	Broadway House, Topsham, Devon
Geo Wood, Esq. F H S	Mechanics	Rochford, Essex
Oct Leefe, Esq.	Mineralogy	Richmond, Yorkshire.
William White, Esq	Entomology	Godalming, Surrey
C. R. Hall, Esq. M D.	Physiology	Holmeschapel, near Middlewitch, Cheshire
W R Callender, jun. Esq.	Chemistry, Geology	Mosley Street, Manchester
C. W. Peach, Esq.	Natural History	Fowey, Cornwall.
V. O Walmesley, Esq.	Natural History	Westwood House, Wigan, Lancashire
Nath. J Holmes, Esq	Mineralogy	Hampstead
Rev. F. Wright, B A	Natural History	St Stythian's, Penryn, Cornwall.
Rev. W. W. Spicer, B.A	Classics	Puttenham, near Guildford, Surrey.
Rev. C Parish, B A	British Botany	West Hatch, Taunton, Somerset
J B Denton, Esq C E	Engineering	Graveley, Herts
W Llewellyn, jun Esq	Geology	The Wern, Pontypool
S. R. Ridgway, Esq	Natural Philosophy	Magdalen House, Exeter
James Ward, Esq	Botany	Richmond, Yorkshire
R T Abraham, Esq	Entomology	Heavitree, near Exeter
Leslie Ogilby, Esq	Botany, Zoology	27 Prussia Street, Dublin
Benj Kennedy, Esq F L S.	Botany	26 Upper Harley Street, London
James Paxton, Esq M D	Anatomy	Rugby
Rev E W Dowell	Ornithology	Morston, Holt, Norfolk.
John Hewson, Esq. F R C S	Anatomy	Lincoln
Jas C Dale, Esq M A	British Entomology	Glanville's Wootton, Dorset
T Nunnelly, Esq F R C S E	Anatomy	Leeds
Jas Thos Bell, Esq	Natural History	10 Northwick Terrace, Maida Hill.
George Bird, Esq	Anatomy	Tillerton, Yorkshire
W. H. Allchin, Esq M B	Natural History, Anatomy	13 Huntley Street, Bedford Square.
Geo W Turner, Esq.	Natural Philosophy	Exeter
J C Pickersgill, Esq.	Mineralogy	31 Tavistock Square
Robert Baker, Esq	Geology, Agriculture, &c.	Writtle, Essex
Amos Beardsley, Esq F G S	Geology, &c.	Langley Heanor, near Derby
J Chippendale, Esq F R C S	Anatomy, &c.	10 New Cavendish St. Portland Place
J. W. G Gutch, Esq.	Medicine, &c	77 Great Portland Street.
†W H F Platé, Esq. LL D	Oriental Languages	5 Montague Place, Kentish Town

London —Printed by George Barclay, 28 Castle Street, Leicester Square